Tales of the Celtic Otherworld

Tales of the Celtic Otherworld

Compiled and edited by

JOHN MATTHEWS

Colour illustrations by Ian Daniels

BLANDFORD

With thanks to Frank Gerace and Cheryl Wanner,
especially for the seafood

A BLANDFORD BOOK

First published in the UK 1998 by Blandford
A Cassell Imprint

Reprinted 1998

Cassell plc
Wellington House
125 Strand
London WC2R 0BB

Distributed in the United States by Sterling Publishing Co., Inc.,
387 Park Avenue South, New York, NY 10016-8810

**A Cataloguing-in-Publication Data entry for this title
is available from the British Library**

ISBN 0-7137-2656-3

Colour plates by Ian Daniels

Designed by Chris Bell

Printed and bound by Kyodo Printing Co., Singapore

Frontispiece: *Ean Chinn-duine – the bird with a human
head, from The Story of Conn-eda; or the Golden Apples
of Loch Erne*

Contents

INTRODUCTION

Immrama –
Journeys to the
Otherworld

VIRTUALLY EVERY CULTURE in the world has a concept of the afterlife, and many revolve around the idea of an Otherworld of one kind or another, from which the spirit comes and where it returns after death. Traditions relating to the Celtic Otherworld are among the most detailed and powerful of any such mythos. This is attested to by the large number of ancient texts that have survived since early times. These describe journeys to the Otherworld, what occurred there and the kind of people likely to be encountered. Indeed a whole genre of works, known in Irish tradition as *Immrama* ('journeys'), was devoted entirely to stories of this kind. The present collection, drawn from a wide range of material from various parts of the Celtic world, includes such celebrated works as 'The Voyage of Bran', 'Cormac's Adventures in the Land of Promise' and 'Pwyll in Annwvyn', as well as a number of lesser known works, including the dazzling folk-tale of 'Gold Apple, Son of the King of Erin'. Together these convey a powerful account of the Celtic Otherworld in all its multifarious aspects. These are colourful, exciting and visionary stories, which have been read and pondered over since they were first written down in the Middle Ages, and they still make exciting reading for today's audience.

When one first looks at these stories, the first impression they make is one of light and vitality. Rather than an ending of life, the Otherworld of the Celts is a gateway into another kind of life. Often this life looks very like the one we experience daily – though it is generally transformed, made 'Other', by the beauty and everlasting quality of its nature. It is a world enhanced by infinite possibilities, by the beauty of its physical manifestation (for this is no misty, insubstantial place, but a world of solids and absolutes) and by the marvellous beings who inhabit it.

These beings, the gods and spirits and wondrous creatures who inhabit the inner life of the Celtic imagination, are present both in the outer world and the inner, where they take on a more powerful presence, becoming more real, as well as more sensuously present. In this collection we shall encounter many such extraordinary beings, here perceived as being every bit as real as ourselves, and as acting according to their own rules and laws of existence. Thus we find Bran, in the story of his voyage to the Otherworld (page 11), encountering the wonderful fairy woman, the sound of whose silvery branch sends him forth into adventures; or in the other great *immram*, 'The Voyage of Maildun' (page 20), a veritable menagerie of curious beasts, strange beings, and wondrous Otherworldly people.

A brief look at just a few of the many descriptions of the Otherworld that are to be found in Celtic literature (more will be found in the stories which follow here) serves to show not only the infinite richness of the Celtic Otherworld tradition, but also something of the mighty array of images which face us when we venture into this enchanted region of the soul.

Perhaps one of the most interesting descriptions comes not from a literary text, or even from a Celtic source, but from a Classical Roman description of Britain – which was, to those living elsewhere, often perceived as being itself a very real and solid bastion of the Otherworld. Thus, when the historian and geographer Procopius wrote his account of the island he called 'Brittia', he made it clear that this was no ordinary place, but an abode of the dead. To this place the people who lived on the opposite coast were given the task of conveying the souls of the dead.

> At a late hour of the night they are conscious of a knocking at their doors and hear an indistinct voice calling them together for their task, and they with no hesitation rise from their beds and walk to the shore, not understanding what necessity leads them to do this, but compelled nevertheless. There they see skiffs in readiness with no man at all in them, not their own skiffs, however, but a different kind, in which they embark and lay hold of the oars. And they are aware that the boats are burdened with large number of passengers and are wet by the waves to the edge of the planks and the oarlocks, having not so much as one finger's breadth above the water; they themselves, however, see no one, but after rowing a single hour they put in at Brittia. And yet when they make the voyage in their own skiffs, not using sails but rowing, they with difficulty make this passage in a night and a day. And when they have reached the island and have been relieved of their burden, they depart with all speed, their boats now becoming suddenly light and rising above the waves, for they sink no further into the water than the keel itself.
>
> *(Translated by A.C. Dewing)*

Procopius is probably conflating several sources here, both those of actual geographical accounts (since lost) and of storytellers eager to add mystery to the 'Islands of the West'. What is interesting is the degree of similarity between this description and others that occur in Celtic literature in both early and more recent times.

A glance at three such descriptions will illustrate the truth of this. The first of these, which comes from the medieval Irish tale 'Cormac's Adventures in the Land of Promise' (page 111), paints an enchanting picture of the magical realm in which the hero finds himself.

> There was a large fortress in the midst of the plain with a wall of bronze around it. In the fortress was a house of white silver, and it was half-thatched with the wings of white birds. A fairy host of horsemen were at the house, with lapfulls

of the wings of white birds in their bosoms to thatch the house. . . . Cormac saw a man kindling a fire, and the thick-boled oak was cast upon it, top and butt. When the man came again with another oak, the burning of the first oak had ended. Then he saw another royal stronghold, and another wall of bronze around it. There were four palaces therein. He entered the fortress and saw the vast palace with its beams of bronze, its wattling of silver, and its thatch of the wings of white birds. Then he saw in the enclosure a shining fountain, with five streams flowing out of it, and the hosts in turn drinking its water. . . . He entered the palace. There was one couple inside awaiting him. The warrior's figure was distinguished owing to the beauty of his shape, the comeliness of his form, and the wonder of his countenance. The girl along with him, mature, yellow-haired, with a golden headdress, was the loveliest of the world's women. Cormac's feet were washed by invisible hands. There was bathing in a pool without the need of attendance. The heated stones themselves went into and came out of the water.

(Translated by C.H. Slover)

This is a place which readily reflects that of the actual world of the early Celts, but enriched, magnified, transformed into something rich and strange. In the second extract, from 'The Voyage of Bran', the hero meets Manannan mac Lir, the god of the sea, who perceives the overlap of the two worlds in a wonderful way:

What is a clear sea
For the prowed skiff in which Bran is,
That is a happy plain with profusion of flowers
To me from the chariot of two wheels.

Bran sees
The number of waves beating across the clear sea:
I myself see in Mag Mon
Red-headed flowers without fault.

Sea-horses glisten in summer
As far as Bran has stretched his glance:
Rivers pour forth a stream of honey
In the land of Manannan son of Ler.

The sheen of the main, on which thou art,
The white hue of the sea, on which thou rowest about,
Yellow and azure are spread out,
It is land, and is not rough.

Speckled salmon leap from the womb
Of the white sea, on which thou lookest:
They are calves, they are coloured lambs
With friendliness, without mutual slaughter.

Though (but) one chariot-rider is seen
In Mag Mell of many flowers,
There are many steeds on its surface,
Though them thou seest not.

(Translated by Kuno Meyer)

Finally, we catch a glimpse into another aspect of the Otherworld, the mysterious place where time is not and where no one grows any older. In the poem 'The Defence of the Chair', by the great Welsh shaman-poet Taliesin, we find the author reflecting upon his own perception of the Otherworld:

> My chair is in Caer Siddi,
> Where no-one is afflicted with age or illness.
> Manawydden and Pryderi have known it well.
> It is surrounded by three circles of fire.
> To the borders of the city come the ocean's flood,
> A fruitful fountain flows before it,
> Whose liquor is sweeter than the finest wine.

(Translated by John Matthews)

This is a simple but telling statement, in keeping with the poet's laconic style, which tells of his own sojourn in the Otherworld, from where the foundation of his poetic spirit (his Chair) comes. It shares some details with the previous examples, both of which are from Irish tradition.

The consensus of descriptions to be found among the vast remains of Celtic literature is that the Otherworld is divided into three levels or 'worlds'. These have many names, but are more often referred to simply as the Upperworld, the Middle World or the Underworld. The latter, which is also the place occupied by the ancestors, is the most often described and its importance to the Celts is clear enough. In numerous instances the hero who visits the Otherworld does so by entering a fairy mound or *sidhe*, beyond which he finds another world within or beneath the earth. In other stories the way is again downward, by way of wells or lakes that offer admittance to an Otherworldly realm.

In addition, the evidence of Celtic folklore and myth is unified in its presentation of the ancient gods (for example the Irish *Tuatha de Danaan*) as retiring beneath the 'hollow hills' after their conquest or expulsion by succeeding tribes who possessed their own families of gods. Thus, when the heroes of Celtic tradition went into the earth, they frequently went to visit the ancestors, who remembered and preserved the traditions of older times. Again and again the ancient dead are recalled to tell of some past great event, or to advise the visitor on the direction of his own life.

The Roman author Tertullian recording, in his book *De Anima*, the words of the older writer Nicander, reports that the Celts spent nights at the tombs of their heroes in order to obtain special oracles. Archaeological evidence abounds for the existence of ancestor 'cults' or 'worship' among the Celts, who made offerings to their great dead in much the same way as to the gods themselves. Indeed, it is even possible that they saw the famous ancestors as, in some senses, attaining the status of gods themselves – or at least as holding a place of honour among the denizens of the Otherworld. R.J. Stewart in his illuminating book *The Underworld Initiation* (London: Thorsons, 1985), places the whole concept on a practical, day-to-day basis, suggesting that the ancient grave sites had guardian spirits attached to them, partly for the purpose of consultation; an idea which seems wholly in keeping with the evidence of folklore and myth.

Nor is the tradition of the Otherworld limited to pagan accounts. In later texts, influenced by Christian writers, we find accounts of visits to the Otherworld that combine Christian imagery with more ancient lore. Thus in the ninth-century 'Vision of Adamnan' we find the following passage, which could have come from either source.

> Now this is the first land to which he came: a land black and burnt, bare and seared, without any torture therein. A glen full of fire on the hither side of it, a vast flame there which comes over its border on every side. Black is its lower part, red its middle and its upper part. Eight monsters there, with their eyes like fiery gledes. And a vast bridge there is over the glen wherein . . . sinners are punished. It stretches from one brink to the other: its ends are low and its middle high. Three hosts are preparing to wend across it, and not all pass.
>
> *(Translated by Whitley Stokes)*

It is to these realms that the human adventurers, whose deeds are narrated hereafter, go in search of wonder and wisdom. And it is from these places that Otherworldly beings come forth to visit our world – always with fascinating results. It is very much two-way traffic, and in many of the following stories it is this very exchange which drives the action. It will be seen that the encounters with Otherworldly beings, both 'here' and 'there', was taken as a natural event, to be accepted as matter-of-factly as meeting another human being.

When all the many and varied accounts of the Otherworld, described in a story tradition which extends from the fifth to the fifteenth centuries, are put together, we find that a significantly unvarying pattern emerges, which enables us to know a good deal about its makeup and constituent parts. The main aspects may be listed as follows:

- the way to the Otherworld is frequently across (or under) water;
- the Otherworld is often characterized as an island;
- the houses are rich and often thatched with gold or bird's wings;
- there are doors and windows of crystal;
- food and drink is always plentiful;
- there are numbers of fairy women of great beauty to be found there;
- Otherworldly birds sing so sweetly that time passes unnoticed; (or)
- time is of a different kind and two days in the Otherworld is sometimes equal to two years here;
- there is no sickness;
- everything is more alive, more beautiful, more noble than in the earthly realm.

These are only some of the factors which characterize the Otherworld of the Celts. There is much more that will be observed from a reading of the stories which follow. Apart from the pleasure of the tales themselves, there is a great deal to be learned about the nature of the Celtic beliefs and practices, which may still offer us valuable insights into our own lives today. A companion volume, *Classic Celtic Fairy Tales* (Blandford, 1997), offers a further selection, many of which contain still more images of the Otherworld.

John Matthews
Oxford, 1997

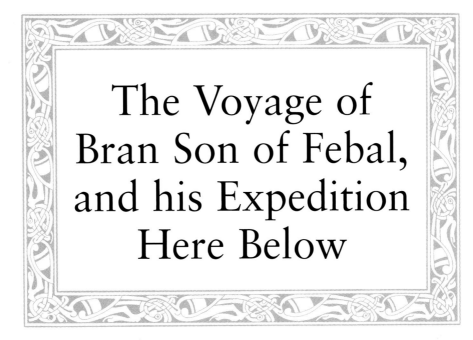

The Voyage of Bran Son of Febal, and his Expedition Here Below

WAS FIFTY QUATRAINS the woman from unknown lands sang on the floor of the house to Bran son of Febal, when the royal house was full of kings, who knew not whence the woman had come, since the ramparts were closed.

This is the beginning of the story. One day, in the neighbourhood of his stronghold, Bran went about alone, when he heard music behind him. As often as he looked back, 'twas still behind him the music was. At last he fell asleep at the music, such was its sweetness. When he awoke from his sleep, he saw close by him a branch of silver with white blossoms, nor was it easy to distinguish its bloom from that branch. Then Bran took the branch in his hand to his royal house. When the hosts were in the royal house, they saw a woman in strange raiment on the floor of the house. 'Twas then she sang the fifty quatrains to Bran, while the host heard her, and all beheld the woman.

And she said:

'A branch of the apple-tree from Emain
I bring, like those one knows;
Twigs of white silver are on it,
Crystal brows with blossoms.

'There is a distant isle,
Around which sea-horses glisten:
A fair course against the white-swelling surge, –
Four feet uphold it.

'A delight of the eyes, a glorious range,
Is the plain on which the hosts hold games:
Coracle contends against chariot
In southern Mag Findargat.

'Feet of white bronze under it
Glittering through beautiful ages.
Lovely land throughout the world's age,
On which the many blossoms drop.

'An ancient tree there is with blossoms,
On which birds call to the Hours.
'Tis in harmony it is their wont
To call together every Hour.

'Splendours of every colour glisten
Throughout the gentle-voiced plains.
Joy is known, ranked around music,
In southern Mag Argatnél.

'Unknown is wailing or treachery
In the familiar cultivated land,
There is nothing rough or harsh,
But sweet music striking on the ear.

'Without grief, without sorrow, without death,
Without any sickness, without debility,
That is the sign of Emain –
Uncommon is an equal marvel.

'A beauty of a wondrous land,
Whose aspects are lovely,
Whose view is a fair country,
Incomparable is its haze.

'Then if Aircthech is seen,
On which dragonstones and crystals drop
The sea washes the wave against the land,
Hair of crystal drops from its mane.

'Wealth, treasures of every hue,
Are in Ciuin, a beauty of freshness,
Listening to sweet music,
Drinking the best of wine.

'Golden chariots in Mag Réin,
Rising with the tide to the sun,
Chariots of silver in Mag Mon,
And of bronze without blemish.

'Yellow golden steeds are on the sward there,
Other steeds with crimson hue,
Others with wool upon their backs
Of the hue of heaven all-blue.

'At sunrise there will come
A fair man illumining level lands;
He rides upon the fair sea-washed plain,
He stirs the ocean till it is blood.

12

'A host will come across the clear sea,
To the land they show their rowing;
Then they row to the conspicuous stone,
From which arise a hundred strains.

'It sings a strain unto the host
Through long ages, it is not sad,
Its music swells with choruses of hundreds –
They look for neither decay nor death.

'Many-shaped Emne by the sea,
Whether it be near, whether it be far,
In which are many thousands of motley women,
Which the clear sea encircles.

'If he has heard the voice of the music,
The chorus of the little birds from Imchiuin,
A small band of women will come from a height
To the plain of sport in which he is.

'There will come happiness with health
To the land against which laughter peals,
Into Imchiuin at every season
Will come everlasting joy.

'It is a day of lasting weather
That showers silver on the lands,
A pure-white cliff on the range of the sea,
Which from the sun receives its heat.

'The host race along Mag Mon,
A beautiful game, not feeble,
In the variegated land over a mass of beauty
They look for neither decay nor death.

'Listening to music at night,
And going into Ildathach,
A variegated land, splendour on a diadem of beauty,
Whence the white cloud glistens.

'There are thrice fifty distant isles
In the ocean to the west of us;
Larger than Erin twice
Is each of them, or thrice.

'A great birth will come after ages,
That will not be in a lofty place,
The son of a woman whose mate will not be known,
He will seize the rule of the many thousands.

'A rule without beginning, without end,
He has created the world so that it is perfect,
Whose are earth and sea,
Woe to him that shall be under His unwill!

"Tis He that made the heavens,
Happy he that has a white heart,
He will purify hosts under pure water,
'Tis He that will heal your sicknesses.

'Not to all of you is my speech,
Though its great marvel has been made known:
Let Bran hear from the crowd of the world
What of wisdom has been told to him.

'Do not fall on a bed of sloth,
Let not thy intoxication overcome thee,
Begin a voyage across the clear sea,
If perchance thou mayst reach the land of women.'

Thereupon the woman went from them, while they knew not whither she went. And she took her branch with her. The branch sprang from Bran's hand into the hand of the woman, nor was there strength in Bran's hand to hold the branch.

Then on the morrow Bran went upon the sea. The number of his men was three companies of nine. One of his foster-brothers and mates was set over each of the three companies of nine. When he had been at sea two days and two nights, he saw a man in a chariot coming towards him over the sea. That man also sang thirty other quatrains to him, and made himself known to him, and said that he was Manannan the son of Ler, and said that it was upon him to go to Ireland after long ages, and that a son would be born to him, even Mongan son of Fiachna – that was the name which would be upon him.

So he sang these thirty quatrains to him:

'Bran deems it a marvellous beauty
In his coracle across the clear sea:
While to me in my chariot from afar
It is a flowery plain on which he rides about.

'What is a clear sea
For the prowed skiff in which Bran is,
That is a happy plain with profusion of flowers
To me from the chariot of two wheels.

'Bran sees
The number of waves beating across the clear sea:
I myself see in Mag Mon
Red-headed flowers without fault.

'Sea-horses glisten in summer
As far as Bran has stretched his glance:
Rivers pour forth a stream of honey
In the land of Manannan son of Ler.

'The sheen of the main, on which thou art,
The white hue of the sea, on which thou rowest about,
Yellow and azure are spread out,
It is land, and is not rough.

*'At sunrise
there will come
A fair man
illumining
level lands;
He rides upon
the fair sea-
washed plain,
He stirs the
ocean till it
is blood'.*

'Speckled salmon leap from the womb
Of the white sea, on which thou lookest:
They are calves, they are coloured lambs
With friendliness, without mutual slaughter.

'Though (but) one chariot-rider is seen
In Mag Mell of many flowers,
There are many steeds on its surface,
Though them thou seest not.

'The size of the plain, the number of the host,
Colours glisten with pure glory,
A fair stream of silver, cloths of gold,
Afford a welcome with all abundance.

'A beautiful game, most delightful,
They play (sitting) at the luxurious wine,
Men and gentle women under a bush,
Without sin, without crime.

'Along the top of a wood has swum
Thy coracle across ridges,
There is a wood of beautiful fruit
Under the prow of thy little skiff.

'A wood with blossom and fruit,
On which is the vine's veritable fragrance,
A wood without decay, without defect,
On which are leaves of golden hue.

'We are from the beginning of creation
Without old age, without consummation of earth,
Hence we expect not that there should be frailty,
The sin has not come to us.

'An evil day when the Serpent went
To the father to his city!
She has perverted the times in this world,
So that there came decay which was not original.

'By greed and lust he has slain us,
Through which he has ruined his noble race:
The withered body has gone to the fold of torment,
And everlasting abode of torture.

'It is a law of pride in this world
To believe in the creatures, to forget God,
Overthrow by diseases, and old age,
Destruction of the soul through deception.

'A noble salvation will come
From the King who has created us,
A white law will come over seas,
Besides being God, He will be man.

'This shape, he on whom thou lookest,
Will come to thy parts;
'Tis mine to journey to her house,
To the woman in Line-mag.

'For it is Moninnan, the son of Ler,
From the chariot in the shape of a man,
Of his progeny will be a very short while
A fair man in a body of white clay.

'Monann, the descendant of Ler, will be
A vigorous bed-fellow to Caintigern:
He shall be called to his son in the beautiful world,
Fiachna will acknowledge him as his son.

'He will delight the company of every fairy-knoll,
He will be the darling of every goodly land,
He will make known secrets – a course of wisdom –
In the world, without being feared.

'He will be in the shape of every beast,
Both on the azure sea and on land,
He will be a dragon before hosts at the onset,
He will be a wolf of every great forest.

'He will be a stag with horns of silver
In the land where chariots are driven,
He will be a speckled salmon in a full pool,
He will be a seal, he will be a fair-white swan.

'He will be throughout long ages
An hundred years in fair kingship,
He will cut down battalions, – a lasting grave –
He will redden fields, a wheel around the track.

'It will be about kings with a champion
That he will be known as a valiant hero,
Into the strongholds of a land on a height
I shall send an appointed end from Islay.

'High shall I place him with princes,
He will be overcome by a son of error;
Moninnan, the son of Ler,
Will be his father, his tutor.

'He will be – his time will be short –
Fifty years in this world:
A dragonstone from the sea will kill him
In the fight at Senlabor.

'He will ask a drink from Loch Ló,
While he looks at the stream of blood,
The white host will take him under a wheel of clouds
To the gathering where there is no sorrow.

'Steadily then let Bran row,
Not far to the Land of Women,
Emne with many hues of hospitality
Thou wilt reach before the setting of the sun.'

Thereupon Bran went from him. And he saw an island. He rows round about it, and a large host was gaping and laughing. They were all looking at Bran and his people, but would not stay to converse with them. They continued to give forth gusts of laughter at them. Bran sent one of his people on the island. He ranged himself with the others, and was gaping at them like the other men of the island. He kept rowing round about the island. Whenever his man came past Bran, his comrades would address him. But he would not converse with them, but would only look at them and gape at them. The name of this island is the Island of Joy. Thereupon they left him there.

It was not long thereafter when they reached the Land of Women. They saw the leader of the women at the port. Said the chief of the women: 'Come hither on land, O Bran son of Febal! Welcome is thy advent!' Bran did not venture to go on shore. The woman throws a ball of thread to Bran straight over his face. Bran put his hand on the ball, which clave to his palm. The thread of the ball was in the woman's hand, and she pulled the coracle towards the port. Thereupon they went into a large house, in which was a bed for every couple, even thrice nine beds. The food that was put on every dish vanished not from them. It seemed a year to them that they were there, – it chanced to be many years. No savour was wanting to them.

Home-sickness seized one of them, even Nechtan the son of Collbran. His kindred kept praying Bran that he should go to Ireland with him. The woman said to them their going would make them rue. However, they went, and the woman said that none of them should touch the land, and that they should visit and take with them the man whom they had left in the Island of Joy.

Then they went until they arrived at a gathering at Srub Brain. The men asked of them who it was came over the sea. Said Bran: 'I am Bran the son of Febal,' saith he. However, the other saith: 'We do not know such a one, though the Voyage of Bran is in our ancient stories.'

The man leaps from them out of the coracle. As soon as he touched the earth of Ireland, forthwith he was a heap of ashes, as though he had been in the earth for many hundred years. 'Twas then that Bran sang this quatrain:

'For Collbran's son great was the folly
To lift his hand against age,
Without any one casting a wave of pure water
Over Nechtan, Collbran's son.'

Thereupon, to the people of the gathering Bran told all his wanderings from the beginning until that time. And he wrote these quatrains in Ogam, and then bade them farewell. And from that hour his wanderings are not known.

 # NOTES

Source: Kuno Meyer (editor and translator), *The Voyage of Bran mac Febal to the Land of the Living . . . with an essay on the Irish Version of the Hay Otherworld by Alfred Nutt*, London: D. Nutt 1895–7 (2 vols).

This is one of the most famous and justly renowned stories of the *immram* type. Dating from around the eighth or ninth centuries, it takes its hero, from the moment when a mysterious fairy woman enters his hall with her magical silver branch, out of the ordinary world and into the realm of the people of the *sidhe*. In the process, it gives us a remarkable range of poetic and visionary descriptions of the Otherworld, both above and beneath the waves. The Silver Branch itself was traditionally used to announce the arrival of a bard or storyteller in the court, though in this, as other stories of this genre, it fulfils the role of placing those who hear it into an enchanted sleep in which they could travel to the Otherworld and remain there for a time that was no time at all in the outer world. Here the mysterious woman brings a branch from Emain Macha, the Otherworld home of the *sidhe* or fairy folk of Ireland. (Only 30 of her 50 quatrains have been included here.) As a result, Bran sets out on a remarkable voyage, and almost at once encounters the sea god Manannan mac Lir, who utters a series of prophecies. Bran then sails on to a rich variety of islands, each of which illustrates another aspect of the endlessly varied Otherworld. The story became a pattern for many other tales, few of which (with the possible exception of 'The Voyage of Maildun') managed to emulate its powerful style and rich magical allusion.

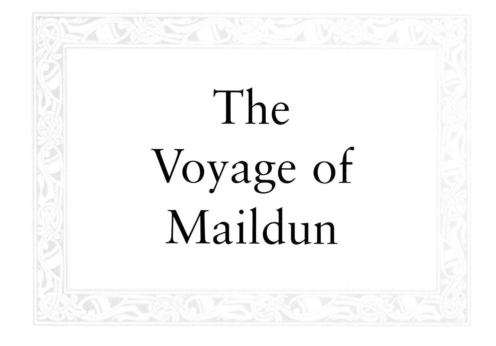

The Voyage of Maildun

MAILDUN'S CHILDHOOD AND YOUTH – HE BEGINS HIS VOYAGE
IN QUEST OF THE PLUNDERERS WHO SLEW HIS FATHER

HERE WAS ONCE an illustrious man of the tribe of Owenaght of Ninus, Allil Ocar Aga by name, a goodly hero, and lord of his own tribe and territory. One time, when he was in his house unguarded, a fleet of plunderers landed on the coast, and spoiled his territory. The chief fled for refuge to the church of Dooclone; but the spoilers followed him thither, slew him, and burned the church over his head.

Not long after Allil's death, a son was born to him. The child's mother gave him the name of Maildun; and, wishing to conceal his birth, she brought him to the queen of that country, who was her dear friend. The queen took him to her, and gave out that he was her own child; and he was brought up with the king's sons, slept in the same cradle with them, and was fed from the same breast and from the same cup. He was a very lovely child; and the people who saw him thought it doubtful if there was any other child living at the time equally beautiful.

As he grew up to be a young man, the noble qualities of his mind gradually unfolded themselves. He was high-spirited and generous, and he loved all sorts of manly exercises. In ball-playing, in running and leaping, in throwing the stone, in chess-playing, in rowing, and in horse-racing, he surpassed all the youths that came to the king's palace, and won the palm in every contest.

One day, when the young men were at their games, a certain youth among them grew envious of Maildun; and he said, in an angry and haughty tone of voice –

'It is a cause of much shame to us that we have to yield in every game, whether of skill or of strength, whether on land or on water, to an obscure youth, of whom no one can tell who is his father or his mother, or what race or tribe he belongs to.'

On hearing this, Maildun ceased at once from play; for until that moment he believed that he was the son of the king of the Owenaght, and of the queen who had nursed him. And going anon to the queen, he told her what had happened; and he said to her –

'If I am not thy son, I will neither eat nor drink till thou tell me who my father and mother are.'

She tried to soothe him, and said, 'Why do you worry yourself searching after this matter? Give no heed to the words of this envious youth. Am I not a mother to you? And in all this country, is there any mother who loves her son better than I love you?'

He answered, 'All this is quite true; yet I pray thee let me know who my parents are.'

The queen then, seeing that he would not be put off, brought him to his mother, and put him into her hands. And when he had spoken with her, he asked her to tell him who his father was.

'You are bent on a foolish quest, my child,' she said; 'for even if you knew all about your father, the knowledge would bring neither advantage nor happiness to you; for he died before you were born.'

'Even so,' he replied, 'I wish to know who he was.'

So his mother told him the truth, saying, 'Your father was Allil Ocar Aga, of the tribe of Owenaght of Ninus.'

Maildun then set out for his father's territory; and his three foster brothers, namely, the king's three sons, who were noble and handsome youths like himself, went with him. When the people of his tribe found out that the strange youth was the son of their chief, whom the plunderers had slain years before, and when they were told that the three others were the king's sons, they gave them all a joyful welcome, feasting them, and showing them much honour; so that Maildun was made quite happy, and soon forgot all the abasement and trouble he had undergone.

Some time after this, it happened that a number of young people were in the churchyard of Dooclone – the same church in which Maildun's father had been slain – exercising themselves in casting a hand-stone. The game was to throw the stone clear over the charred roof of the church that had been burned; and Maildun was there contending among the others. A foul-tongued fellow named Brickna, a servant of the people who owned the church, was standing by; and he said to Maildun –

'It would better become you to avenge the man who was burned to death here, than to be amusing yourself casting a stone over his bare, burnt bones.'

'Who was he?' inquired Maildun.

'Allil Ocar Aga, your father,' replied the other.

'Who slew him?' asked Maildun.

'Plunderers from a fleet slew him and burned him in this church,' replied Brickna; 'and the same plunderers are still sailing in the same fleet.'

Maildun was disturbed and sad after hearing this. He dropped the stone that he held in his hand, folded his cloak round him, and buckled on his shield. And he left the company, and began to inquire of all he met, the road to the plunderers' ships. For a long time he could get no tidings of them; but at last some persons, who knew where the fleet lay, told him that it was a long way off, and that there was no reaching it except by sea.

Now Maildun was resolved to find out these plunderers, and to avenge on them the death of his father. So he went without delay into Corcomroe, to the druid Nuca, to seek his advice about building a curragh, and to ask also for a charm to protect him, both while building it, and while sailing on the sea afterwards.

The druid gave him full instructions. He told him the day he should begin to build his curragh, and the exact day on which he was to set out on his voyage; and he was very particular about the number of the crew, which, he said, was to be sixty chosen men, neither more nor less.

So Maildun built a large triple-hide curragh, following the druid's directions in every particular; chose his crew of sixty, among whom were his two friends, Germane and Diuran Lekerd; and on the day appointed put out to sea.

When he had got only a very little way from the land, he saw his three foster brothers running down to the shore, signalling and calling out to him to return and take them on board; for they said they wished to go with him.

'We shall not turn back,' said Maildun; 'and you cannot come with us; for we have already got our exact number.'

'We will swim after you in the sea till we are drowned, if you do not return for us,' replied they; and so saying, the three plunged in and swam after the curragh.

When Maildun saw this, he turned his vessel towards them, and took them on board rather than let them be drowned.

THE FIRST ISLAND – TIDINGS OF THE PLUNDERERS

They sailed that day and night, as well as the whole of next day, till darkness came on again; and at midnight they saw two small bare islands, with two great houses on them near the shore. When they drew near, they heard the sounds of merriment and laughter, and the shouts of revellers intermingled with the loud voices of warriors boasting of their deeds. And listening to catch the conversation, they heard one warrior say to another –

'Stand off from me, for I am a better warrior than thou; it was I who slew Allil Ocar Aga, and burned Dooclone over his head; and no one has ever dared to avenge it on me. Thou hast never done a great deed like that!'

'Now surely,' said Germane and Diuran to Maildun, 'Heaven has guided our ship to this place! Here is an easy victory. Let us now sack this house, since God has revealed our enemies to us, and delivered them into our hands!'

While they were yet speaking, the wind arose, and a great tempest suddenly broke on them. And they were driven violently before the storm, all that night and a part of next day, into the great and boundless ocean; so that they saw neither the islands they had left nor any other land; and they knew not whither they were going.

Then Maildun said, 'Take down your sail and put by your oars, and let the curragh drift before the wind in whatsoever direction it pleases God to lead us;' which was done.

He then turned to his foster brothers, and said to them, 'This evil has befallen us because we took you into the curragh, thereby violating the druid's directions; for he forbade me to go to sea with more than sixty men for my crew, and we had that number before you joined us. Of a surety more evil will come of it.'

His foster brothers answered nothing to this, but remained silent.

THE ISLAND OF THE MONSTROUS ANTS

For three days and three nights they saw no land. On the morning of the fourth day, while it was yet dark, they heard a sound to the north-east; and Germane said –

'This is the voice of the waves breaking on the shore.'

As soon as it was light they saw land and made towards it. While they were casting lots to know who should go and explore the country, they saw great flocks of ants coming down to the beach, each of them as large as a foal. The people judged by their numbers, and by their eager and hungry look, that they were bent on eating both ship and crew; so they turned their vessel round and sailed quickly away.

> Their multitudes countless, prodigious their size;
>   Were never such ants seen or heard of before.
> They struggled and tumbled and plunged for the prize,
> And fiercely the famine fire blazed from their eyes,
>   As they ground with their teeth the red sand of the shore!

THE TERRACED ISLE OF BIRDS

Again for three days and three nights they saw no land. But on the morning of the fourth day they heard the murmur of the waves on the beach; and as the day dawned, they saw a large high island, with terraces all round it, rising one behind another. On the terraces grew rows of tall trees, on which were perched great numbers of large, bright-coloured birds.

When the crew were about to hold council as to who should visit the island and see whether the birds were tame, Maildun himself offered to go. So he went with a few companions; and they viewed the island warily, but found nothing to hurt or alarm them; after which they caught great numbers of the birds and brought them to their ship.

> A shield-shaped island, with terraces crowned,
> And great trees circling round and round:
> From the summit down to the wave-washed rocks,
> There are bright-coloured birds in myriad flocks –
> Their plumes are radiant; but hunger is keen;
>   So the birds are killed,
>   Till the curragh is filled,
> And the sailors embark on the ocean green!

A MONSTER

They sailed from this, and on the fourth day discovered a large, sandy island, on which, when they came near, they saw a huge, fearful animal standing on the beach, and looking at them very attentively. He was somewhat like a horse in shape; but his legs were like the legs of a dog; and he had great, sharp claws of a blue colour.

23

Maildun, having viewed this monster for some time, liked not his look; and, telling his companions to watch him closely, for that he seemed bent on mischief, he bade the oarsmen row very slowly towards land.

The monster seemed much delighted when the ship drew nigh the shore, and gambolled and pranced about with joy on the beach, before the eyes of the voyagers; for he intended to eat the whole of them the moment they landed.

'He seems not at all sorry to see us coming,' said Maildun; 'but we must avoid him and put back from the shore.'

This was done. And when the animal observed them drawing off, he ran down in a great rage to the very water's edge, and digging up large, round pebbles with his sharp claws, he began to fling them at the vessel; but the crew soon got beyond his reach, and sailed into the open sea.

A horrible monster, with blazing eyes,
In shape like a horse and tremendous in size,
    Awaiting the curragh, they saw;
        With big bony jaws
        And murderous claws,
    That filled them with terror and awe:
        How gleeful he dances,
        And bellows and prances,
    As near to the island they draw;
        Expecting a feast –
        The bloodthirsty beast –
With his teeth like edge of a saw:
        Then he ran to the shore,
        With a deafening roar,
Intending to swallow them raw:
        But the crew, with a shout,
        Put their vessel about,
And escaped from his ravenous maw!

THE DEMON HORSE-RACE

After sailing a long distance, they came in view of a broad, flat island. It fell to the lot of Germane to go and examine it, and he did not think the task a pleasant one. Then his friend Diuran said to him –

'I will go with you this time; and when next it falls to my lot to visit an island, you shall come with me.' So both went together.

They found the island very large; and some distance from the shore they came to a broad green race-course, in which they saw immense hoof-marks, the size of a ship's sail, or of a large dining-table. They found nut-shells, as large as helmets, scattered about; and although they could see no one, they observed all the marks and tokens that people of huge size were lately employed there at sundry kinds of work.

Seeing these strange signs, they became alarmed, and went and called their companions from the boat to view them. But the others, when they had seen them, were also struck with fear, and all quickly retired from the place and went on board their curragh.

When they had got a little way from the land, they saw dimly, as it were through a mist, a vast multitude of people on the sea, of gigantic size and demoniac look, rushing along the crests of the waves with great outcry. As soon as this shadowy host had landed, they went to the green, where they arranged a horse-race.

The horses were swifter than the wind; and as they pressed forward in the race, the multitudes raised a mighty shout like thunder, which reached the crew as if it were beside them. Maildun and his men, as they sat in their curragh, heard the strokes of the whips and the cries of the riders; and though the race was far off, they could distinguish the eager words of the spectators: – 'Observe the grey horse!' 'See that chestnut horse!' 'Watch the horse with the white spots!' 'My horse leaps better than yours!'

After seeing and hearing these things, the crew sailed away from the island as quickly as they were able, into the open ocean, for they felt quite sure that the multitude they saw was a gathering of demons.

A spacious isle of meadowy plains, with a broad and sandy shore:
Two bold and trusty spies are sent, its wonders to explore.
Mysterious signs, strange, awful sights, now meet the wanderers' eyes:
Vast hoof-marks, and the traces dire of men of monstrous size:
And lo! on the sea, in countless hosts, their shadowy forms expand;
They pass the affrighted sailors by, and like demons they rush to land;
They mount their steeds, and the race is run, in the midst of hell's uproar:
Then the wanderers quickly raise their sails, and leave the accursèd shore.

THE PALACE OF SOLITUDE

They suffered much from hunger and thirst this time, for they sailed a whole week without making land; but at the end of that time they came in sight of a high island, with a large and very splendid house on the beach near the water's edge. There were two doors – one turned inland, and the other facing the sea; and the door that looked towards the sea was closed with a great flat stone. In this stone was an opening, through which the waves, as they beat against the door every day, threw numbers of salmon into the house.

The voyagers landed, and went through the whole house without meeting any one. But they saw in one large room an ornamented couch, intended for the head of the house, and in each of the other rooms was a larger one for three members of the family: and there was a cup of crystal on a little table before each couch. They found abundance of food and ale, and they ate and drank till they were satisfied, thanking God for having relieved them from hunger and thirst.

> Aloft, high towering o'er the ocean's foam,
> The spacious mansion rears its glittering dome.
> Each day the billows, through the marble door,
> Shoot living salmon floundering on the floor.
> Couches that lure the sailors to recline,
> Abundant food, brown ale, and sparkling wine;
> Tables and chairs in order duly placed,
> With crystal cups and golden goblets graced.
> But not a living soul the wanderers found;
> 'Twas silence all and solitude profound.
> They eat and drink, give thanks, then hoist their sail,
> And skim the deep once more, obedient to the gale.

THE ISLAND OF THE WONDERFUL APPLE TREE

After leaving this, they suffered again from hunger, till they came to an island with a high hill round it on every side. A single apple tree grew in the middle, very tall and slender, and all its branches were in like manner exceedingly slender, and of wonderful length, so that they grew over the hill and down to the sea.

When the ship came near the island, Maildun caught one of the branches in his hand. For three days and three nights the ship coasted the island, and during all this time he held the branch, letting it slide through his hand, till on the third day he found a cluster of seven apples on the very end. Each of these apples supplied the travellers with food and drink for forty days and forty nights.

THE ISLAND OF BLOODTHIRSTY QUADRUPEDS

A beautiful island next came in view, in which they saw, at a distance, multitudes of large animals shaped like horses. The voyagers, as they drew near, viewed them attentively, and soon observed that one of them opened his mouth and bit a great piece out of the side of the animal that stood next him, bringing away skin and flesh. Immediately after, another did the same to the nearest of his fellows. And, in short, the voyagers saw that all the animals in the island kept worrying and tearing each other from time to time in this manner; so that the ground was covered far and wide with the blood that streamed from their sides.

> In needless strife they oft contend,
>   A cruel, mutual-mangling brood;
> Their flesh with gory tusks they rend,
>   And crimson all the isle with blood.

AN EXTRAORDINARY MONSTER

The next island had a wall all round it. When they came near the shore, an animal of vast size, with a thick, rough skin, started up inside the wall, and ran round the island with the swiftness of the wind. When he had ended his race, he went to a high point, and standing on a large, flat stone, began to exercise himself according to his daily custom, in the following manner. He kept turning himself completely round and round in his skin, the bones and flesh moving, while the skin remained at rest.

When he was tired of this exercise, he rested a little; and he then began turning his skin continually round his body, down at one side and up at the other like a mill-wheel; but the bones and flesh did not move.

After spending some time at this sort of work, he started and ran round the island as at first, as if to refresh himself. He then went back to the same spot, and this time, while the skin that covered the lower part of his body remained without motion, he whirled the skin of the upper part round and round like the movement of a flat-lying millstone. And it was in this manner that he spent most of his time on the island.

Maildun and his people, after they had seen these strange doings, thought it better not to venture nearer. So they put out to sea in great haste. The monster, observing them about to fly, ran down to the beach to seize the ship; but finding that they had got out of his reach, he began to fling round stones at them with great force and an excellent aim. One of them struck Maildun's shield and went quite through it, lodging in the keel of the curragh; after which the voyagers got beyond his range and sailed away.

In a wall-circled isle a big monster they found,
    With a hide like an elephant, leathery and bare;
He threw up his heels with a wonderful bound,
    And ran round the isle with the speed of a hare.

But a feat more astounding has yet to be told:
    He turned round and round in his leathery skin;
His bones and his flesh and his sinews he rolled –
    He was resting outside while he twisted within!

Then, changing his practice with marvellous skill,
    His carcase stood rigid and round went his hide;
It whirled round his bones like the wheel of a mill –
    He was resting within while he twisted outside!

Next, standing quite near on a green little hill,
    After galloping round in the very same track,
While the skin of his belly stood perfectly still,
    Like a millstone he twisted the skin of his back!

But Maildun and his men put to sea in their boat,
    For they saw his two eyes looking over the wall;
And they knew by the way that he opened his throat,
    He intended to swallow them, curragh and all!

Not daring to land on this island, they turned away hurriedly, much disheartened, not knowing whither to turn or where to find a resting-place. They sailed for a long time, suffering much from hunger and thirst, and praying fervently to be relieved from their distress. At last, when they were beginning to sink into a state of despondency, being quite worn out with toil and hardship of every kind, they sighted land.

It was a large and beautiful island, with innumerable fruit trees scattered over its surface, bearing abundance of gold-coloured apples. Under the trees they saw herds of short, stout animals, of a bright red colour, shaped somewhat like pigs; but coming nearer, and looking more closely, they perceived with astonishment that the animals were all fiery, and that their bright colour was caused by the red flames which penetrated and lighted up their bodies.

The voyagers now observed several of them approach one of the trees in a body, and striking the trunk all together with their hind legs, they shook down some of the apples and ate them. In this manner the animals employed themselves every day, from early morning till the setting of the sun, when they retired into deep caves, and were seen no more till next morning.

Numerous flocks of birds were swimming on the sea, all round the island. From morning till noon, they continued to swim away from the land, farther and farther out to sea; but at noon they turned round, and from that to sunset they swam back towards the shore. A little after sunset, when the animals had retired to their caves, the birds flocked in on the island, and spread themselves over it, plucking the apples from the trees and eating them.

Maildun proposed that they should land on the island, and gather some of the fruit, saying that it was not harder or more dangerous for them than for the birds; so two of the men were sent beforehand to examine the place. They found the ground hot under their feet, for the fiery animals, as they lay at rest, heated the earth all around and above their caves; but the two scouts persevered notwithstanding, and brought away some of the apples.

When morning dawned, the birds left the island and swam out to sea; and the fiery animals, coming forth from their caves, went among the trees as usual, and ate the apples till evening. The crew remained in their curragh all day; and as soon as the animals had gone into their caves for the night, and the birds had taken their place, Maildun landed with all his men. And they plucked the apples till morning, and brought them on board, till they had gathered as much as they could stow into their vessel.

THE PALACE OF THE LITTLE CAT

After rowing for a long time, their store of apples failed them, and they had nothing to eat or drink; so that they suffered sorely under a hot sun, and their mouths and nostrils were filled with the briny smell of the sea. At last they came in sight of land – a little island with a large palace on it. Around the palace was a wall, white all over, without stain or flaw, as if it had been built of burnt lime, or carved out of one unbroken rock of chalk; and where it looked towards the sea it was so lofty that it seemed almost to reach the clouds.

The gate of this outer wall was open, and a number of fine houses, all snowy white, were ranged round on the inside, enclosing a level court in the middle, on which all the houses opened. Maildun and his people entered the largest of them, and walked through several rooms without meeting with any one. But on reaching the principal apartment, they saw in it a small cat, playing among a number of low, square, marble pillars, which stood ranged in a row; and his play was, leaping continually from the top of one pillar to the top of another. When the men entered the room, the cat looked at them for a moment, but returned to his play anon, and took no further notice of them.

Looking now to the room itself, they saw three rows of precious jewels ranged round the wall from one door-jamb to the other. The first was a row of brooches of gold and silver, with their pins fixed in the wall, and their heads outwards; the second, a row of torques of gold and silver; and the third, a row of great swords, with hilts of gold and silver.

Round the room were arranged a number of couches, all pure white and richly ornamented. Abundant food of various kinds was spread on tables, among which they observed a boiled ox and a roast hog; and there were many large drinking-horns, full of good, intoxicating ale.

'Is it for us that this food has been prepared?' said Maildun to the cat.

The cat, on hearing the question, ceased from playing, and looked at him; but he recommenced his play immediately. Whereupon Maildun told his people that the dinner was meant for them; and they all sat down, and ate and drank till they were satisfied, after which they rested and slept on the couches.

When they awoke, they poured what was left of the ale into one vessel; and they gathered the remnants of the food to bring them away. As they were about to go, Maildun's eldest foster brother asked him –

'Shall I bring one of those large torques away with me?'

'By no means,' said Maildun; 'it is well that we have got food and rest. Bring nothing away, for it is certain that this house is not left without some one to guard it.'

The young man, however, disregarding Maildun's advice, took down one of the torques and brought it away. But the cat followed him, and overtook him in the middle of the court, and, springing on him like a blazing, fiery arrow, he went through his body, and reduced it in a moment to a heap of ashes. He then returned to the room, and, leaping up on one of the pillars, sat upon it.

Maildun turned back, bringing the torque with him, and, approaching the cat, spoke some soothing words; after which he put the torque back to the place from which it had been taken. Having done this, he collected the ashes of his foster brother, and, bringing them to the shore, cast them into the sea. They all then went on board the curragh, and continued their voyage, grieving for their lost companion, but thanking God for His many mercies to them.

AN ISLAND THAT DYED BLACK AND WHITE

On the morning of the third day, they came to another island, which was divided into two parts by a wall of brass running across the middle. They saw two great flocks of sheep, one on each side of the wall; and all those at one side were black, while those at the other side were white.

A very large man was employed in dividing and arranging the sheep; and he often took up a sheep and threw it with much ease over the wall from one side to the other. When he threw over a white sheep among the black ones, it became black immediately; and in like manner, when he threw a black sheep over, it was instantly changed to white.

The travellers were very much alarmed on witnessing these doings; and Maildun said –

'It is very well that we know so far. Let us now throw something on shore, to see whether it also will change colour; if it does, we shall avoid the island.'

So they took a branch with black-coloured bark and threw it towards the white sheep, and no sooner did it touch the ground than it became white. They then threw a white-coloured branch on the side of the black sheep, and in a moment it turned black.

'It is very lucky for us,' said Maildun, 'that we did not land on the island, for doubtless our colour would have changed like the colour of the branches.'

So they put about with much fear, and sailed away.

THE ISLAND OF THE BURNING RIVER

On the third day, they came in view of a large, broad island, on which they saw a herd of gracefully shaped swine; and they killed one small porkling for food. Towards the centre rose a high mountain, which they resolved to ascend, in order to view the island; and Germane and Diuran Lekerd were chosen for this task.

When they had advanced some distance towards the mountain, they came to a broad, shallow river; and sitting down on the bank to rest, Germane dipped the point of his lance into the water, which instantly burned off the top, as if the lance had been thrust into a furnace. So they went no farther.

On the opposite side of the river, they saw a herd of animals like great horn-less oxen, all lying down; and a man of gigantic size near them: and Germane began to strike his spear against his shield, in order to rouse the cattle.

'Why are you frightening the poor young calves in that manner?' demanded the big shepherd, in a tremendous voice.

Germane, astonished to find that such large animals were nothing more than calves, instead of answering the question, asked the big man where the mothers of those calves were.

'They are on the side of yonder mountain,' he replied.

Germane and Diuran waited to hear no more; but, returning to their companions, told them all they had seen and heard; after which the crew embarked and left the island.

THE MILLER OF HELL

The next island they came to, which was not far off from the last, had a large mill on it; and near the door stood the miller, a huge-bodied, strong, burly man. They saw numberless crowds of men and horses laden with corn, coming towards the mill; and when their corn was ground they went away towards the west. Great herds of all kinds of cattle covered the plain as far as the eye could reach, and among them many wagons laden with every kind of wealth that is produced on the ridge of the world. All these the miller put into the mouth of his mill to be ground; and all, as they came forth, went westwards.

Maildun and his people now spoke to the miller, and asked him the name of the mill, and the meaning of all they had seen on the island. And he, turning quickly towards them, replied in few words –

'This mill is called the Mill of Inver-tre-Kenand, and I am the miller of hell. All the corn and all the riches of the world that men are dissatisfied with, or which they complain of in any way, are sent here to be ground; and also every precious article, and every kind of wealth, which men try to conceal from God. All these I grind in the Mill of Inver-tre-Kenand, and send them afterwards away to the west.'

He spoke no more, but turned round and busied himself again with his mill. And the voyagers, with much wonder and awe in their hearts, went to their curragh and sailed away.

THE ISLE OF WEEPING

After leaving this, they had not been long sailing when they discovered another large island, with a great multitude of people on it. They were all black, both skin and clothes, with black head-dresses also; and they kept walking about, sighing and weeping and wringing their hands, without the least pause or rest.

It fell to the lot of Maildun's second foster brother to go and examine the island. And when he went among the people, he also grew sorrowful, and fell to weeping and wringing his hands, with the others. Two of the crew were sent to bring him back; but they were unable to find him among the mourners; and, what was worse, in a little time they joined the crowd, and began to weep and lament like all the rest.

Maildun then chose four men to go and bring back the others by force, and he put arms in their hands, and gave them these directions –

'When you land on the island, fold your mantles round your faces, so as to cover your mouths and noses, that you may not breathe the air of the country; and look neither to the right nor to the left, neither at the earth nor at the sky, but fix your eyes on your own men till you have laid hands on them.'

They did exactly as they were told, and having come up with their two companions, namely, those who had been sent after Maildun's foster brother, they seized them and brought them back by force. But the other they could not find. When these two were asked what they had seen on the island, and why they began to weep, their only reply was –

'We cannot tell; we only know that we did what we saw the others doing.'

And after this the voyagers sailed away from the island, leaving Maildun's second foster brother behind.

THE ISLE OF THE FOUR PRECIOUS WALLS

The next was a high island, divided into four parts by four walls meeting in the centre. The first was a wall of gold; the second, a wall of silver; the third, a wall of copper; and the fourth, a wall of crystal. In the first of the four divisions were kings; in the second, queens; in the third, youths; and in the fourth, young maidens.

When the voyagers landed, one of the maidens came to meet them, and leading them forward to a house, gave them food. This food, which she dealt out to them from a small vessel, looked like cheese, and whatever taste pleased each person best, that was the taste he found on it. And after they had eaten till they were satisfied, they slept in a sweet sleep, as if gently intoxicated, for three days and three nights. When they awoke on the third day, they found themselves in their curragh on the open sea; and there was no appearance in any direction either of the maiden or of the island.

THE PALACE OF THE CRYSTAL BRIDGE

They came now to a small island, with a palace on it, having a copper chain in front, hung all over with a number of little silver bells. Straight before the door there was a fountain, spanned by a bridge of crystal, which led to the palace. They walked towards the bridge, meaning to cross it, but every time they stepped on it they fell backwards flat on the ground.

After some time, they saw a very beautiful young woman coming out of the palace, with a pail in her hand; and she lifted a crystal slab from the bridge, and, having filled her vessel from the fountain, she went back into the palace.

'This woman has been sent to keep house for Maildun,' said Germane.

'Maildun indeed!' said she, as she shut the door after her.

After this they began to shake the copper chain, and the tinkling of the silver bells was so soft and melodious that the voyagers gradually fell into a gentle, tranquil sleep, and slept so till next morning. When they awoke, they saw the same young woman coming forth from the palace, with the pail in her hand; and she lifted the crystal slab as before, filled her vessel, and returned into the palace.

'This woman has certainly been sent to keep house for Maildun,' said Germane.

'Wonderful are the powers of Maildun!' said she, as she shut the door of the court behind her.

They stayed in this place for three days and three nights, and each morning the maiden came forth in the same manner, and filled her pail. On the fourth day, she came towards them, splendidly and beautifully dressed, with her bright yellow hair bound by a circlet of gold, and wearing silver-work shoes on her small, white feet. She had a white mantle over her shoulders, which was fastened in front by a silver brooch studded with gold; and under all, next her soft, snow-white skin, was a garment of fine white silk.

'My love to you, Maildun, and to your companions,' she said; and she mentioned them all, one after another, calling each by his own proper name. 'My love to you,' said she. 'We knew well that you were coming to our island, for your arrival has long been foretold to us.'

The beautiful, young woman lifted a crystal slab from the bridge and filled her vessel from the fountain.

Then she led them to a large house standing by the sea, and she caused the curragh to be drawn high up on the beach. They found in the house a number of couches, one of which was intended for Maildun alone, and each of the others for three of his people. The woman then gave them, from one vessel, food which was like cheese; first of all ministering to Maildun, and then giving a triple share to every three of his companions; and whatever taste each man wished for, that was the taste he found on it. She then lifted the crystal slab at the bridge, filled her pail, and dealt out drink to them; and she knew exactly how much to give, both of food and of drink, so that each had enough and no more.

'This woman would make a fit wife for Maildun,' said his people. But while they spoke, she went from them with her pail in her hand.

When she was gone, Maildun's companions said to him, 'Shall we ask this maiden to become thy wife?'

He answered, 'What advantage will it be to you to ask her?'

She came next morning, and they said to her, 'Why dost thou not stay here with us? Wilt thou make friendship with Maildun; and wilt thou take him for thy husband?'

She replied that she and all those that lived on the island were forbidden to marry with the sons of men; and she told them that she could not disobey, as she knew not what sin or transgression was.

She then went from them to her house; and on the next morning, when she returned, and after she had ministered to them as usual, till they were satisfied with food and drink, and were become cheerful, they spoke the same words to her.

'To-morrow,' she replied, 'you will get an answer to your question;' and so saying, she walked towards her house, and they went to sleep on their couches.

When they awoke next morning, they found themselves lying in their curragh on the sea, beside a great high rock; and when they looked about, they saw neither the woman, nor the palace of the crystal bridge, nor any trace of the island where they had been sojourning.

THE ISLE OF SPEAKING BIRDS

One night, soon after leaving this, they heard in the distance, towards the northeast, a confused murmur of voices, as if from a great number of persons singing psalms. They followed the direction of the sound, in order to learn from what it proceeded; and at noon the next day, they came in view of an island, very hilly and lofty. It was full of birds, some black, some brown, and some speckled, who were all shouting and speaking with human voices; and it was from them that the great clamour came.

THE AGED HERMIT, AND THE HUMAN SOULS

At a little distance from this they found another small island, with many trees on it, some standing singly, and some in clusters, on which were perched great numbers of birds. They also saw an aged man on the island, who was covered thickly all over with long, white hair, and wore no other dress. And when they landed, they spoke to him, and asked him who he was and what race he belonged to.

'I am one of the men of Erin,' he replied. 'On a certain day, a long, long time ago, I embarked in a small curragh, and put out to sea on a pilgrimage; but I had got only a little way from shore, when my curragh became very unsteady, as if it were about to overturn. So I returned to land, and, in order to steady my boat, I placed under my feet at the bottom, a number of green surface sods, cut from one of the grassy fields of my own country, and began my voyage anew. Under the guidance of God, I arrived at this spot; and He fixed the sods in the sea for me, so that they formed a little island. At first I had barely room to stand; but every year, from that time to the present, the Lord has added one foot to the length and breadth of my island, till in the long lapse of ages it has grown to its present size.

And on one day in each year, He has caused a single tree to spring up, till the island has become covered with trees. Moreover, I am so old that my body, as you see, has become covered with long, white hair, so that I need no other dress.

'And the birds that ye see on the trees,' he continued, 'these are the souls of my children, and of all my descendants, both men and women, who are sent to this little island to abide with me according as they die in Erin. God has caused a well of ale to spring up for us on the island; and every morning the angels bring me half a cake, a slice of fish, and a cup of ale from the well; and in the evening the same allowance of food and ale is dealt out to each man and woman of my people. And it is in this manner that we live, and shall continue to live till the end of the world; for we are all awaiting here the day of judgment.'

Maildun and his companions were treated hospitably on the island by the old pilgrim for three days and three nights; and when they were taking leave of him, he told them that they should all reach their own country except one man.

THE ISLAND OF THE BIG BLACKSMITHS

When they had been for a long time tossed about on the waters, they saw land in the distance. On approaching the shore, they heard the roaring of a great bellows, and the thundering sound of smiths' hammers striking a large glowing mass of iron on an anvil; and every blow seemed to Maildun as loud as if a dozen men had brought down their sledges all together.

When they had come a little nearer, they heard the big voices of the smiths in eager talk.

'Are they near?' asked one.

'Hush! Silence!' says another.

'Who are they that you say are coming?' inquired a third.

'Little fellows, that are rowing towards our shore in a pigmy boat,' says the first.

When Maildun heard this, he hastily addressed the crew –

'Put back at once, but do not turn the curragh: reverse the sweep of your oars, and let her move stern forward, so that those giants may not perceive that we are flying!'

The crew at once obey, and the boat begins to move away from the shore, stern forward, as he had commanded.

The first smith again spoke. 'Are they near enough to the shore?' said he to the man who was watching.

'They seem to be at rest,' answered the other; 'for I cannot perceive that they are coming closer, and they have not turned their little boat to go back.'

In a short time the first smith asks again, 'What are they doing now?'

'I think,' said the watcher, 'they are flying; for it seems to me that they are now farther off than they were a while ago.'

At this the first smith rushed out of the forge – a huge, burly giant – holding, in the tongs which he grasped in his right hand, a vast mass of iron sparkling and glowing from the furnace; and, running down to the shore with long, heavy strides, he flung the red-hot mass with all his might after the curragh. It fell a little short, and plunged down just near the prow, causing the whole sea to hiss and boil and heave up around the boat. But they plied their oars, so that they quickly got beyond his reach, and sailed out into the open ocean.

35

THE CRYSTAL SEA

After a time, they came to a sea like green crystal. It was so calm and transparent that they could see the sand at the bottom quite clearly, sparkling in the sunlight. And in this sea they saw neither monsters, nor ugly animals, nor rough rocks; nothing but the clear water and the sunshine and the bright sand. For a whole day they sailed over it, admiring its splendour and beauty.

A LOVELY COUNTRY BENEATH THE WAVES

After leaving this they entered on another sea, which seemed like a clear, thin cloud; and it was so transparent, and appeared so light, that they thought at first it would not bear up the weight of the curragh.

Looking down, they could see, beneath the clear water, a beautiful country, with many mansions surrounded by groves and woods. In one place was a single tree; and, standing on its branches, they saw an animal fierce and terrible to look upon.

Round about the tree was a great herd of oxen grazing, and a man stood near to guard them, armed with shield and spear and sword; but when he looked up and saw the animal on the tree, he turned anon and fled with the utmost speed. Then the monster stretched forth his neck, and, darting his head downward, plunged his fangs into the back of the largest ox of the whole herd, lifted him off the ground into the tree, and swallowed him down in the twinkling of an eye; whereupon the whole herd took to flight.

When Maildun and his people saw this, they were seized with great terror; for they feared they should not be able to cross the sea over the monster, on account of the extreme mist-like thinness of the water; but after much difficulty and danger they got across it safely.

AN ISLAND GUARDED BY A WALL OF WATER

When they came to the next island, they observed with astonishment that the sea rose up over it on every side, steep and high, standing, as it were, like a wall all round it. When the people of the island saw the voyagers, they rushed hither and thither, shouting, 'There they are, surely! There they come again for another spoil!'

Then Maildun's people saw great numbers of men and women, all shouting and driving vast herds of horses, cows, and sheep. A woman began to pelt the crew from below with large nuts; she flung them so that they alighted on the waves round the boat, where they remained floating; and the crew gathered great quantities of them and kept them for eating.

When they turned to go away, the shouting ceased; and they heard one man calling aloud, 'Where are they now?' and another answering him, 'They are gone away!'

From what Maildun saw and heard at this island, it is likely that it had been foretold to the people that their country should some day be spoiled by certain marauders; and that they thought Maildun and his men were the enemies they expected.

A WATER-ARCH IN THE AIR

On the next island they saw a very wonderful thing, namely, a great stream of water which, gushing up out of the strand, rose into the air in the form of a rainbow, till it crossed the whole island and came down on the strand at the other side. They walked under it without getting wet; and they hooked down from it many large salmon. Great quantities of salmon of a very great size fell also out of the water over their heads down on the ground; so that the whole island smelled of fish, and it became troublesome to gather them on account of their abundance.

From the evening of Sunday till the evening of Monday, the stream never ceased to flow, and never changed its place, but remained spanning the island like a solid arch of water. Then the voyagers gathered the largest of the salmon, till they had as much as the curragh would hold; after which they sailed out into the great sea.

THE SILVER PILLAR OF THE SEA

The next thing they found after this was an immense silver pillar standing in the sea. It had eight sides, each of which was the width of an oar-stroke of the curragh, so that its whole circumference was eight oar-strokes. It rose out of the sea without any land or earth about it, nothing but the boundless ocean; and they could not see its base deep down in the water, neither were they able to see the top on account of its vast height.

A silver net hung from the top down to the very water, extending far out at one side of the pillar; and the meshes were so large that the curragh in full sail went through one of them. When they were passing through it, Diuran struck the mesh with the edge of his spear, and with the blow cut a large piece off it.

'Do not destroy the net,' said Maildun; 'for what we see is the work of great men.'

'What I have done,' answered Diuran, 'is for the honour of my God, and in order that the story of our adventures may be more readily believed; and I shall lay this silver as an offering on the altar of Armagh, if I ever reach Erin.'

That piece of silver weighed two ounces and a half, as it was reckoned afterwards by the people of the church of Armagh.

After this they heard some one speaking on the top of the pillar, in a loud, clear, glad voice; but they knew neither what he said, nor in what language he spoke.

AN ISLAND STANDING ON ONE PILLAR

The island they saw after this was named Encos ['one foot']; and it was so called because it was supported by a single pillar in the middle. They rowed all round it, seeking how they might get into it; but could find no landing-place. At the foot of the pillar, however, down deep in the water, they saw a door securely closed and locked, and they judged that this was the way into the island. They called aloud, to find out if any persons were living there; but they got no reply. So they left it, and put out to sea once more.

THE ISLAND QUEEN DETAINS THEM WITH HER
MAGIC THREAD-CLEW

The next island they reached was very large. On one side rose a lofty, smooth, heath-clad mountain, and all the rest of the island was a grassy plain. Near the sea-shore stood a great high palace, adorned with carvings and precious stones, and strongly fortified with a high rampart all round. After landing, they went towards the palace, and sat to rest on the bench before the gateway leading through the outer rampart; and, looking in through the open door, they saw a number of beautiful young maidens in the court.

After they had sat for some time, a rider appeared at a distance, coming swiftly towards the palace; and on a near approach, the travellers perceived that it was a lady, young and beautiful and richly dressed. She wore a blue, rustling silk head-dress; a silver-fringed purple cloak hung from her shoulders; her gloves were embroidered with gold thread; and her feet were laced becomingly in close-fitting scarlet sandals. One of the maidens came out and held her horse, while she dismounted and entered the palace; and soon after she had gone in, another of the maidens came towards Maildun and his companions and said –

'You are welcome to this island. Come into the palace; the queen has sent me to invite you, and is waiting to receive you.'

They followed the maiden into the palace; and the queen bade them welcome, and received them kindly. Then, leading them into a large hall in which a plentiful dinner was laid out, she bade them sit down and eat. A dish of choice food and a crystal goblet of wine were placed before Maildun; while a single dish and a single drinking-bowl, with a triple quantity of meat and drink, were laid before each three of his companions. And having eaten and drunk till they were satisfied, they went to sleep on soft couches till morning.

Next day, the queen addressed Maildun and his companions –

'Stay now in this country, and do not go a-wandering any longer over the wide ocean from island to island. Old age or sickness shall never come upon you; but you shall be always as young as you are at present, and you shall live for ever a life of ease and pleasure.'

'Tell us,' said Maildun, 'how you pass your life here.'

'That is no hard matter,' answered the queen. 'The good king who formerly ruled over this island was my husband, and these fair young maidens that you see are our children. He died after a long reign, and as he left no son, I now reign, the sole ruler of the island. And every day I go to the Great Plain, to administer justice and to decide causes among my people.'

'Wilt thou go from us to-day?' asked Maildun.

'I must needs go even now,' she replied, 'to give judgments among the people; but as to you, you will all stay in this house till I return in the evening, and you need not trouble yourselves with any labour or care.'

They remained in that island during the three months of winter. And these three months appeared to Maildun's companions as long as three years, for they began to have an earnest desire to return to their native land. At the end of that time, one of them said to Maildun –

'We have been a long time here; why do we not return to our own country?'

'What you say is neither good nor sensible,' answered Maildun, 'for we shall not find in our own country anything better than we have here.'

But this did not satisfy his companions, and they began to murmur loudly. '38 'It is quite clear,' said they, 'that Maildun loves the queen of this island;

and as this is so, let him stay here; but as for us, we will return to our own country.'

Maildun, however, would not consent to remain after them, and he told them that he would go away with them.

Now, on a certain day, not long after this conversation, as soon as the queen had gone to the Great Plain to administer justice, according to her daily custom, they got their curragh ready and put out to sea. They had not gone very far from land when the queen came riding towards the shore; and, seeing how matters stood, she went into the palace and soon returned with a ball of thread in her hand.

Walking down to the water's edge, she flung the ball after the curragh, but held the end of the thread in her hand. Maildun caught the ball as it was passing, and it clung to his hand; and the queen, gently pulling the thread towards her, drew back the curragh to the very spot from which they had started in the little harbour. And when they had landed, she made them promise that if ever this happened again, some one should always stand up in the boat and catch the ball.

The voyagers abode on the island, much against their will, for nine months longer. For every time they attempted to escape, the queen brought them back by means of the clew, as she had done at first, Maildun always catching the ball.

At the end of the nine months, the men held council, and this is what they said –

'We know now that Maildun does not wish to leave the island; for he loves this queen very much, and he catches the ball whenever we try to escape, in order that we may be brought back to the palace.'

Maildun replied, 'Let some one else attend to the ball next time, and let us try whether it will cling to his hand.'

They agreed to this, and, watching their opportunity, they again put off towards the open sea. The queen arrived, as usual, before they had gone very far, and flung the ball after them as before. Another man of the crew caught it, and it clung as firmly to his hand as to Maildun's; and the queen began to draw the curragh towards the shore. But Diuran, drawing his sword, cut off the man's hand, which fell with the ball into the sea; and the men gladly plying their oars, the curragh resumed her outward voyage.

When the queen saw this, she began to weep and lament, wringing her hands and tearing her hair with grief; and her maidens also began to weep and cry aloud and clap their hands, so that the whole palace was full of grief and lamentation. But none the less did the men bend to their oars, and the curragh sailed away; and it was in this manner that the voyagers made their escape from the island.

THE ISLE OF INTOXICATING WINE-FRUITS

They were now a long time tossed about on the great billows, when at length they came in view of an island with many trees on it. These trees were somewhat like hazels, and they were laden with a kind of fruit which the voyagers had not seen before, extremely large, and not very different in appearance from apples, except that they had a rough, berry-like rind.

After the crew had plucked all the fruit off one small tree, they cast lots who should try them, and the lot fell on Maildun. So he took some of them, and, squeezing the juice into a vessel, drank it. It threw him into a sleep of intoxication so deep that he seemed to be in a trance rather than in a natural slumber, without breath or motion, and with the red foam on his lips. And from that hour till the same hour next day, no one could tell whether he was living or dead.

When he awoke next day, he bade his people to gather as much of the fruit as they could bring away with them; for the world, as he told them, never produced anything of such surpassing goodness. They pressed out the juice of the fruit till they had filled all their vessels; and so powerful was it to produce intoxication and sleep, that, before drinking it, they had to mix a large quantity of water with it to moderate its strength.

THE ISLE OF THE MYSTIC LAKE

The island they came to next was larger than most of those they had seen. On one side grew a wood of yew trees and great oaks; and on the other side was a grassy plain, with one small lake in the midst. A noble-looking house stood on the near part of the plain, with a small church not far off; and numerous flocks of sheep browsed over the whole island.

The travellers went to the church, and found in it a hermit, with snow-white beard and hair, and all the other marks of great old age. Maildun asked who he was, and whence he had come.

He replied, 'I am one of the fifteen people, who, following the example of our master, Brendan of Birra, sailed on a pilgrimage out into the great ocean. After many wanderings, we settled on this island, where we lived for a long time; but my companions died one after another, and of all who came hither, I alone am left.'

The old pilgrim then showed them Brendan's satchel, which he and his companions had brought with them on their pilgrimage; and Maildun kissed it, and all bowed down in veneration before it. And he told them that as long as they remained there, they might eat of the sheep and of the other food of the island; but to waste nothing.

One day, as they were seated on a hill, gazing out over the sea, they saw what they took to be a black cloud coming towards them from the south-west. They continued to view it very closely as it came nearer and nearer; and at last they perceived with amazement that it was an immense bird, for they saw quite plainly the slow, heavy flapping of his wings. When he reached the island, he alighted on a little hillock over the lake; and they felt no small alarm, for they thought, on account of his vast size, that if he saw them, he might seize them in his talons, and carry them off over the sea. So they hid themselves under trees and in the crannies of rocks; but they never lost sight of the bird, for they were bent on watching his movements.

He appeared very old, and he held in one claw a branch of a tree, which he had brought with him over the sea, larger and heavier than the largest full-grown oak. It was covered with fresh, green leaves, and was heavily laden with clusters of fruit, red and rich-looking like grapes, but much larger.

He remained resting for a time on the hill, being much wearied after his flight, and at last he began to eat the fruit off the branch. After watching him for some time longer, Maildun ventured warily towards the hillock, to see whether he was inclined to mischief; but the bird showed no disposition to harm him. This emboldened the others, and they all followed their chief.

The whole crew now marched in a body round the bird, headed by Maildun, with their shields raised; and as he still made no stir, one of the men, by Maildun's directions, went straight in front of him, and brought away some of the fruit from the branch which he still held in his talons. But the bird went on plucking and eating his fruit, and never took the least notice.

On the evening of that same day, as the men sat looking over the sea to the south-west, where the great bird first appeared to them, they saw in the distance two others, quite as large, coming slowly towards them from the very same point. On they came, flying at a vast height, nearer and nearer, till at last they swooped down and alighted on the hillock in front of the first bird, one on each side.

Although they were plainly much younger than the other, they seemed very tired, and took a long rest. Then, shaking their wings, they began picking the old bird all over, body, wings, and head, plucking out the old feathers and the decayed quill points, and smoothing down his plumage with their great beaks. After this had gone on for some time, the three began plucking the fruit off the branch, and they ate till they were satisfied.

Next morning, the two birds began at the very same work, picking and arranging the feathers of the old bird as before; and at midday they ceased, and began again to eat the fruit, throwing the stones and what they did not eat of the pulp, into the lake, till the water became red like wine. After this the old bird plunged into the lake and remained in it, washing himself, till evening, when he again flew up on the hillock, but perched on a different part of it, to avoid touching and defiling himself with the old feathers and the other traces of age and decay, which the younger birds had removed from him.

On the morning of the third day, the two younger birds set about arranging his feathers for the third time; and on this occasion they applied themselves to their task in a manner much more careful and particular than before, smoothing the plumes with the nicest touches, and arranging them in beautiful lines and glossy tufts and ridges. And so they continued without the least pause till midday, when they ceased. Then, after resting for a little while, they opened their great wings, rose into the air, and flew away swiftly towards the south-west, till the men lost sight of them in the distance.

Meantime the old bird, after the others had left, continued to smooth and plume his feathers till evening; then, shaking his wings, he rose up, and flew three times round the island, as if to try his strength. And now the men observed that he had lost all the appearances of old age: his feathers were thick and glossy, his head was erect and his eye bright, and he flew with quite as much power and swiftness as the others. Alighting for the last time on the hillock, after resting a little, he rose again, and turning his flight after the other two, to the point from which he had come, he was soon lost to view, and the voyagers saw no more of him.

It now appeared very clear to Maildun and his companions that this bird had undergone a renewal of youth from old age, according to the word of the prophet, which says, 'Thy youth shall be renewed as the eagle.' Diuran, seeing this great wonder, said to his companions –

'Let us also bathe in the lake, and we shall obtain a renewal of youth like the bird.'

But they said, 'Not so, for the bird has left the poison of his old age and decay in the water.'

Diuran, however, would have his own way; and he told them he was resolved to try the virtue of the water, and that they might follow his example or not, whichever they pleased. So he plunged in and swam about for some time, after which he took a little of the water and mixed it in his mouth; and in the end he swallowed a small quantity. He then came out perfectly sound and whole; and he remained so ever after, for as long as he lived he never lost a tooth or had a grey hair, and he suffered not from disease or bodily weakness of any kind. But none of the others ventured in.

The voyagers, having remained long enough on this island, stored in their currogh a large quantity of the flesh of the sheep; and after bidding farewell to the ancient cleric, they sought the ocean once more.

Now once again, when winds and tide combine,
The flying curragh cleaves the crested brine.
Far to the west an island rose to view,
With verdant plains, clear streams, and mountains blue.
An aged hermit, bred in Erin's land,
Welcomed and blessed the chieftain and his band;
Brought food and drink, and bade them rest awhile,
And view the wonders of that lovely isle.
   Lo, from the sea, three birds of monstrous size,
With vast wings slowly moving, cleave the skies;
And as they nearer drew, the sailors saw
One held a fruit branch firmly in his claw.
Down by the clear, mysterious lake they light,
Eat from the branch, and rest them from their flight.
   The aged bird, with plumes decayed and thin,
Paused on the brink awhile, then, plunging in,
He bath'd and smooth'd his feathers o'er and o'er,
Shook his great wings and rested on the shore.
   Now while the other two his plumes arrange,
Through all his frame appears a wondrous change:
His eyes grow bright, his head erect and bold,
His glossy plumage shines like burnished gold;
Free from old age, his glorious form expands;
In radiant youth and beauty proud he stands!
   Such was the gift that lake of wonder gave;
Such was the virtue of its mystic wave.

THE ISLE OF LAUGHING

They next came to an island with a great plain extending over its whole surface. They saw a vast multitude of people on it, engaged in sundry youthful games, and all continually laughing. The voyagers cast lots who should go to examine the island; and the lot fell upon Maildun's third foster brother.

The moment he landed he went among the others and joined in their pastimes and in their laughter, as if he had been among them all his life. His companions waited for him a very long time, but were afraid to venture to land after him; and at last, as there seemed no chance of his returning, they left him and sailed away.

THE ISLE OF THE BLEST

They came now to a small island with a high wall of fire all round it, and there was a large open door in the wall at one side near the sea. They sailed backward and forward many times, and always paused before the door; for whenever they came right in front of it, they could see almost the whole island through it.

And this is what they saw: a great number of people, beautiful and glorious-looking, wearing rich garments adorned and radiant all over, feasting joyously, and drinking from embossed vessels of red gold which they held in their hands. The voyagers heard also their cheerful, festive songs; and they marvelled greatly, and their hearts were full of gladness at all the happiness they saw and heard. But they did not venture to land.

THE HERMIT OF THE SEA-ROCK

A little time after leaving this, they saw something a long way off towards the south, which at first they took to be a large white bird floating on the sea, and rising and falling with the waves; but on turning their curragh towards it for a nearer view, they found that it was a man. He was very old, so old that he was covered all over with long, white hair, which grew from his body; and he was standing on a broad, bare rock, and kept continually throwing himself on his knees, and never ceased praying.

When they saw that he was a holy man, they asked and received his blessing; after which they began to converse with him; and they inquired who he was, and how he had come to that rock. Then the old man gave them the following account: –

'I was born and bred in the island of Tory. When I grew up to be a man, I was cook to the brotherhood of the monastery; and a wicked cook I was; for every day I sold part of the food entrusted to me, and secretly bought many choice and rare things with the money. Worse even than this I did; I made secret passages underground into the church and into the houses belonging to it, and I stole from time to time great quantities of golden vestments, book-covers adorned with brass and gold, and other holy and precious things.'

'I soon became very rich, and had my rooms filled with costly couches, with clothes of every colour, both linen and woollen, with brazen pitchers and caldrons, and with brooches and armlets of gold. Nothing was wanting in my house, of furniture and ornament, that a person in a high rank of life might be expected to have; and I became very proud and overbearing.'

'One day, I was sent to dig a grave for the body of a rustic that had been brought from the mainland to be buried on the island. I went and fixed on a spot in the little graveyard; but as soon as I had set to work, I heard a voice speaking down deep in the earth beneath my feet –

"Do not dig this grave!"

'I paused for a moment, startled; but, recovering myself, I gave no further heed to the mysterious words, and again I began to dig. The moment I did so, I heard the same voice, even more plainly than before –

"Do not dig this grave! I am a devout and holy person, and my body is lean and light; do not put the heavy, pampered body of that sinner down upon me!"

'But I answered, in the excess of my pride and obstinacy, "I will certainly dig this grave; and I will bury this body down on you!"'

'"If you put that body down on me, the flesh will fall off your bones, and you will die, and be sent to the infernal pit at the end of three days; and, moreover, the body will not remain where you put it."'

'"What will you give me," I asked, "if I do not bury the corpse on you?"'

'"Everlasting life in heaven," replied the voice.

'"How do you know this; and how am I to be sure of it?"' I inquired.

'And the voice answered me, "The grave you are digging is clay. Observe now whether it will remain so, and then you will know the truth of what I tell you. And you will see that what I say will come to pass, and that you cannot bury that man on me, even if you should try to do so."'

'These words were scarce ended, when the grave was turned into a mass of white sand before my face. And when I saw this, I brought the body away, and buried it elsewhere.'

'It happened, some time after, that I got a new curragh made, with the hides painted red all over; and I went to sea in it. As I sailed by the shores and islands, I was so pleased with the view of the land and sea from my curragh that I resolved to live altogether in it for some time; and I brought on board all my treasures – silver cups, gold bracelets, and ornamented drinking-horns, and everything else, from the largest to the smallest article.'

'I enjoyed myself for a time, while the air was clear and the sea calm and smooth. But one day, the winds suddenly arose and a storm burst upon me, which carried me out to sea, so that I quite lost sight of land, and I knew not in what direction the curragh was drifting. After a time, the wind abated to a gentle gale, the sea became smooth, and the curragh sailed on as before, with a quiet, pleasant movement.'

'But suddenly, though the breeze continued to blow, I thought I could perceive that the curragh ceased moving, and, standing up to find out the cause, I saw with great surprise an old man not far off, sitting on the crest of a wave.'

'He spoke to me; and, as soon as I heard his voice, I knew it at once, but I could not at the moment call to mind where I had heard it before. And I became greatly troubled, and began to tremble, I knew not why.'

'"Whither art thou going?" he asked.'

'"I know not," I replied; "but this I know, I am pleased with the smooth, gentle motion of my curragh over the waves."'

'"You would not be pleased," replied the old man, "if you could see the troops that are at this moment around you."'

'"What troops do you speak of?" I asked. And he answered –'

'"All the space round about you, as far as your view reaches over the sea, and upwards to the clouds, is one great towering mass of demons, on account of your avarice, your thefts, your pride, and your other crimes and vices."'

'He then asked, "Do you know why your curragh has stopped?"'

'I answered, "No;" and he said, "It has been stopped by me; and it will never move from that spot till you promise me to do what I shall ask of you."'

'I replied that perhaps it was not in my power to grant his demand.'

'"It is in your power," he answered; "and if you refuse me, the torments of hell shall be your doom."'

'He then came close to the curragh, and, laying his hands on me, he made me swear to do what he demanded.'

'"What I ask is this," said he; "that you throw into the sea this moment all the ill-gotten treasures you have in the curragh."'

'This grieved me very much, and I replied, "It is a pity that all these costly things should be lost."'

'To which he answered, "They will not go to loss; a person will be sent to take charge of them. Now do as I say."'

'So, greatly against my wishes, I threw all the beautiful precious articles overboard, keeping only a small wooden cup to drink from.'

'"You will now continue your voyage," he said; "and the first solid ground your curragh reaches, there you are to stay."'

'He then gave me seven cakes and a cup of watery whey as food for my voyage; after which the curragh moved on, and I soon lost sight of him. And now I all at once recollected that the old man's voice was the same as the voice that I had heard come from the ground, when I was about to dig the grave for the body of the rustic. I was so astonished and troubled at this discovery, and so disturbed at the loss of all my wealth, that I threw aside my oars, and gave myself up altogether to the winds and currents, not caring whither I went; and for a long time I was tossed about on the waves, I knew not in what direction.'

'At last it seemed to me that my curragh ceased to move; but I was not sure about it, for I could see no sign of land. Mindful, however, of what the old man had told me, that I was to stay wherever my curragh stopped, I looked round more carefully; and at last I saw, very near me, a small rock level with the surface, over which the waves were gently laughing and tumbling. I stepped on to the rock; and the moment I did so, the waves seemed to spring back, and the rock rose high over the level of the water; while the curragh drifted by and quickly disappeared, so that I never saw it after. This rock has been my abode from that time to the present day.'

'For the first seven years, I lived on the seven cakes and the cup of whey given me by the man who had sent me to the rock. At the end of that time the cakes were all gone; and for three days I fasted, with nothing but the whey to wet my mouth. Late in the evening of the third day, an otter brought me a salmon out of the sea; but though I suffered much from hunger, I could not bring myself to eat the fish raw, and it was washed back again into the waves.'

'I remained without food for three days longer; and in the afternoon of the third day, the otter returned with the salmon. And I saw another otter bring firewood; and when he had piled it up on the rock, he blew it with his breath till it took fire and lighted up. And then I broiled the salmon and ate till I had satisfied my hunger.'

'The otter continued to bring me a salmon every day, and in this manner I lived for seven years longer. The rock also grew larger and larger daily, till it became the size you now see it. At the end of seven years, the otter ceased to bring me my salmon, and I fasted for three days. But at the end of the third day, I was sent half a cake of fine wheaten flour and a slice of fish; and on the same day my cup of watery whey fell into the sea, and a cup of the same size, filled with good ale, was placed on the rock for me.'

'And so I have lived, praying and doing penance for my sins to this hour. Each day my drinking-vessel is filled with ale, and I am sent half a wheatflour cake and a slice of fish; and neither rain nor wind, nor heat, nor cold, is allowed to molest me on this rock.'

This was the end of the old man's history. In the evening of that day, each man of the crew received the same quantity of food that was sent to the old hermit himself, namely, half a cake and a slice of fish; and they found in the vessel as much good ale as served them all.

The next morning he said to them, 'You shall all reach your own country in safety. And you, Maildun, you shall find in an island on your way, the very man that slew your father; but you are neither to kill him nor take revenge on him in any way. As God has delivered you from the many dangers you have passed through, though you were very guilty, and well deserved death at His hands; so you forgive your enemy the crime he committed against you.'

After this they took leave of the old man and sailed away.

SIGNS OF HOME

Soon after they saw a beautiful verdant island, with herds of oxen, cows, and sheep browsing all over its hills and valleys; but no houses nor inhabitants were to be seen. And they rested for some time on this island, and ate the flesh of the cows and sheep.

One day, while they were standing on a hill, a large falcon flew by; and two of the crew, who happened to look closely at him, cried out, in the hearing of Maildun –

'See that falcon! He is surely like the falcons of Erin!'

'Watch him closely,' cried Maildun; 'and observe exactly in what direction he is flying!'

And they saw that he flew to the south-east, without turning or wavering.

They went on board at once; and, having unmoored, they sailed to the south-east after the falcon. After rowing the whole day, they sighted land in the dusk of the evening, which seemed to them like the land of Erin.

MAILDUN MEETS HIS ENEMY, AND ARRIVES HOME

On a near approach, they found it was a small island; and now they recognized it as the very same island they had seen in the beginning of their voyage, in which they had heard the man in the great house boast that he had slain Maildun's father, and from which the storm had driven them out into the great ocean.

They turned the prow of their vessel to the shore, landed, and went towards the house. It happened that at this very time the people of the house were seated at their evening meal; and Maildun and his companions, as they stood outside, heard a part of their conversation.

Said one to another, 'It would not be well for us if we were now to see Maildun.'

'As to Maildun,' answered another, 'it is very well known that he was drowned long ago in the great ocean.'

'Do not be sure,' observed a third; 'perchance he is the very man that may waken you up some morning from your sleep.'

'Supposing he came now,' asks another, 'what should we do?'

The head of the house now spoke in reply to the last question; and Maildun at once knew his voice –

'I can easily answer that,' said he. 'Maildun has been for a long time suffering great afflictions and hardships; and if he were to come now, though we were enemies once, I should certainly give him a welcome and a kind reception.'

When Maildun heard this he knocked at the door, and the door-keeper asked who was there; to which Maildun made answer –

'It is I, Maildun, returned safely from all my wanderings.'

The chief of the house then ordered the door to be opened; and he went to meet Maildun, and brought himself and his companions into the house. They were joyfully welcomed by the whole household; new garments were given to them; and they feasted and rested, till they forgot their weariness and their hardships.

They related all the wonders God had revealed to them in the course of their voyage, according to the word of the sage who says, 'It will be a source of pleasure to remember these things at a future time.'

After they had remained here for some days, Maildun returned to his own country. And Diuran Lekerd took the five half-ounces of silver he had cut down from the great net at the Silver Pillar, and laid it, according to his promise, on the high altar of Armagh.

# NOTES

Source: P.W. Joyce, *Old Celtic Romances,* London: Kegan Paul, 1894.

This ninth-century text, the second of the great *immrama*, begins as a quest for vengeance against the raiders who had slain the hero's father. It soon develops into a marvellous series of adventures on different islands, each of which is both a description of an aspect of the Other-world and a representation of a different stage in the soul's journey through life. The work had been justly described as a Celtic 'Book of the Dead' for this reason. The poetry and wonder of the descriptions of the islands makes it a unique example of the visionary journey, and, in the end, Maildun (also known as Maelduin) is so changed by his experiences in the Otherworld that he no longer desires vengeance.

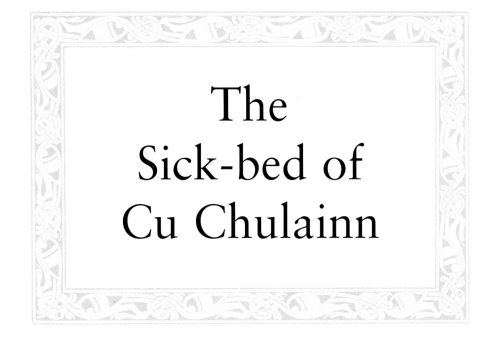

The Sick-bed of Cu Chulainn

VERY YEAR THE MEN of Ulster were accustomed to hold festival together; and the time when they held it was for three days before Samain, and for three days after that day, and upon Samain itself. And the time that is spoken of is that when the men of Ulster used to assemble in Mag Muirthemne, and there they used to hold the festival every year; nor was there anything in the world that they would do at that time except sports, and marketings, and splendors, and pomps, and feasting and eating; and it is from that custom of theirs that the Festival of Samain was descended, that is now held throughout the whole of Ireland.

Now once upon a time the men of Ulster held festival in Mag Muirthemne, and the reason that this festival was held was that every man of them should every Samain give account of the combats he had made and of his valor. It was their custom to hold that festival in order to give account of these combats, and the manner in which they gave that account was this: each man used to cut off the tip of the tongue of a foe whom he had killed, and carry it with him in a pouch. Moreover, in order to make more great the numbers of their contests, some used to bring with them the tips of the tongues of beasts, and each man publicly declared the fights he had fought, one man of them after the other. And they did this also: they laid their swords over their thighs when they related their combats, and their own swords used to turn against them when the strife that they declared was false; nor was this to be wondered at, for at that time it was customary for demons to scream from the weapons of men, so that for this cause their weapons might be the more able to guard them.

To that festival then came all the men of Ulster except two alone, and these two were Fergus mac Roig, and Conall the Victorious.

'Let the festival be held!' cried the men of Ulster.

'Nay,' said Cu Chulainn, 'it shall not be held until Conall and Fergus come,' and this he said because Fergus was the foster-father of Cu Chulainn, and Conall was his comrade.

Then said Sencha, 'Let us for the present engage in games of chess; and let the druids sing, and let the jugglers perform their feats'; and it was done as he had said.

Now while they were thus employed a flock of birds came down and hovered over a neighbouring lake; never were seen in Ireland more beautiful birds than these. And a longing that these birds should be given to them seized upon the women who were there; and each of them began to boast of the prowess of her husband at bird-catching.

'How I wish,' said Ethne, Conchobar's wife, 'that I could have two of those birds, one of them upon each of my two shoulders.'

'It is what we all long for,' said the women.

'If any should have this gift, I should be the first one to have it,' said Ethne Inguba, the wife of Cu Chulainn.

'What are we to do now?' said the women.

'It is easy to answer you,' said Leborcham, the daughter of Oa and Adarc; 'I will go now with a message from you, and will seek for Cu Chulainn.' She then went to Cu Chulainn.

'The women of Ulster would be well pleased,' she said, 'if yonder birds were given to them by thy hand.'

Cu Chulainn reached for his sword to unsheathe it against her. 'Cannot the women of Ulster find any other but us,' he said, 'to give them their bird-hunt to-day?'

'It is not seemly for thee to rage thus against them,' said Leborcham, 'for it is on thy account that the women of Ulster have assumed one of their three blemishes, even the blemish of blindness.' For there were three blemishes that the women of Ulster assumed, that of crookedness of gait, and that of a stammering in their speech, and that of blindness. Each of the women who loved Conall the Victorious had assumed a crookedness of gait; each woman who loved Cuscraid Menn, the Stammerer of Macha, Conchobar's son, stammered in her speech; each woman in like manner who loved Cu Chulainn, had assumed a blindness of her eyes, in order to resemble Cu Chulainn; for he, when his mind was angry within him, was accustomed to draw in one of his eyes so far that a crane could not reach it in his head, and would thrust out the other so that it was as great as a cauldron in which a calf is cooked.

'Yoke for us the chariot, O Loeg!' said Cu Chulainn. At that Loeg yoked the chariot, and Cu Chulainn went into the chariot, and he cast his sword at the birds with a cast like the cast of a boomerang, so that they flapped against the water with their claws and wings. And they seized upon all the birds, and they gave them and distributed them among the women; nor was there any one of the women, except Ethne alone, who had not a pair of those birds.

Then Cu Chulainn returned to his wife.

'Thou art angry,' said he to her.

'I am in no way angry,' answered Ethne, 'for I deem it as being by me that the distribution was made. And thou hast done what was fitting,' she said, 'for there is not one of these women but loves thee; none in whom thou hast no share; but for myself, none has any share in me but thou alone.'

'Be not angry,' said Cu Chulainn, 'if in the future any birds come to Mag Muirthemne or to the Boyne, the two birds that are the most beautiful among those that come shall be thine.'

A little while after this they saw two birds flying over the lake, linked together by a chain of red gold. They sang a gentle song, and a sleep fell upon all the men who were there except Cu Chulainn. Cu Chulainn rose up to pursue the birds.

49

'If thou wilt listen to me,' said Loeg (and so also said Ethne), 'thou wilt not go against them; behind those birds is some special power. Other birds may be taken by thee at some future day.'

'Is it possible that such claim as this should be made upon me?' said Cu Chulainn. 'Place a stone in my sling, O Loeg!'

Loeg thereon took a stone, and he placed it in the sling, and Cu Chulainn launched the stone at the birds, but the cast missed. 'Alas!' said he. He took another stone, and he launched this also at the birds, but the stone flew past them.

'Wretch that I am,' he cried; 'since the very first day that I assumed arms, I have never missed a cast until this day!' And he threw his spear at them, and the spear went through the shield of the wing of one of the birds, and the birds flew away, and went beneath the lake.

After this Cu Chulainn departed, and he rested his back against a stone pillar, and his soul was angry within him, and sleep fell upon him. Then saw he two women come to him; the one of them had a green mantle upon her, and upon the other was a purple mantle folded in five folds. And the woman in the green mantle approached him, and she laughed a laugh at him, and she gave him a stroke with a horsewhip. And then the other approached him, and she also laughed at him, and she struck him in the same way; and for a long time were they thus, each of them in turn coming to him and striking him, until he was all but dead; and then they departed from him.

Now the men of Ulster perceived the state in which Cu Chulainn was, and they cried out that he should be awakened; but 'Nay,' said Fergus, 'you shall not move him, for he is seeing a vision'; and a little after that Cu Chulainn arose from his sleep.

'What has happened to thee?' said the men of Ulster; but he had no power to bid greeting to them.

'Let me be carried,' he said, 'to the sick-bed that is in Tete Brecc; not to Dun Imrith, nor yet to Dun Delgan.'

'Wilt thou not be carried to Dun Delgan, thy stronghold, to seek for Emer?' said Loeg.

'Nay,' said he, 'my word is for Tete Brecc'; and thereon they bore him from that place, and he was in Tete Brecc until the end of one year, and during all that time he had speech with no one.

Now upon a certain day before the next Samain, at the end of a year, when the men of Ulster were in the house where Cu Chulainn was, Fergus being at the side-wall, and Conall the Victorious at his head, and Lugaid Red-Stripes at his pillow, and Ethne Inguba at his feet; – when they were there in this manner, a man came to them, and he seated himself near the entrance of the chamber in which Cu Chulainn lay.

'What has brought thee here?' said Conall the Victorious.

'No hard question to answer,' said the man. 'If the man who lies yonder were in health, he would be a good protection to all of Ulster; in the weakness and the sickness in which he now is, so much the more great is the protection that they have from him. I have no fear of any of you,' he said, 'for it is to give to this man a greeting that I come.'

'Welcome to thee, then, and fear nothing,' said the men of Ulster; and the man rose to his feet, and he sang them the following verses:

O, Cu Chulainn! of thy illness
Not great will be the length.
They would heal thee if they were here,
The daughters of Aed Abrat.

Thus spoke Liban in Mag Cruach,
By the side of Labraid the Swift:
Love holds Fann's heart;
She longs to be joined to Cu Chulainn.

Goodly in truth would be the day
When Cu Chulainn comes to my land.
If he comes he shall have silver and gold;
He shall have much wine to drink.

Could he but love me enough for that,
Cu Chulainn son of Sualtam!
I have seen him in slumber,
Without his arms, in very truth.

'Tis to Mag Muirthemne thou shouldst go,
On the night of Samain, without injury to thyself.
I will send thee Liban,
To heal thy sickness, O Cu Chulainn!

O, Cu Chulainn! of thy illness,
Not great will be the length.
They would heal thee if they were here,
The daughters of Aed Abrat.

'Who art thou, then, thyself?' said the men of Ulster.

'I am Angus, the son of Aed Abrat,' he answered; and the man then left them, nor did any of them know whence it was he had come, nor whither he went.

Then Cu Chulainn sat up, and he spoke to them. 'Fortunate indeed is this!' said the men of Ulster; 'tell us what it is that has happened to thee.'

'Upon Samain night last year,' he said, 'I indeed saw a vision'; and he told them of all he had seen.

'What should now be done, Father Conchobar?' said Cu Chulainn.

'This hast thou to do,' answered Conchobar; 'rise, and go to the pillar where thou wert before.'

Then Cu Chulainn went forth to the pillar, and then saw he the woman in the green mantle come to him. 'This is good, O Cu Chulainn!' said she.

'It is no good thing in my thought,' said Cu Chulainn. 'Wherefore camest thou to me last year?'

'It was indeed to do no injury to thee that we came,' said the woman, 'but to seek for thy friendship. I have come to greet thee,' she said, 'from Fann, the daughter of Aed Abrat; her husband, Manannan mac Lir (Son of the Sea), has abandoned her, and she has thereon set her love on thee. My own name is Liban, and I have brought to thee a message from my husband, Labraid the Swift Sword-Wielder, that he will give thee the woman Fann in exchange for one day's service to him in battle against Senach Siaborthe, and against Eochaid Iuil, and against Eogan Inber.'

'I am in no fit state,' he said, 'to contend with men to-day.'

'That will last but a little while,' she said; 'thou shalt be whole, and all that thou hast lost of thy strength shall be increased to thee. Labraid shall bestow on thee that gift, for he is the best of all warriors that are in the world.'

'Where is it that Labraid dwells?' asked Cu Chulainn.

'In Mag Mell, the Plain of Delight,' said Liban; 'and now I desire to go to that other land,' said she.

'Let Loeg go with thee,' said Cu Chulainn, 'that he may learn of the land from which thou hast come.'

'Let him come, then,' said Liban.

She and Loeg departed after that, and they went forward toward Mag Mell, the place where Fann was. And Liban turned to seek for Loeg, and she placed him beside her shoulder. 'Thou wouldst never go hence, O Loeg!' said Liban, 'wert thou not under a woman's protection.'

'It is not a thing that I have most been accustomed to up to this time,' said Loeg, 'to be under a woman's guard.'

'Shame, and everlasting shame,' said Liban, 'that Cu Chulainn is not where thou art.'

'It were well for me,' answered Loeg, 'if it were indeed he who is here.'

They passed on then, and went forward until they came opposite to the shore of an island, and there they saw a skiff of bronze lying upon the lake before them. They entered into the skiff, and they crossed over to the island, and came to the palace door, and there they saw a man, and he came towards them. And thus spoke Liban to the man whom they saw there:

Where is Labraid, the swift sword-handler,
The head of victorious troops?
Victory is in his strong chariot;
He stains with red the points of his spears.

And the man replied to her thus:

Labraid, the swift sword-handler –
He is not slow: he will be strong.
They are gathering for the battle;
They are making ready for the slaughter
That will fill Mag Fidga.

They entered into the palace, and they saw there thrice fifty couches within the palace, and three times fifty women upon the couches; and the women all bade Loeg welcome, and it was in these words that they addressed him:

Welcome to thee, O Loeg,
Because of thy quest:
Loeg, we also
Hail thee as our guest!

'What wilt thou do now?' said Liban; 'wilt thou go on without a delay, and hold speech with Fann?'

'I will go,' he answered, 'if I may know the place where she is.'

'That is no hard matter to tell,' she answered; 'she is in her chamber apart.' They went there, and they greeted Fann, and she welcomed Loeg in the same fashion as the others had done.

Fann was the daughter of Aed Abrat; Aed means fire, and he is the fire of the eye: that is, of the eye's pupil: Fann moreover is the name of the tear that runs from the eye; it was on account of the clearness of her beauty that she was so named, for there is nothing else in the world except a tear to which her beauty could be likened.

Now, while they were thus in that place, they heard the rattle of Labraid's chariot as he approached the island, driving across the water. 'The spirit of Labraid is gloomy to-day,' said Liban; 'I will go and greet him.' And she went out, and she bade welcome to Labraid, and she spoke as follows:

> Hail to Labraid, swift sword-handler!
> Heir to an army – small and armed with javelins.
> He hacks the shields – he scatters the spears,
> He cleaves the bodies – he slaughters free men;
> He seeks for bloodshed – bright is he in the conflict:
> To thee, who war against the hosts, Labraid, hail!
>
> Hail to Labraid, the swift sword-handler!
> Heir to an army – small and armed with javelins.

Labraid did not reply to her, and the lady spoke again thus:

> Hail to Labraid, swift sword-handler!
> Ready in giving, – generous to all, – eager for combat;
> Scarred thy side, – fair thy speech, – strong thy hand,
> Kindly in ruling, – hardy in judgments, – powerful in vengeance.
> He fights off the hosts. – Hail, Labraid!
>
> Hail to Labraid, swift handler of the battle-sword!

Labraid still made no answer, and she sang another lay thus:

> Hail, Labraid, swift sword-handler!
> Bravest of warriors, – more proud than the sea!
> He routs the armies, – he joins the combats;
> He tests the soldiers, – he raises up the weak,
> He humbles the strong. Hail, Labraid!
>
> Hail, Labraid, swift sword-handler!

'Thou speakest not rightly, O woman,' said Labraid; and he then addressed her thus:

> There is no pride or arrogance in me, oh wife!
> And no deluding spell can weaken my judgment.
> We are going now into a conflict of doubtful issue, decisive and severe,
> Where red swords strike in powerful hands,
> Against the multitudinous and united hosts of Eochaid Iuil.
> There is no presumption in me – no pride and no arrogance in me, oh wife!

'Let now thy mind be appeased,' said the woman Liban to him. 'Loeg, the charioteer of Cu Chulainn, is here; and Cu Chulainn has sent word to thee that he will come to join thy hosts.'

Then Labraid bade welcome to Loeg, and he said to him: 'Welcome, O Loeg! For the sake of the lady with whom thou comest, and for the sake of him from whom thou hast come. Go now to thine own land, O Loeg!' said Labraid, 'and Liban shall accompany thee.'

Then Loeg returned to Emain, and he gave news of what he had seen to Cu Chulainn, and to all others beside; and Cu Chulainn rose up, and he passed his hand over his face, and he greeted Loeg brightly, and his mind was strengthened within him for the news that Loeg had brought him.

Now as to Cu Chulainn, it has to be related thus: he called upon Loeg to come to him; and 'Go, O Loeg!' said Cu Chulainn, 'to the place where Emer is; and say to her that fairy women have come upon me, and that they have destroyed my strength; and say also to her that it goes better with me from hour to hour, and bid her to come and see me'; and the young man Loeg then spoke these words in order to hearten the mind of Cu Chulainn:

> Little indeed is its use to a warrior –
> The bed where he lies in sickness.
> His illness is the work of the fairy folk,
> Of the women of Mag Trogach.

> They have beaten thee,
> They have put thee into captivity;
> They have led thee off the track.
> The power of the women has rendered thee impotent.

> Awake from the sleep in which thou art fighting
> Against beings who are not soldiers;
> The hour has come for thee to take thy place
> Among heroes who drive their chariots to battle.

> Place thyself upon the seat of thy war chariot.
> Then will come the chance
> To cover thyself with wounds,
> To do great deeds.

> When Labraid shows his power,
> When the splendor of his glory shines,
> Then must thou arise,
> Then wilt thou be great.

> Little indeed is its use to a warrior –
> The bed where he lies in sickness.
> His illness is the work of the fairy folk,
> Of the women of Mag Trogach.

And Loeg, after that heartening, departed; and he went to the place where Emer was; and he told her of the state of Cu Chulainn.

'Ill has it been what thou hast done, O youth!' she said; 'for although thou art known as one who dost wander in the lands where the fairy folk dwell, yet no virtue of healing hast thou found there and brought for the cure of thy lord. Shame upon the men of Ulster!' she said, 'for they have not sought to do a great deed, and to heal him. Yet, had Conchobar thus been fettered, had it been Fergus who lost his sleep, had it been Conall the Victorious to whom wounds had been dealt, Cu Chulainn would have saved them.' And she then sang a song, and in this fashion she sang it:

O Loeg mac Riangabra! Alas!
Thou hast searched fairyland many times in vain;
Thou tarriest long in bringing thence
The healing of the son of Dechtire.

Woe to the high-souled Ulstermen!
Neither foster-father or foster-brother of Cu Chulainn
Has made a search through the wide world
To find the cure for his brave comrade.

If Fergus, foster-father of Cu Chulainn, were under this spell,
And if, to heal him, there was needed the knowledge of a druid,
The son of Dechtire would never take repose
Until Fergus had found a druid who could heal him.

If it were the foster-brother of Cu Chulainn, Conall the Victorious,
Who was afflicted with wounds,
Cu Chulainn would search through the whole world
Until he found a physician to heal him.

If Loegaire the Triumphant
Had been overborne in rugged combat,
Cu Chulainn would have searched through the green meads of all Ireland
To find a cure for the son of Connad mac Iliach.

Alas! Sickness seizes upon me, too,
Because of Cu Chulainn, the Hound of Conchobar's smith!
The sickness that I feel at my heart creeps over my whole body!
Would that I might find a physician to heal thee!

Alas! Death is at my heart!
For sickness has checked the warrior who rode his chariot across the plain,
And now he goes no more
To the assembly of Muirthemne.

Why does he go forth no more from Emain?
It is because of the fairy folk that he lingers.
My voice grows weak and dies.

Month, season, year, all have gone by,
And yet sleep has not taken up its accustomed course.
There is no one by him. Not one fair word
Doth ever come to his ears, O Loeg mac Riangabra.

And, after that she had sung that song, Emer went forward to Emain that she might visit Cu Chulainn; and she seated herself in the chamber where Cu Chulainn was, and thus she addressed him: 'Shame upon thee!' she said, 'to lie thus prostrate for a woman's love! Well may this long sick-bed of thine cause thee to ail!' And it was in this fashion that she addressed him, and she chanted this lay:

> Arise, hero of Ulster!
> Awake joyful and sound.
> Look upon the king of Ulster, how great he is!
> Long enough hast thou slept.

> It is ill sleeping too deep;
> It is the weakness that follows defeat;
> Sleeping too long is like milk to repletion;
> It is the lieutenant of death; it has all death's power.

> Awake! Sleep is the repose of the sot;
> Throw it off with burning energy.
> I have spoken much, but it is love that inspires me.
> Arise, hero of Ulster!

> Arise, hero of Ulster!
> Awake joyful and sound.
> Look upon the king of Ulster, how great he is!
> Long enough hast thou slept.

And Cu Chulainn at her word stood up; and he passed his hand over his face, and he cast all his heaviness and his weariness away from him, and then he arose, and went on his way before him until he came to the enclosure that he sought; and in that enclosure Liban appeared to him. And Liban spoke to him, and she strove to lead him into fairyland; but 'What place is that in which Labraid dwells?' said Cu Chulainn. 'It is easy for me to tell thee!' she said:

> Labraid's home is over a pure lake,
> Where troops of women congregate.
> Easy for thee to go there,
> If thou wilt know swift Labraid.

> His skilled arm strikes down hundreds;
> Wise are they who describe his deeds:
> Beautifully purple the colors
> Which are on the cheeks of Labraid.

> He shakes his head like a wolf in the battle
> Before the thin blood-stained swords.
> He shatters the arms of his impotent enemies;
> He shatters the bucklers of the warriors.

'I will not go thither at a woman's invitation,' said Cu Chulainn.

'Let Loeg go then,' said the woman, 'and let him bring to thee tidings of all that is there.'

'Let him depart, then,' said Cu Chulainn; and Loeg rose up and departed with Liban, and they came to Mag Luada, and to Bile Buada, and over the fair green of Emain, and over the fair green of Fidga, and in that place dwelt Aed Abrat, and with him his daughters.

Then Fann bade welcome to Loeg, and 'How is it,' said she, 'that Cu Chulainn has not come with thee?'

'It pleased him not,' said Loeg, 'to come at a woman's call; moreover, he desired to know whether it was indeed from thee that had come the message, and to have full knowledge of everything.'

'It was indeed from me that the message was sent,' she said; 'and let now Cu Chulainn come swiftly to seek us, for it is for to-day that the strife is set.'

Then Loeg went back to the place where he had left Cu Chulainn, and Liban with him; and 'How appears this quest to thee, O Loeg?' said Cu Chulainn.

And Loeg answered, 'In a happy hour shalt thou go,' said he, 'for the battle is set for to-day'; and it was in this manner that he spake, and described the fairy world thus:

I went in the twinkling of an eye
Into a marvellous country where I had been before.
I reached a cairn of twenty armies,
And there I found Labraid of the long hair.

I found him sitting on the cairn,
A great multitude of arms about him.
On his head his beautiful fair hair
Was decked with an apple of gold.

Although the time was long since my last visit
He recognized me by my five-fold purple mantle.
Said he, 'Wilt thou come with me
Into the house where dwells Failbe the Fair?'

Two kings are in the house,
Failbe the Fair and Labraid.
Three fifties of warriors are about them.
For all their great number they live in the one house.

On the right are fifty beds,
And on the beds, as many warriors;
On the left, fifty beds,
And a warrior on every bed.

The beds have round columns,
Beautiful posts, adorned with gold.
They gleam brightly in the light
Which comes from a stone, precious and brilliant.

At the door toward the west
On the side toward the setting sun,
There is a troop of grey horses with dappled manes,
And another troop of horses, purple-brown.

At the door toward the east
Are three trees of purple glass.
From their tops a flock of birds sing a sweetly drawn-out song
For the children who live in the royal stronghold.

At the entrance to the enclosure is a tree
From whose branches there comes beautiful and harmonious music.
It is a tree of silver, which the sun illumines;
It glistens like gold.

There are thrice fifty trees.
At times their leaves mingle, at times, not.
Each tree feeds three hundred people
With abundant food, without rind.

There is a well in that noble palace of the fairy-mound.
There you will find thrice fifty splendid cloaks,
With a brooch of shining gold
To fasten each of the cloaks.

There is a cauldron of invigorating mead,
For the use of the inmates of the house.
It never grows less; it is a custom
That it should be full forever.

There is a woman in the noble palace.
There is no woman like her in Erin.
When she goes forth you see her fair hair.
She is beautiful and endowed with many gifts.

Her words, when she speaks to anyone,
Have a marvellous charm.
She wounds every man to the heart
With the love she inspires.

The noble lady said,
'Who is the youth whom we do not know?
Come hither if it be thou
That art the servant of the warrior of Muirthemne.'

I yielded to her request with reluctance;
I feared for my honor.
She said to me, 'Will he come,
The only son of the excellent Dechtire?'

It is a pity that thou hast not gone, O Cu Chulainn!
Everyone asks for you.
You yourself should see how it is built,
The grand palace that I have seen.

If I owned the whole of Erin,
With supreme sovereignty over its fair inhabitants,
I would give it up – the temptation would be irresistible –
I would go and live in the country where I have just been.

I went in the twinkling of an eye
Into a country where I had been before.
I reached a cairn of twenty armies,
And there I found Labraid of the long hair.

'The quest then is a good one,' said Cu Chulainn.

'It is goodly indeed,' said Loeg, 'and it is right that thou shouldst go to attain it, and all things in that land are good.' And thus further also spoke Loeg, as he told of the loveliness of the fairy dwelling:

> They are beautiful women, victorious, never knowing the sorrow of the
>   vanquished,
> The daughters of Aed Abrat.
> The beauty of Fann deserves glittering renown;
> No king or queen is her equal.
>
> I repeat what has been said to me:
> She is a mortal daughter of Adam, without sin.
> The beauty of Fann in our days,
> Is beyond comparison.
>
> I saw the glorious warriors
> Armed with trenchant weapons,
> With garments of bright colors;
> These were not the garments of underlings.
>
> I saw the women, joyous at the feast;
> I saw the troop of maidens;
> I saw the handsome boys
> Walking about the trees on the hill.
>
> In the house I heard the musicians
> Playing for Fann.
> If I had not made haste to go away
> I would have got my hurt from that music.
>
> I saw the hill where the house stands.
> Ethne Inguba is a fair woman,
> But the woman I speak of now,
> Would drive entire armies to madness.

And Cu Chulainn, when he had heard that report, went on with Liban to that land, and he took his chariot with him. And they came to the island of Labraid, and there Labraid and all the women that were there bade them welcome; and Fann gave an especial welcome to Cu Chulainn.

'What is there now set for us to do?' said Cu Chulainn.

'No hard matter to answer,' said Labraid; 'we must go forth and make a circuit about the army.'

They went out then, and they came to the army, and they let their eyes wander over it; and the host seemed to them to be innumerable. 'Arise, and go hence for the present,' said Cu Chulainn to Labraid; and Labraid departed, and Cu Chulainn remained confronting the army. And there were two ravens there, who spake, and revealed druid secrets, but the armies who heard them laughed.

'It must surely be the madman from Ireland who is there,' said the army; 'it is he whom the ravens would make known to us'; and the armies chased them away so that they found no resting-place in that land.

Now at early morn Eochaid Iuil went out in order to bathe his hands in the spring, and Cu Chulainn saw his shoulder through the hood of his tunic, and he hurled his spear at him, and he pierced him. And he by himself slew thirty-three of them, and then Senach Siaborthe assailed him, and a great fight was fought between them, and Cu Chulainn slew him; and after that Labraid approached, and he broke before him those armies.

Then Labraid entreated Cu Chulainn to stay his hand from the slaying; and 'I fear now,' said Loeg, 'that the man will turn his wrath upon us; for he has not found a combat to suffice him. Go now,' said Loeg, 'and let there be brought three vats of cold water to cool his heat. The first vat into which he goes will boil over; after he has gone into the second vat, none will be able to bear the heat of it: after he has gone into the third vat, its water will have but a moderate heat.'

And when the women saw Cu Chulainn's return, Fann sang thus:

> Stately the charioteer that steps the road;
> If he be beardless it is because he is young.
> Splendid the course he drives over the plain,
> At eve on Aenach Fidgai.
>
> There is in each of his two cheeks
> A red dimple like red blood,
> A green dimple, a brown dimple,
> A crimson dimple of light color.
>
> There are seven lights in his eye, –
> It is a fact not to be left unspoken, –
> Eyebrows brown, of noblest set,
> Eyelashes of chafer black.
>
> He outstrips all men in every slaughter;
> He traverses the battle to the place of danger;
> There is not one with a high hardy blade,
> Not one like Cu Chulainn.
>
> Cu Chulainn it is that comes hither,
> The young champion from Muirthemne;
> They who have brought him from afar
> Are the daughters of Aed Abrat.
>
> Dripping blood in long red streams,
> To the sides of lofty spears he brings;
> Haughty, proud, high for valor,
> Woe be to him against whom he becomes angered.

Liban, moreover, bade a welcome to Cu Chulainn, and she sang as follows:

> Welcome to Cu Chulainn;
> Relieving king;
> A great prince of Mag Muirthemne;
> Great his noble mind;
> A battle-victorious champion;
> A strong valor-stone;
> Blood-red of anger;

61

Ready to arrange the champions of valor of Ulster;
Beautiful his complexion;
Dazzler of the eyes to maidens;
He is welcome.

'Tell us now of the deeds thou hast done, O Cu Chulainn!' cried Liban; and Cu
Chulainn replied to her thus:

I threw a cast of my spear
Into the court of Eogan Inber.
I do not know – path of fame –
Whether it is good I have done, or evil.

A host fair, red-complexioned, on backs of steeds,
They pierced me upon all sides;
The people of Manannan son of Lir,
Invoked by Eogan Inber.

I heard the groan of Eochaid Iuil;
It is in good friendship his lips speak.
If the man has spoken true, it certainly won the battle,
The throw that I threw.

Now, after all these things had passed, Cu Chulainn slept with Fann, and he
abode for a month in her company, and at the end of the month he came to bid
her farewell. 'Tell me,' she said, 'to what place I may go for our tryst, and I will
be there'; and they made tryst at the yew tree by the strand that is known as Iubar
Cinn Trachta (Newry).

Now word was brought to Emer of that tryst, and knives were whetted by
Emer to slay the fairy woman; and she came to the place of the tryst, and fifty
women were with her. And there she found Cu Chulainn and Loeg, and they were
engaged in the chess-play, so that they did not perceive the women's approach.
But Fann marked it, and she cried out to Loeg: 'Look now, O Loeg!' she said,
'and mark that sight that I see.'

'What sight is that of which thou speakest?' said Loeg, and he looked and saw
it, and thus it was that Fann addressed him:

Loeg! Look behind thee!
   Close at hand
Wise, well-ranked women
   Press on us;
Bright on each bosom
   Shines the gold clasp;
Knives, with green edges
   Whetted, they hold.
As for the slaughter chariot chiefs race,
Comes Forgall's daughter; changed is her countenance.

'Have no fear,' said Cu Chulainn, 'thou shalt meet no foe;
Enter thou my strong car, with its bright seat:
I will set thee before me, will guard thee from harm
Against women, that swarm from Ulster's four quarters:

*Cu Chulainn
at battle with
the armies on
the island of
Labraid.*

63

Though the daughter of Forgall vows war against thee,
Though her dear foster-sisters she rouses against thee,
Bold Emer will dare no deed of destruction,
Though she rageth against thee, for I will protect thee.'

Moreover to Emer he said:

I avoid thee, O lady, as heroes
    Avoid to meet friends in battle;
The hard spear thy hand shakes cannot injure,
    Nor the blade of thy thin gleaming knife;
For the wrath that rages within thee
    Is but weak, nor can cause me fear:
It were hard if the war my might wages
    Must be quenched by a weak woman's power.

'Speak! And tell me, Cu Chulainn,' said Emer,
    'Why thou wouldst lay this shame on my head?
I stand dishonored before the women of Ulster,
And all women who dwell in Erin,
    And all folk who love honor beside:
Though I came on thee secretly,
    Though I remain oppressed by thy might,
And though great is thy pride in the battle,
    If thou leavest me, naught is thy gain:
Why, dear youth, dost thou make such attempt?'

'Speak thou, Emer, and say,' said Cu Chulainn,
    'Should I not remain with this lady?
For she is fair, pure and bright, and well skilled,
A fit mate for a monarch, filled with beauty,
    And can ride the waves of ocean:
She is lovely in countenance, lofty in race,
And skilled in handicraft, can do fine needlework,
    Has a mind that can guide with firmness.'

'Truly,' answered Emer, 'the woman to whom thou dost cling is in no way better than am I myself! Yet fair seems all that's red; what's new seems glittering; and bright what's set o'erhead; and sour are things well known! Men worship what they lack; and what they have seems weak; in truth thou has all the wisdom of the time! O youth!' she said, 'once we dwelled in honor together, and we would so dwell again, if only I could find favor in thy sight!' and her grief weighted heavily upon her.

'By my word,' said Cu Chulainn, 'thou dost find favor, and thou shalt find it as long as I am in life.'

'Desert me, then!' cried Fann.

'No,' said Emer, 'it is more fitting that I should be the deserted one.'

'Not so, indeed,' said Fann. 'It is I who must go, and danger rushes upon me from afar.' And an eagerness for lamentation seized upon Fann, and her soul was great within her, for it was shame to her to be deserted and straightway to return to her home; moreover, the mighty love that she bore to Cu Chulainn was tumultuous in her, and in this fashion she lamented, and lamenting sang this song:

I it is that will go on the journey;
I give assent with great affliction;
Though there is a man of equal fame,
I would prefer to remain.

I would rather be here,
To be subject to thee, without grief,
Than to go, though you may wonder at it,
To the sunny palace of Aed Abrat.

O Emer! The man is thine,
And well mayst thou wear him, thou good woman, –
What my arm cannot reach,
That I am forced to wish well.

Many were the men that were asking for me,
Both in the court and in the wilderness;
Never with those did I hold a meeting,
Because I it was that was righteous.

Woe! To give love to a person,
If he does not take notice of it;
It is better for a person to turn away
Unless he is loved as he loves.

With fifty women hast thou come hither,
O Emer of the yellow hair,
To capture Fann – it was not well –
And to kill her in her misery.

There are thrice fifty, during my days,
Of women, beautiful and unwedded,
With me in my court together;
They would not abandon me.

Now upon this it was discerned by Manannan that Fann the daughter of Aed
Abrat was engaged in unequal warfare with the women of Ulster, and that she
was like to be left by Cu Chulainn. And thereon Manannan came from the east
to seek for Fann, and he was perceived by her, nor was there any other conscious
of his presence saving Fann alone. And when she saw Manannan, Fann was
seized by great bitterness of mind and by grief, and being thus, she made this
song:

Behold the valiant son of Lir,
From the plains of Eogan Inber, –
Manannan, lord over the world's fair hills,
There was a time when he was dear to me.

Even if to-day he were nobly constant,
My mind loves not jealousy.
Affection is a subtle thing;
It makes its way without labor.

65

One day I was with the son of Lir,
In the sunny palace of Dun Inber;
We then thought, without doubt,
That we should never be separated.

When Manannan, the great one, espoused me,
I was a worthy wife for him;
For his life he could not win from me
The odd game at chess.

When Manannan the great married me,
I was a wife worthy of him;
A wristband of doubly-tested gold
He gave to me as the price of my blushes.

I had with me at going over the sea
Fifty maidens of many gifts.
I gave to them fifty men,
Without reproach, as their companions.

Four fifties, without deceit,
That was the assembly of one house;
Twice fifty men, happy and perfect,
Twice fifty women, fair and healthy.

I see coming over the sea hither –
No erring person sees him –
The horseman of the crested wave;
He stays not on his long boats.

At thy coming, no one yet sees,
Anyone but a dweller in the fairy-mound;
Thy good sense is magnified by every gentle host,
Though they be far away from thee.

As for me, I would have cause for anger,
Because the minds of women are silly;
The person whom I loved exceedingly
Has placed me here at a disadvantage.

I bid thee farewell, O beautiful Cu;
We depart from thee with a good heart;
Though we return not, be thy good will with us;
Everything is good, compared with going away.

It is now time for me to take my departure;
There is a person to whom it is not a grief;
It is, however, a great disgrace,
O Loeg, son of Riangabra.

I shall go with my own husband,
Because he will not show me disobedience.
Now that you may not say it is a secret departure,
If you desire it, now behold me.

Then Fann rose behind Manannan as he passed, and Manannan greeted her: 'O woman!' he said, 'Which wilt thou do? Wilt thou depart with me, or abide here until Cu Chulainn comes to thee?'

'In truth,' answered Fann, 'either of the two of you would be a fitting husband to adhere to; and neither of you is better than the other; yet, Manannan, it is with thee that I go, nor will I wait for Cu Chulainn, for he has betrayed me; and there is another matter, moreover, that weigheth with me, O noble prince!' said she, 'and that is that thou hast no consort who is of worth equal to thine, but such a one hath Cu Chulainn already.'

And Cu Chulainn saw Fann as she went from him to Manannan, and he cried out to Loeg: 'What does this mean that I see?'

"Tis no hard matter to answer,' said Loeg. 'Fann is going away with Manannan mac Lir, since she hath not pleased thee!'

Then Cu Chulainn bounded three times high into the air, and he made three great leaps towards the south, and thus he came to Tara Luachra, and there he abode for a long time, having no meat and no drink, dwelling upon the mountains, and sleeping upon the high-road that runs through the midst of Luachra.

Then Emer went on to Emain, and there she sought out king Conchobar, and she told him of Cu Chulainn's state, and Conchobar sent out his learned men and his people of skill, and the druids of Ulster, to find Cu Chulainn, and to bind him fast, and bring him with them to Emain. And Cu Chulainn tried to kill the people of skill, but they chanted wizard and fairy spells against him, and they bound fast his feet and his hands until he came a little to his senses. Then he begged for a drink at their hands, and the druids gave him a drink of forgetfulness, so that afterwards he had no more remembrance of Fann nor of anything else that he had then done; and they also gave a drink of forgetfulness to Emer that she might forget her jealousy, for her state was in no way better than the state of Cu Chulainn. And Manannan shook his cloak between Cu Chulainn and Fann, so that they might never meet together again throughout eternity.

NOTES

Source: Tom Peete Cross and Clark Harris Slover (editors), *Ancient Irish Tales*, Dublin: Figgis, 1936.

This remarkable story is part of a cycle which revolves around the great Ultonian hero Chuclainn (Cu Chulainn), whose deeds are as remarkable as any hero in any culture. Here he is shown to be as subject to the power of the Otherworld as any man. Like many of the truly ancient stories of Ireland, this one bears the marks of having been edited together from several other texts. The basic story is that of the mortal who, having fallen beneath the spell of the fairy people, is healed of a malady and assisted by them in the settling of a tribal feud. The doubling of various events in this version of the story – the two visits of the fairy messengers to Chuclainn and the doubling of Loeg's account of his visit to the Otherworld – is a further indication of the age of the story. There are various inconsistencies, such as the early disappearance of Ethne from the story to be replaced by Chuclainn's wife Emer, and the fact that he seems to move from Tete Brecc to Emain Macha; but these do nothing to hold up the story, which still makes up for these occasional lapses with its poetry and extraordinary detailed account of the Otherworld.

The Adventures of Connla the Fair

HY WAS ART THE LONE ONE so called? Not hard to say.

One day as Connla the Bold, son of Conn the Hundred-Fighter, was with his father on the Hill of Usnech he saw a woman in unfamiliar dress. Said Connla, 'Where do you come from, O woman?'

The woman answered, 'I come from the Lands of the Living, where there is neither death nor want nor sin. We keep perpetual feast without need for service. Peace reigns among us without strife. A great fairy-mound (*sid*) it is, in which we live; wherefore we are called "folk of the fairy-mound" (*aes side*).'

'Who is it you are speaking to?' Conn asked his son; for none could see the woman save Connla alone.

The woman answered, 'He is speaking to a young and beautiful woman of noble descent, who will know neither death nor old age. Long have I loved Connla, and I summon him to Mag Mell, where Boadach the Eternal is king, a king in whose realm there has been no weeping and no sorrow since he began his rule.

'Come with me, O bold Connla, with rosy neck, gleaming like a candle. The fair crown that sits above thy ruddy countenance is a token of thy royalty. If thou wilt follow me thy form shall never decrease in youth or beauty, even to the marvellous Day of Judgment.'

Then Conn spoke to his druid (Corann was his name), for they had all heard everything the woman had said, although they did not see her:

The fairy woman summons Connla to Mag Mell.

I appeal to you, Corann,
Skilled in song, skilled in arts!
A power has come over me
Too great for my skill,
Too great for my strength;
A battle has come upon me
Such as I have not met since I took the sovereignty.

68

By a treacherous attack the unseen shape overpowers me,
To rob me of my fair son,
With heathen words of magic.
He is snatched from my royal side
By women's words of magic.

Whereupon the druid sang a magic incantation against the voice of the woman, so that no one could hear her voice, and Connla saw no more of her at that time. But as the woman departed before the potent chanting of the druid, she threw Connla an apple.

Connla remained to the end of a month without food or drink, for no nourishment seemed to him worthy to be consumed save only the apple. What he ate of the apple never diminished it, but it remained always unconsumed.

Longing seized upon Connla for the woman he had seen. On the day when the month was completed Connla was seated with his father in Mag Archommin, and he saw the same woman coming toward him. She spoke to him thus:

A woeful seat where Connla sits!
Among short-lived mortals,
Awaiting only dreadful death.
The living, the immortal call to you;
They summon you to the people of Tethra
Who behold you every day
In the assemblies of your native land,
Among your beloved kinsmen.

When Conn heard the voice of the woman, he called to his attendants, 'Summon me the druid. I see that her tongue is loosed to-day.'

Then said the woman:

O Conn the Hundred-Fighter,
Thou shouldst not cling to druidry!
It will not be long before there will come
To give judgments on our broad strand
A righteous one, with many wonderful companies
Soon his law will reach you.
He will annihilate the false law of the druids
In the sight of the black magic demon.

Then Conn wondered why Connla made no answer except when the woman came. 'Has it touched your heart, what the woman says, O Connla?' asked Conn.

Then said Connla, 'It is not easy for me. Although I love my people, longing for the woman has seized me.'

The woman said:

Thou strivest – most difficult of wishes to fulfill –
Against the wave of longing which drives thee hence.
That land we may reach in my crystal boat,
The fairy-mound of Boadach.

70

There is yet another land
That is no worse to reach;
I see it, now the sun sinks.
Although it is far, we may reach it before night.

That is the land which rejoices
The heart of everyone who wanders therein;
No other sex lives there
Save women and maidens.

Then Connla gave a leap into the woman's crystal boat. The people saw him going away. Hardly could their eyes follow Connla and the maiden as they fared forth over the sea. From that day forward they were never seen again. And then said Conn as he gazed upon his other son Art, 'To-day is Art left the lone one.' Hence he came to be called 'Art the Lone One' *(Art Oenfer)*.

NOTES

Source: Tom Peete Cross and Clark Harris Slover (editors and translators), *Ancient Irish Tales*, London: Figgis, 1936.

Several of the Otherworldly tales in this book concern the love of mortal men for fairy women and vice versa (less often, curiously, is it men who long for immortal women). In this story, as in the one that follows, we see this happen in dramatic circumstances which have an effect both on our own world and on the realm of the *sidhe*. 'The Adventures of Connla the Fair' is one of the oldest stories in this collection, dating from the eighth century, although not written down until some time after. It is cast in the form of a *dinnsencha*, or tale of landlore. There exists a vast body of such tales, all relating to places in Ireland where famous heroes or heroines are said to have lived. This is not a genuine *dinnsencha*, however, but simply a literary device. As its translators note, it is a nice touch to place the prediction of the coming of the 'righteous one', St Patrick (arch enemy of the pagans in Ireland), in the mouth of one of the fairy folk. Conn the Hundred Fighter (also known as Conn of the Hundred Battles), Connla's father, was one of the earliest recorded High Kings of Ireland, who flourished during the latter half of the second century AD.

Pwyll in Annwvyn

WYLL PRINCE OF DYVED was lord of the seven Cantrevs of Dyved; and once upon a time he was at Narberth his chief palace, and he was minded to go and hunt, and the part of his dominions in which it pleased him to hunt was Glyn Cuch. So he set forth from Narbeth that night, and went as far as Llwyn Diarwyd. And that night he tarried there, and early on the morrow he rose and came to Glyn Cuch, when he let loose the dogs in the wood, and sounded the horn, and began the chase. And as he followed the dogs, he lost his companions; and whilst he listened to the hounds, he heard the cry of other hounds, a cry different from his own, and coming in the opposite direction.

And he beheld a glade in the wood forming a level plain, and as his dogs came to the edge of the glade, he saw a stag before the other dogs. And lo, as it reached the middle of the glade, the dogs that followed the stag overtook it and brought it down. Then looked he at the colour of the dogs, staying not to look at the stag, and of all the hounds that he had seen in the world, he had never seen any that were like unto these. For their hair was of a brilliant shining white, and their ears were red; and as the whiteness of their bodies shone, so did the redness of their ears glisten. And he came towards the dogs, and drove away those that had brought down the stag, and set his own dogs upon it.

And as he was setting on his dogs he saw a horseman coming towards him upon a large light-grey steed, with a hunting horn round his neck, and clad in garments of grey woollen in the fashion of a hunting garb. And the horseman drew near and spoke unto him thus. 'Chieftain,' said he, 'I know who thou art, and I greet thee not.' 'Peradventure,' said Pwyll, 'thou art of such dignity that thou shouldest not do so.' 'Verily,' answered he, 'it is not my dignity that prevents me.' 'What is it then, O Chieftain?' asked he. 'By Heaven, it is by reason of thine own ignorance and want of courtesy.' 'What discourtesy, Chieftain, hast thou seen in me?' 'Greater discourtesy saw I never in man,' said he, 'than to drive away the dogs that were killing the stag and to set upon it thine own. This was discourteous, and though I may not be revenged upon thee, yet I declare to Heaven that I will do thee more dishonour than the value of an hundred stags.' 'O Chieftain,' he replied, 'if I have done ill I will redeem thy friendship.' 'How wilt thou redeem it?' 'According as thy dignity may be, but I know not who thou art?' 'A crowned king am I in the land whence I come.' 'Lord,' said he, 'may the day prosper with thee, and from what land comest thou?' 'From Annwvyn,' answered he; 'Arawn, a King of Annwvyn, am I.' 'Lord,' said he, 'how may I gain thy friendship?' 'After this manner mayest thou,' he said. 'There is a man whose dominions are opposite to mine, who is ever warring against me, and he is Havgan, a King of Annwvyn, and by ridding me of this oppression, which thou canst easily do, shalt thou gain my friendship.' 'Gladly will I do this,' said he. 'Show me how I may.' 'I will show thee. Behold thus it is thou mayest. I will make firm friendship with thee; and this will I do. I will send thee to Annwvyn in my stead, and I will give thee the fairest lady thou didst ever behold to be thy companion, and I will put my form and semblance upon thee, so that not a page of the chamber, nor an officer, nor any other man that has always followed me shall know that it is not I. And this shall be for the space of a year from to-morrow, and then we will meet in this place.' 'Yes,' said he; 'but when I shall have been there for the space of a year, by what means shall I discover him of whom thou speakest?' 'One year from this night,' he answered, 'is the time fixed between him and me that we should meet at the Ford; be thou there in my likeness, and with one stroke that thou givest him, he shall no longer live. And if he ask thee to give him another, give it not, how much soever he may entreat thee, for when I did so he fought with me next day as well as ever before.' 'Verily,' said Pwyll, 'what shall I do concerning my kingdom?' Said Arawn, 'I will cause that no one in all thy dominions, neither man nor woman, shall know that I am not thou, and I will go there in thy stead.' 'Gladly then,' said Pwyll, 'will I set forward.' 'Clear shall be thy path, and nothing shall detain thee, until thou come into my dominions, and I myself will be thy guide!'

So he conducted him until he came in sight of the palace and its dwellings. 'Behold,' said he, 'the Court and the kingdom in thy power. Enter the Court, there is no one there who will know thee, and when thou seest what service is done there, thou wilt know the customs of the Court.'

So he went forward to the Court, and when he came there, he beheld sleeping-rooms, and halls, and chambers, and the most beautiful buildings ever seen. And he went into the hall to disarray, and there came youths and pages and disarrayed him, and all as they entered saluted him. And two knights came and drew his hunting-dress from about him, and clothed him in a vesture of silk and gold. And the hall was prepared, and behold he saw the household and the host enter in, and the host was the most comely and the best equipped that he had ever seen. And with them came in likewise the Queen, who was the fairest woman that he had ever yet beheld. And she had on a yellow robe of shining satin; and they washed and went to the table, and sat, the Queen upon one side of him, and one who seemed to be an Earl on the other side.

And he began to speak with the Queen, and he thought, from her speech, that she was the seemliest and most noble lady of converse and of cheer that ever was. And they partook of meat, and drink, with songs and with feasting; and of all the Courts upon the earth, behold this was the best supplied with food and drink, and vessels of gold and royal jewels.

And the year he spent in hunting, and minstrelsy, and feasting, and diversions, and discourse with his companions until the night that was fixed for the conflict. And when that night came, it was remembered even by those who lived in the furthest part of his dominions, and he went to the meeting, and the nobles of the kingdom with him. And when he came to the Ford, a knight arose and spake thus. 'Lords,' said he, 'listen well. It is between two kings that this meeting is, and between them only. Each claimeth of the other his land and territory, and do all of you stand aside and leave the fight to be between them.'

Thereupon the two kings approached each other in the middle of the Ford, and encountered, and at the first thrust, the man who was in the stead of Arawn struck Havgan on the centre of the boss of his shield, so that it was cloven in twain, and his armour was broken, and Havgan himself was borne to the ground an arm's and a spear's length over the crupper of his horse, and he received a deadly blow. 'O Chieftain,' said Havgan, 'what right hast thou to cause my death? I was not injuring thee in anything, and I know not wherefore thou wouldest slay me. But, for the love of Heaven, since thou hast begun to slay me, complete thy work.' 'Ah, Chieftain,' he replied, ' I may yet repent doing that unto thee, slay thee who may, I will not do so.' 'My trusty Lords,' said Havgan, 'bear me hence. My death has come. I shall be no more able to uphold you.' 'My Nobles,' also said he who was in the semblance of Arawn, 'take counsel and know who ought to be my subjects.' 'Lord,' said the Nobles, 'all should be, for there is no king over the whole of Annwvyn but thee.' 'Yes,' he replied, 'it is right that he who comes humbly should be received graciously, but he that doth not come with obedience, shall be compelled by the force of swords.'

And thereupon he received the homage of the men, and he began to conquer the country; and the next day by noon the two kingdoms were in his power. And thereupon he went to keep his tryst, and came to Glyn Cuch.

And when he came there, the King of Annwvyn was there to meet him, and each of them was rejoiced to see the other. 'Verily,' said Arawn, 'may Heaven reward thee for thy friendship towards me. I have heard of it. When thou comest thyself to thy dominions,' said he, 'thou wilt see that which I have done for thee.' 'Whatever thou hast done for me, may Heaven repay it thee.'

Then Arawn gave to Pwyll Prince of Dyved his proper form and semblance, and he himself took his own; and Arawn set forth towards the Court of Annwvyn; and he was rejoiced when he beheld his hosts, and his household, whom he had not seen so long; but they had not known of his absence, and wondered no more at his coming than usual. And that day was spent in joy and merriment; and he sat and conversed with his wife and his nobles. And when it was time for them rather to sleep than to carouse, they went to rest.

Pwyll Prince of Dyved came likewise to his country and dominions, and began to inquire of the nobles of the land, how his rule had been during the past year, compared with what it had been before. 'Lord,' said they, 'thy wisdom was never so great, and thou wast never so kind or so free in bestowing thy gifts, and thy justice was never more worthily seen than in this year.' 'By Heaven,' said he, 'for all the good you have enjoyed, you should thank him who hath been with you; for behold, thus hath this matter been.' And thereupon Pwyll related the whole unto them. 'Verily, Lord,' said they, 'render thanks unto Heaven that thou hast such a fellowship, and withhold not from us the rule which we have enjoyed for this year past.' 'I take Heaven to witness that I will not withhold it,' answered Pwyll.

And thenceforth they made strong the friendship that was between them, and each sent unto the other horses, and greyhounds, and hawks, and all such jewels as they thought would be pleasing to each other. And by reason of his having dwelt that year in Annwvyn, and having ruled there so prosperously, and united the two kingdoms in one day by his valour and prowess, he lost the name of Pwyll Prince of Dyved, and was called Pwyll Chief of Annwvyn from that time forward.

Once upon a time, Pwyll was at Narberth his chief palace, where a feast had been prepared for him, and with him was a great host of men. And after the first meal, Pwyll arose to walk, and he went to the top of a mound that was above the palace, and was called Gorsedd Arberth. 'Lord,' said one of the Court, 'it is peculiar to the mound that whosoever sits upon it cannot go thence, without either receiving wounds or blows, or else seeing a wonder.' 'I fear not to receive wounds and blows in the midst of such a host as this, but as to the wonder, gladly would I see it. I will go therefore and sit upon the mound.'

And upon the mound he sat. And while he sat there, they saw a lady, on a pure white horse of large size, with a garment of shining gold around her, coming along the highway that led from the mound; and the horse seemed to move at a slow and even pace, and to be coming up towards the mound. 'My men,' said Pwyll, 'is there any among you who knows yonder lady?' 'There is not, Lord,' said they. 'Go one of you and meet her, that we may know who she is.' And one of them arose, and as he came upon the road to meet her, she passed by, and he followed as fast as he could, being on foot; and the greater was his speed, the further was she from him. And when he saw that it profited him nothing to follow her, he returned to Pwyll, and said unto him, 'Lord, it is idle for any one in the world to follow her on foot.' 'Verily,' said Pwyll, 'go unto the palace, and take the fleetest horse that thou seest, and go after her.'

And he took a horse and went forward. And he came to an open level plain, and put spurs to his horse; and the more he urged his horse, the further was she from him. Yet she held the same pace as at first. And his horse began to fail; and when his horse's feet failed him, he returned to the place where Pwyll was. 'Lord,' said he, 'it will avail nothing for any one to follow yonder lady. I know of no horse in these realms swifter than this, and it availed me not to pursue her.' 'Of a truth,' said Pwyll, 'there must be some illusion here. Let us go towards the palace.' So to the palace they went, and they spent that day. And the next day they arose, and that also they spent until it was time to go to meat. And after the first meal, 'Verily,' said Pwyll, 'we will go the same party as yesterday to the top of the mound. And do thou,' said he to one of his young men, 'take the swiftest horse that thou knowest in the field.' And thus did the young man. And they went towards the mound, taking the horse with them. And as they were sitting down they beheld the lady on the same horse, and in the same apparel, coming along the same road. 'Behold,' said Pwyll, 'here is the lady of yesterday. Make ready, youth, to learn who she is.' 'My lord,' said he, 'that will I gladly do.' And thereupon the lady came opposite to them. So the youth mounted his horse; and before he had settled himself in his saddle, she passed by, and there was a clear space between them. But her speed was no greater than it had been the day before. Then he put his horse into an amble, and thought that notwithstanding the gentle pace at which his horse went, he should soon overtake her. But this availed him not; so he gave his horse the reins. And still he came no nearer to her than when he went at a foot's pace. And the more he urged his horse, the further was she from him. Yet she rode not faster than before. When he saw that it availed not to follow her, he returned to the place where Pwyll was. 'Lord,' said he, 'the horse can no more than thou hast seen.' 'I see indeed that it avails not that any one should follow her. And by Heaven,' said he, 'she must needs have an errand to some one in this plain, if her haste would allow her to declare it. Let us go back to the palace.' And to the palace they went, and they spent that night in songs and feasting, as it pleased them.

And the next day they amused themselves until it was time to go to meat. And when meat was ended, Pwyll said, 'Where are the hosts that went yesterday and the

day before to the top of the mound?' 'Behold, Lord, we are here,' said they. 'Let us go,' said he, 'to the mound, to sit there. And do thou,' said he to the page who tended his horse, 'saddle my horse well, and hasten with him to the road, and bring also my spurs with thee.' And the youth did thus. And they went and sat upon the mound; and ere they had been there but a short time, they beheld the lady coming by the same road, and in the same manner, and at the same pace. 'Young man,' said Pwyll, 'I see the lady coming; give me my horse.' And no sooner had he mounted his horse than she passed him. And he turned after her and followed her. And he let his horse go bounding playfully, and thought that at the second step or the third he should come up with her. But he came no nearer to her than at first. Then he urged his horse to his utmost speed, yet he found that it availed nothing to follow her. Then said Pwyll, 'O maiden, for the sake of him whom thou best lovest, stay for me.' 'I will stay gladly,' said she, 'and it were better for thy horse hadst thou asked it long since.' So the maiden stopped, and she threw back that part of her headdress which covered her face. And she fixed her eyes upon him, and began to talk with him. 'Lady,' asked he, 'whence comest thou, and whereunto dost thou journey?' 'I journey on mine own errand,' said she, 'and right glad am I to see thee.' 'My greeting be unto thee,' said he. Then he thought that the beauty of all the maidens, and all the ladies that he had ever seen, was as nothing compared to her beauty. 'Lady,' he said, 'wilt thou tell me aught concerning thy purpose?' 'I will tell thee,' said she. 'My chief quest was to seek thee.' 'Behold,' said Pwyll, 'this is to me the most pleasing quest on which thou couldst have come; and wilt thou tell me who thou art?' 'I will tell thee, Lord,' said she. 'I am Rhiannon, the daughter of Heveydd Hên, and they sought to give me to a husband against my will. But no husband would I have, and that because of my love for thee, neither will I yet have one unless thou reject me. And hither have I come to hear thy answer.' 'By Heaven,' said Pwyll, 'behold this is my answer. If I might choose among all the ladies and damsels in the world, thee would I choose.' 'Verily,' said she, 'if thou art thus minded, make a pledge to meet me ere I am given to another.' 'The sooner I may do so, the more pleasing will it be unto me,' said Pwyll, 'and wheresoever thou wilt, there will I meet with thee.' 'I will that thou meet me this day twelvemonth at the palace of Heveydd. And I will cause a feast to be prepared, so that it be ready against thou come.' 'Gladly,' said he, 'will I keep this tryst.' 'Lord,' said she, 'remain in health, and be mindful that thou keep thy promise; and now I will go hence.' So they parted, and he went back to his hosts and to them of his household. And whatsoever questions they asked him respecting the damsel, he always turned the discourse upon other matters. And when a year from that time was gone, he caused a hundred knights to equip themselves and to go with him to the palace of Heveydd Hên. And he came to the palace, and there was great joy concerning him, with much concourse of people and great rejoicing, and vast preparations for his coming. And the whole Court was placed under his orders.

And the hall was garnished and they went to meat, and thus did they sit; Heveydd Hên was on one side of Pwyll, and Rhiannon on the other. And all the rest according to their rank. And they ate and feasted and talked one with another, and at the beginning of the carousal after the meat, there entered a tall auburn-haired youth, of royal bearing, clothed in a garment of satin. And when he came into the hall, he saluted Pwyll and his companions. 'The greeting of Heaven be unto thee, my soul,' said Pwyll, 'come thou and sit down.' 'Nay,' said he, 'a suitor am I, and I will do mine errand.' 'Do so willingly,' said Pwyll. 'Lord,' said he, 'my errand is unto thee, and it is to crave a boon of thee that I come.' 'What boon soever thou mayest ask of me, as far as I am able, thou shalt have.' 'Ah,' said Rhiannon, 'where-

Arawn riding with his hunting dogs.

fore didst thou give that answer?' 'Has he not given it before the presence of these nobles?' asked the youth. 'My soul,' said Pwyll, 'what is the boon thou askest?' 'The lady whom best I love is to be thy bride this night; I come to ask her of thee with the feast and the banquet that are in this place.' And Pwyll was silent because of the answer which he had given. 'Be silent as long as thou wilt,' said Rhiannon. 'Never did man make worse use of his wits than thou hast done.' 'Lady,' said he, 'I knew not who he was.' 'Behold this is the man to whom they would have given me against my will,' said she. 'And he is Gwawl the son of Clud, a man of great power and wealth, and because of the word thou hast spoken, bestow me upon him lest shame befall thee.' 'Lady,' said he, 'I understand not thine answer. Never can I do as thou sayest.' 'Bestow me upon him,' said she, 'and I will cause that I shall never be his.' 'By what means will that be?' asked Pwyll. 'In thy hand will I give thee a small bag,' said she. 'See that thou keep it well, and he will ask of thee the banquet, and the feast, and the preparations which are not in thy power. Unto the hosts and the household will I give the feast. And such will be thy answer respecting this. And as concerns myself, I will engage to become his bride this night twelvemonth. And at the end of the year be thou here,' said she, 'and bring this bag with thee, and let thy hundred knights be in the orchard up yonder. And when he is in the midst of joy and feasting, come thou in by thyself, clad in ragged garments, and holding thy bag in thy hand, and ask nothing but a bagful of food, and I will cause that if all the meat and liquor that are in these seven Cantrevs were put into it, it would be no fuller than before. And after a great deal has been put therein, he will ask thee whether thy bag will ever be full. Say thou then that it never will, until a man of noble birth and of great wealth arise and press the food in the bag with both his feet, saying, "Enough has been put therein"; and I will cause him to go and tread down the food in the bag, and when he does so, turn thou the bag, so that he shall be up over his head in it, and then slip a knot upon the thongs of the bag. Let there be also a good bugle horn about thy neck, and as soon as thou hast bound him in the bag, wind thy horn, and let it be a signal between thee and thy knights. And when they hear the sound of the horn, let them come down upon the palace.' 'Lord,' said Gwawl, 'it is meet that I have an answer to my request.' 'As much of that thou hast asked as it is in my power to give, thou shalt have,' replied Pwyll. 'My soul,' said Rhiannon unto him, 'as for the feast and the banquet that are here, I have bestowed them upon the men of Dyved, and the household, and the warriors that are with us. These can I not suffer to be given to any. In a year from to-night a banquet shall be prepared for thee in this palace, that I may become thy bride.'

So Gwawl went forth to his possessions, and Pwyll went also back to Dyved. And they both spent that year until it was the time for the feast at the palace of Heveydd Hên. Then Gwawl the son of Clud set out to the feast that was prepared for him, and he came to the palace, and was received there with rejoicing. Pwyll, also, the Chief of Annwvyn, came to the orchard with his hundred knights, as Rhiannon had commanded him, having the bag with him. And Pwyll was clad in coarse and ragged garments, and wore large clumsy old shoes upon his feet. And when he knew that the carousal after the meat had begun, he went towards the hall, and when he came into the hall, he saluted Gwawl the son of Clud, and his company, both men and women. 'Heaven prosper thee,' said Gwawl, 'and the greeting of Heaven be unto thee.' 'Lord,' said he, 'may Heaven reward thee, I have an errand unto thee.' 'Welcome be thine errand, and if thou ask of me that which is just, thou shalt have it gladly.' 'It is fitting,' answered he. 'I crave but from want, and the boon that I ask is to have this small bag that thou seest filled with meat.' 'A request within reason is this,' said he, 'and gladly shalt thou have it. Bring him food.' A great number of attendants arose and began to fill the bag, but for all that they put into it, it was no fuller than at first. 'My soul,' said Gwawl, 'will thy bag be ever full?' 'It will not, I declare to Heaven,' said he, 'for all that may be put into it, unless one possessed of lands, and domains, and treasure, shall rise and tread down with both his feet the food that is within the bag, and shall say, "Enough has been put therein."' Then said Rhiannon unto Gwawl the son of Clud, 'Rise up quickly.' 'I will willingly arise,' said he. So he rose up, and put his two feet into the bag. And Pwyll turned up the sides of the bag, so that Gwawl was over his head in it. And he shut it up quickly and slipped a knot upon the thongs, and blew his horn. And thereupon behold his household came down upon the palace. And they seized all the host that had come with Gwawl, and cast them into his own prison. And Pwyll threw off his rags, and his old shoes, and his tattered array; and as they came in, every one of Pwyll's knights struck a blow upon the bag, and asked, 'What is here?' 'A Badger,' said they. And in this manner they played, each of them striking the bag, either with his foot or with a staff. And thus played they with the bag. Every one as he came in asked, 'What game are you playing at thus?' 'The game of Badger in the Bag,' said they. And then was the game of Badger in the Bag first played.

'Lord,' said the man in the bag, 'if thou wouldest but hear me, I merit not to be slain in a bag.' Said Heveydd Hên, 'Lord, he speaks truth. It were fitting that thou listen to him, for he deserves not this.' 'Verily,' said Pwyll, 'I will do thy counsel concerning him.' 'Behold this is my counsel then,' said Rhiannon; 'thou art now in a position in which it behoves thee to satisfy suitors and minstrels; let him give unto them in thy stead, and take a pledge from him that he will never seek to revenge that which has been done to him. And this will be punishment enough.' 'I will do this gladly,' said the man in the bag. 'And gladly will I accept it,' said Pwyll, 'since it is the counsel of Heveydd and Rhiannon.' 'Such then is our counsel,' answered they. 'I accept it,' said Pwyll. 'Seek thyself sureties.' 'We will be for him,' said Heveydd, 'until his men be free to answer for him.' And upon this he was let out of the bag, and his liegemen were liberated. 'Demand now of Gwawl his sureties,' said Heveydd, 'we know which should be taken for him.' And Heveydd numbered the sureties. Said Gwawl, 'Do thou thyself draw up the covenant.' 'It will suffice me that it be as Rhiannon said,' answered Pwyll. So unto that covenant were the sureties pledged. 'Verily, Lord,' said Gwawl, 'I am greatly hurt, and I have many bruises. I have need to be anointed; with thy leave I will go forth. I will leave nobles in my stead, to answer for me in all that thou shalt require.' 'Willingly,' said Pwyll, 'mayest thou do thus.' So Gwawl went towards his own possessions.

And the hall was set in order for Pwyll and the men of his host, and for them also of the palace, and they went to the tables and sat down. And as they had sat that time twelvemonth, so sat they that night. And they ate, and feasted, and spent the night in mirth and tranquillity. And the time came that they should sleep, and Pwyll and Rhiannon went to their chamber.

And next morning at the break of day, 'My Lord,' said Rhiannon, 'arise and begin to give thy gifts unto the minstrels. Refuse no one to-day that may claim thy bounty.' 'Thus shall it be gladly,' said Pwyll, 'both to-day and every day while the feast shall last.' So Pwyll arose, and he caused silence to be proclaimed, and desired all the suitors and the minstrels to show and to point out what gifts were to their wish and desire. And this being done, the feast went on, and he denied no one while it lasted. And when the feast was ended, Pwyll said unto Heveydd, 'My Lord, with thy permission I will set out for Dyved to-morrow.' 'Certainly,' said Heveydd, 'may Heaven prosper thee. Fix also a time when Rhiannon may follow thee.' 'By Heaven,' said Pwyll, 'we will go hence together.' 'Willest thou this, Lord?' said Heveydd. 'Yes, by Heaven,' answered Pwyll.

And the next day, they set forward towards Dyved, and journeyed to the palace of Narberth, where a feast was made ready for them. And there came to them great numbers of the chief men and the most noble ladies of the land, and of these there was none to whom Rhiannon did not give some rich gift, either a bracelet, or a ring, or a precious stone. And they ruled the land prosperously both that year and the next.

And in the third year the nobles of the land began to be sorrowful at seeing a man whom they loved so much, and who was moreover their lord and their foster-brother, without an heir. And they came to him. And the place where they met was Preseleu, in Dyved. 'Lord,' said they, 'we know that thou art not so young as some of the men of this country, and we fear that thou mayest not have an heir of the wife whom thou hast taken. Take therefore another wife of whom thou mayest have heirs. Thou canst not always continue with us, and though thou desire to remain as thou art, we will not suffer thee.' 'Truly,' said Pwyll, 'we have not long been joined together, and many things may yet befall. Grant me a year from this time, and for the space of a year we will abide together, and after that I will do according to your wishes. So they granted it. And before the end of a year a son was born unto him. And in Narberth was he born; and on the night that he was born, women were brought out to watch the mother and the boy. And the women slept, as did also Rhiannon, the mother of the boy. And the number of the women that were brought into the chamber was six. And they watched for a good portion of the night, and before midnight every one of them fell asleep, and towards break of day they awoke; and when they awoke, they looked where they had put the boy, and behold he was not there. 'Oh,' said one of the women, 'the boy is lost!' 'Yes,' said another, 'and it will be small vengeance if we are burnt or put to death because of the child.' Said one of the women, 'Is there any counsel for us in the world in this matter?' 'There is,' answered another, 'I offer you good counsel.' 'What is that?' asked they. 'There is here a stag-hound bitch, and she has a litter of whelps. Let us kill some of the cubs, and rub the blood on the face and hands of Rhiannon, and lay the bones before her, and assert that she herself hath devoured her son, and she alone will not be able to gainsay us six.' And according to this counsel it was settled. And towards morning Rhiannon awoke, and she said, 'Women, where is my son?' 'Lady,' said they, 'ask us not concerning thy son, we have nought but the blows and the bruises we got by struggling with thee, and of a truth we never saw any woman so violent as thou, for it was of no avail to contend with thee. Hast thou not thyself devoured thy son? Claim him not therefore of us.' 'For pity's sake,' said Rhiannon; 'the Lord God knows all things. Charge me not falsely. If you tell me this from fear, I assert before Heaven that I will defend you.' 'Truly,' said they, 'we would not bring evil on ourselves for any one in the world.' 'For pity's sake,' said Rhiannon, 'you will receive no evil by telling the truth.' But for all her words, whether fair or harsh, she received but the same answer from the women.

And Pwyll the chief of Annwvyn arose, and his household, and his hosts. And this occurrence could not be concealed, but the story went forth throughout the land, and all the nobles heard it. Then the nobles came to Pwyll, and besought him to put away his wife, because of the great crime which she had done. But Pwyll answered them, that they had no cause wherefore they might ask him to put away his wife, save for her having no children. 'But children has she now had, therefore will I not put her away; if she has done wrong, let her do penance for it.'

So Rhiannon sent for the teachers and the wise men, and as she preferred doing penance to contending with the women, she took upon her a penance. And the penance that was imposed upon her was, that she should remain in that palace of Narberth until the end of seven years, and that she should sit every day near unto a horse-block that was without the gate. And that she should relate the story to all who should come there, whom she might suppose not to know it already; and that she should offer the guests and strangers, if they would permit her, to carry them upon her back into the palace. But it rarely happened that any would permit. And thus did she spend part of the year.

Now at that time Teirnyon Twryv Vliant was Lord of Gwent Is Coed, and he was the best man in the world. And unto his house there belonged a mare, than which neither mare nor horse in the kingdom was more beautiful. And on the night of every first of May she foaled, and no one ever knew what became of the colt. And one night Teirnyon talked with his wife: 'Wife,' said he, 'it is very simple of us that our mare should foal every year, and that we should have none of her colts.' 'What can be done in the matter?' said she. 'This is the night of the first of May,' said he. 'The vengeance of Heaven be upon me, if I learn not what it is that takes away the colts.' So he caused the mare to be brought into a house, and he armed himself, and began to watch that night. And in the beginning of the night, the mare foaled a large and beautiful colt. And it was standing up in the place. And Teirnyon rose up and looked at the size of the colt, and as he did so he heard a great tumult, and after the tumult behold a claw came through the window into the house, and it seized the colt by the mane. Then Teirnyon drew his sword, and struck off the arm at the elbow, so that portion of the arm together with the colt was in the house with him. And then did he hear a tumult and wailing, both at once. And he opened the door, and rushed out in the direction of the noise, and he could not see the cause of the tumult because of the darkness of the night, but he rushed after it and followed it. Then he remembered that he had left the door open, and he returned. And at the door behold there was an infant boy in swaddling-clothes, wrapped around in a mantle of satin. And he took up the boy, and behold he was very strong for the age that he was of.

Then he shut the door, and went into the chamber where his wife was. 'Lady,' said he, 'art thou sleeping?' 'No, lord,' said she, 'I was asleep, but as thou camest in I did awake.' 'Behold, here is a boy for thee if thou wilt,' said he, 'since thou hast never had one.' 'My lord,' said she, 'what adventure is this?' 'It was thus,' said Teirnyon; and he told her how it all befell. 'Verily, lord,' said she, 'what sort of garments are there upon the boy?' 'A mantle of satin,' said he. 'He is then a boy of gentle lineage,' she replied. 'My lord,' she said, 'if thou wilt, I shall have great diversion and mirth. I will call my women unto me, and tell them that I have been pregnant.' 'I will readily grant thee to do this,' he answered. And thus did they, and they caused the boy to be baptized, and the ceremony was performed there; and the name which they gave unto him was Gwri Wallt Euryn, because what hair was upon his head was as yellow as gold. And they had the boy nursed in the Court until he was a year old. And before the year was over he could walk stoutly. And he was larger than a boy of three years old, even one of great growth and size. And the boy was nursed the second year, and then he was as large as a child six years old. And before the end of the fourth year, he would bribe the grooms to allow him to take the horses to water. 'My lord,' said his wife unto Teirnyon, 'where is the colt which thou didst save on the night that thou didst find the boy?' 'I have commanded the grooms of the horses,' said he, 'that they take care of him.' 'Would it not be well, lord,' said she, 'if thou wert to cause him to be broken in, and given to the boy, seeing that on the same night that thou didst find the boy, the colt was foaled and thou didst save him?' 'I will not oppose thee in this matter,' said Teirnyon. 'I will allow thee to give him the colt.' 'Lord,' said she, 'may Heaven reward thee; I will give it him.' So the horse was given to the boy. Then she went to the grooms and those who tended the horses, and commanded them to be careful of the horse, so that he might be broken in by the time that the boy could ride him.

And while these things were going forward, they heard tidings of Rhiannon and her punishment. And Teirnyon Twryv Vliant, by reason of the pity that he felt on hearing this story of Rhiannon and her punishment, inquired closely concerning it, until he had heard from many of those who came to his court. Then did Teirnyon, often lamenting the sad history, ponder within himself, and he looked steadfastly on the boy, and as he looked upon him, it seemed to him that he had never beheld so great a likeness between father and son, as between the boy and Pwyll the Chief of Annwvyn. Now the semblance of Pwyll was well known to him, for he had of yore been one of his followers. And thereupon he became grieved for the wrong that he did, in keeping with him a boy whom he knew to be the son of another man. And the first time that he was alone with his wife, he told her that it was not right that they should keep the boy with them, and suffer so excellent a lady as Rhiannon to be punished so greatly on his account, whereas the boy was the son of Pwyll the Chief of Annwvyn. And Teirnyon's wife agreed with him, that they should send the boy to Pwyll. 'And three things, lord,' said she, 'shall we gain thereby. Thanks and gifts for releasing Rhiannon from her punishment; and thanks from Pwyll for nursing his son and restoring him unto him; and thirdly, if the boy is of gentle nature, he will be our foster-son, and he will do for us all the good in his power.' So it was settled according to this counsel.

And no later than the next day was Teirnyon equipped, and two other knights with him. And the boy, as a fourth in their company, went with them upon the horse which Teirnyon had given him. And they journeyed towards Narberth, and it was not long before they reached that place. And as they drew near to the palace, they beheld Rhiannon sitting beside the horse-block. And when they were opposite to her, 'Chieftain,' said she, 'go not further thus, I will bear every one of you into the palace, and this is my penance for slaying my own son and devouring him.' 'Oh, fair lady,' said Teirnyon, 'think not that I will be one to be carried upon thy back.' 'Neither will I,' said the boy. 'Truly, my soul,' said Teirnyon, 'we will not go.' So they went forward to the palace, and there was great joy at their coming. And at the palace a feast was prepared, because Pywll was come back from the confines of Dyved. And they went into the hall and washed, and Pwyll rejoiced to see Teirnyon. And in this order they sat. Teirnyon between Pwyll and Rhiannon, and Teirnyon's two companions on the other side of Pwyll, with the boy between them. And after meat they began to carouse and to discourse. And Teirnyon's discourse was concerning the adventure of the mare and the boy, and how he and his wife had nursed and reared the child as their own. 'And behold here is thy son, lady,' said Teirnyon. 'And whosoever told that lie concerning thee, has done wrong. And when I heard of thy sorrow, I was troubled and grieved. And I believe that there is none of this host who will not perceive that the boy is the son of Pwyll,' said Teirnyon. 'There is none,' said they all, 'who is not certain thereof.' 'I declare to Heaven,' said Rhiannon, 'that if this be true, there is indeed an end to my trouble.' 'Lady,' said Pendaran Dyved, 'well hast thou named thy son Pryderi, and well becomes him the name of Pryderi son of Pwyll Chief of Annwvyn.' 'Look you,' said Rhiannon, 'will not his own name become him better?' 'What name has he?' asked Pendaran Dyved. 'Gwri Wallt Euryn is the name that we gave him.' 'Pryderi,' said Pendaran, 'shall his name be.' 'It were more proper,' said Pwyll, 'that the boy should take his name from the word his mother spoke when she received the joyful tidings of him.' And thus was it arranged.

'Teirnyon,' said Pwyll, 'Heaven reward thee that thou hast reared the boy up to this time, and, being of gentle lineage, it were fitting that he repay thee for it.' 'My lord,' said Teirnyon, 'it was my wife who nursed him, and there is no one in the world so afflicted as she at parting with him. It were well that he should bear in mind what I and my wife have done for him.' 'I call Heaven to witness,' said Pwyll, 'that while I live I will support thee and thy possessions, as long as I am able to preserve my own. And when he shall have power, he will more fitly maintain them than I. And if this counsel be pleasing unto thee, and to my nobles, it shall be that, as thou hast reared him up to the present time, I will give him to be brought up by Pendaran Dyved, from henceforth. And you shall be companions, and shall both be foster-fathers unto him.' 'This is good counsel,' said they all. So the boy was given to Pendaran Dyved, and the nobles of the land were sent with him. And Teirnyon Twryv Vliant, and his companions, set out for his country, and his possessions, with love and gladness. And he went not without being offered the fairest jewels and the fairest horses, and the choicest dogs; but he would take none of them.

Thereupon they all remained in their own dominions. And Pryderi, the son of Pwyll the Chief of Annwvyn, was brought up carefully as was fit, so that he became the fairest youth, and the most comely, and the best skilled in all good games, of any in the kingdom. And thus passed years and years, until the end of Pwyll the Chief of Annwvyn's life came, and he died.

And Pryderi ruled the seven Cantrevs of Dyved prosperously, and he was beloved by his people, and by all around him. And at length he added unto them the three Cantrevs of Ystrad Tywi, and the four Cantrevs of Cardigan; and these were called the Seven Cantrevs of Seissyllwch. And when he made this addition, Pryderi the son of Pwyll the Chief of Annwvyn desired to take a wife. And the wife he chose was Kicva, the daughter of Gwynn Gohoyw, the son of Gloyw Wallt Lydan, the son of Prince Casnar, one of the nobles of this Island.

And thus ends this portion of the Mabinogion.

 # NOTES

Source: Lady Charlotte Guest (translator), *The Mabinogion*, London: J.M. Dent, 1937.

As in 'The Adventures of Connla the Fair', 'Pwyll in Annwvyn' begins with the meeting between a mortal and a fairy in this case no lesser person than the Lord of Annwvyn (or Annwn) – the Welsh underworld. But in this tale, one of the finest from the great medieval myth-book known as *The Mabinogion*, we learn of the effects of this meeting, and of the complex effects which came about as a result of Pwyll's changing places with Arawn. It is also the story of Rhiannon, one of the most complex and vital characters in the entire range of Celtic myth and romance, and it ends not only with her vindication but also with the establishing of another great Welsh hero-figure, Pryderi, whose name, meaning 'anxiety', gives one more than a small clue as to his future. The story was written down in the thirteenth century, but had certainly been circulating for far longer than this as a bardic tale.

The Story of Bóänd

OETS OF PLEASANT IRELAND, if any of ye should demand it of me: know ye the trick whereby Óengus obtained the Brug in perpetuity?

The mansion where the Dagda, who lacked not cunning, dwelt, ay and the possessions that were Fíacc's; what then caused it, that Óengus came by the white Brug?

Bóänd, wife of fierce Nechtan, came without sorrow thither, to the house of Elcmaire of the steeds, he who gave his judgments from the Brug.

Bóänd fair of bloom from the Brí was at the Brug, in her own brother's dwelling, when the Dagda cast eyes on her, and was seized by desire for her.

Thrice sent the stern Dagda to whom all Banba belonged, and besought proud Elcmaire for the lady who was in his northern dwelling.

Pleasantly spake her brother to fair and slender Bóänd of the *Sídh:* 'Long or short be thy stay here, I will stay at leisure in mine abode.'

The three druids of the noble Dagda return across Ath Gabla's grey river, to tell the king how he might meet the fair and lovely lady.

'Send thou the strong Elcmaire,' quoth the keen soft-voiced druid, 'to go a journey from his house; then lie thou with the woman.'

The Dagda answered angrily: 'Let Elcmaire be sent, 'twill be a fierce triumph! He will not be to his knowledge a pleasant night absent from his stronghold at our bidding.'

'Send thou him forth upon the level road, though he raise neither cess nor tribute, let him be nine months abroad.'

'For I will keep the sun in the lofty ridge of the heavens till the end of nine months ripening the strong grass.'

Elcmaire of the fords was summoned, for he was envoy to the peoples: the king said to him: 'Go speedily on an errand for me!'

'Loth am I to go on thy hest into the country: this I conceal not, O Chief who controllest territories: for since my sister is come from the south, I cannot win gain nor pleasure.'

Bóänd beneath the river.

84

'Thine errand is to go into the country,' answered he who held the feasting of Fál: 'Sleep not at night abroad, till thou reach the white Brug.'

'If he has accepted thy mission,' spoke the druid softly, 'let entertainment deftly prepared await him in the house to which he goes.'

'When he reaches the silent echoing house, let strong new ale be poured out for him: let him be summoned to prove the good faith of the deeds (*sc. the errand*) if he will but arrive at the king's house.'

'Tell me thy proud message,' quoth the swift-footed chief from the hillside. 'Wilt thou go when day comes to seek me a stainless wife?'

Elcmaire of the strong Brug answered: 'If I can go with thy message, tell me, O king chaste and without guile, of whom wouldst thou seek a fair woman?'

'Seek me a woman wise and strong, who can watch over my northern household, from the king of cool Mag Inis, what time thou hast sought him out in his *síd*-dwelling.

Elcmaire rises and fares eastward, as an envoy with his hest: when he reached the king's dwelling, mead and wine were poured out for him.

For such time as the fair hero stayed at his ale without wrongful tarrying, the Dagda lay with his sister, heeding not point of honour, nor deed of war.

The strong hospitaller girds himself, and turns homeward across the hills, till the completion of nine months, when the sun at last went down.

As he approached the yellow stronghold of the Brug, seeing that none came to meet him, and that a strange ripeness was across the fields, he resented what had been done to him.

For the keen Elcmaire marked how upon the lofty mountain beyond him, the bloom of all the flowers had changed, by the time he reached the Brug.

'Ay,' said Bóänd of the strong Brug to the tall king of Ross: 'the quern of the strong hills will find me out, and he will burn me head and foot.'

'Hide thy fault and I will conceal it,' *answered the Dagda*, 'deny it and I will do the same: 'twere ill that thine unfaithfulness should be cast up to thy face.'

Birthpangs seize the woman in that strong hill-fortress in the north: on a site of bright auspice, she brought forth a goodly son.

She spoke: 'Since I yielded to happiness, he is my sole valour (*óen-gus*): *but* so long as earth is strong, I shall not bring him with me to my house.'

'Young (*óc*) is the child (*in mac*),' answered the swart Dagda, 'who sets his foot on Banba's soil: *Óengus in Mac Óc*, let him be called, whosoever would call him a pleasant name.'

Then fear came upon them over the grey estuary, as the warrior *Elcmaire* came home to his *liss*: they parted before him to south and north, and left the child unknown upon the cold plain.

It chanced that crafty Midir was at hand in his *síd*-mansion by the wayside; he brought the child home to his dwelling, where he grew to strength and fame.

Seven years dwelt he in the Brí, and trod that land of warriors: he thought that it was his father who had fostered him, and that he was son of the woman there.

Lads had Midir with him, a merry bright-haired troop: he was wont to have about him, as he feasted in his soldier's house, this little childish company.

One day as they held deedfully their sports upon the ample lawn of the *liss*, they spoke with rash malice to fair and active Óengus.

'Though the kindly Midir has cherished thee here after the manner of sons of kings, thy race and parentage are unknown, although thou hast been reared yonder in the *síd*.'

Bitter to the upright and noble boy, what was said to him in the hospitable

86

síd-dwelling, 'Thine origin and its value is not known,' quoth the noble lads therein.

The boy goes from them homewards: his noble mantle was a burden to him: presently he proclaims his grief loudly through the house.

'Let us hear this cause, a bitter truth, with which thou imprudently reproachest me: come, lad!' spoke Midir to him, 'tell me wherein is thy grief.'

'Since it has cast thee into pain and sorrow,' said Óengus, 'I shall tell thee: I know not my race to proclaim it, that truly grieves me.'

'I will tell thee eagerly what intrigues thee: behold Ireland from the east unto the west, her king is thy father, nor small his renown abroad.'

'I will go with thee on thy road,' quoth stately Midir, 'that thou mayest be stablished safely: that I may leave thee in a fitting mansion in the keen Dagda's house at the feast.'

'I shall bring ale and food to the stronghold, where bides the hero, great and noble: what time his copious ale is prepared, I shall make known to him his fair and noble son.'

'Lad,' spoke Midir of the mead-cups, 'poets will praise thee at the feast; and if he will grant thee a royal boon, what shall we ask for our ale-feast?'

'Be this the plan right purposeful – for not scant is our claim on his possessions – if the grim Dagda would grant a boon, ask boldly for his own fortress!'

The brilliant feast is held: noble it was upon Mag Breg of the kine: the king's household assembled full many throughout the day.

Famed warriors of Banba, they came to the strong Dagda's dwelling; all that found not room in the *dún* bided without at the walls.

'A lad have I,' quoth courteous Midir, 'whom I have brought safely with me all the way: a son whom we have fostered in our *síd* for the king of the fair Isle of Fál.'

Then spoke the stern Dagda, he who held unsorrowing Banba: 'O Midir of the plain of diadems, what seekest thou for thine ample ale-feast?'

'When the ale-feast of the warriors is made ready,' answered Midir, 'I conceal not, O fairhaired King of poets, that I shall not claim thy cattle, but I will accept thy Brug in perpetuity.'

'Seek not heedlessly for my Brug: I will not have it laid under tribute: nay, man, I shall not grant it to thee for all that is beneath the sky.'

'Then, though thou grant no more, for thou art sovereign across every highway; a day and night's loan without fail of the house wherein thou stayest.'

'Give me thy bonds, O prince of Rí, thou who wieldest an accustomed spear, swear to me by moon and sun, as all true men must swear according to cause.'

The Dagda vacated his mansion: 'twas a compromise without value: Óengus and pleasant Midir had overreached the king.

Ere the third day was come, the chieftain returned to them, and even before help could come unto them, the hero ordered them forth forever.

'Sire,' quoth Midir proudly, 'if thou wouldst permit our rightful compact; King of just purposes, night and day are not yet ended.'

In this wise was the Dagda cozened of the fruitful lands of his right: it cast him into sevenfold grief, lest any should divine his secret.

Historians of the wide world, O famed and glorious company: relate to me of the mother of Mac Ind Óc, and under what sod she lies.

I will make known to ye in measured verse, for I am learned by plain and wave: Bóänd pleasant spouse of Nechtan, that is her name in lovely Leth Cuind.

Forty years that were her age, a glorious vision, until she bore the king his son.

Stately Námu's son, he who had reached Fánat of the warriors, perceived that his lady who held his proud residence, had lain there with the swift Dagda.

As the Dagda, not lacking in cunning hastened across the withered plain of the roads, stately Námu's son said to her 'twould profit her little to make lying protest.

'A blessing upon thee,' quoth the lady, 'it will not be hard' . . .

'Yonder rise the springs of Segais . . . whosoever approaches them with a lie, goes not from them in like guise' . . .

'There the cupbearers dispense the cold water of the well, no arduous tale is this, the four of them pace round, guarding it.'

'I will make my way to the pleasing Segais to prove my chastity beyond doubt; thrice shall I walk widdershins around the living water, inviolate!'

But the dire well burst forth towards her – true is my tale: with a cry she lamented her dishonour, when she found not protection in her undertaking.

Fast fled she, and the stream pursued her across the land: nor was more seen of the lovely lady, till she reached the sea.

And the stream keeps fast her name, for as long as the hills shall stand: Bóänd is the swift water's name by every reach in its flowing course.

The period of mighty Nechtan's spouse, Cináed hath rightly established it: the woman's age, until (the river) extinguished her life, in this body she was five years and five times seven.

 # NOTES

Source: Lucius Gwynn (translator), in *ERIU*, Vol. 7 (1914), 230–36.

This poem tells a tale of Otherworldly and mortal love, which takes place in a kind of Otherworldly dimension of Ireland, where the gods Dagda and Midir exist side by side with their human counterparts. The story, of the desire of Dagda (the father god of Irish tradition) for the beautiful maiden Bóänd, reminds one of the Greek tales of Zeus' amorous dallying. The result in this instance is the birth of Oengus mac ind Oc, who is later recognized as the god of love. I have omitted the first nine verses of the poem, which add nothing to the story and are difficult to understand. The manuscript in which the poem appears is unfortunately corrupt, and where the meaning is unclear, and the original translator failed to do so, I have silently amended the text for sense. The same story, in a much reworked and developed version which adds a great deal to the part printed here, will be found in 'The Wooing of Étaín' (page 163).

The Story of Conn-eda; or, The Golden Apples of Loch Erne

T WAS LONG BEFORE the time the western districts of *Innis Fodhla* ['Island of Fate', possibly an old name for Ireland] had any settled name, but were indiscriminately called after the person who took possession of them, and whose name they retained only as long as his sway lasted, a powerful king reigned over this part of the sacred island. He was a puissant warrior, and no individual was found able to compete with him either on land or sea, or question his right to the conquest he made by strength of his manly right hand, the point of his glittering javelin, and keen edge of his blue sword. The great king of the west held uncontrolled sway from the island of Rathlin to the mouth of the Shannon by sea, and far as the glittering Shannon wound its sinuous length by land. The ancient king of the west, whose name was Conn, was good as well as great, and passionately loved by his people. His queen was a *Breaton* (British) princess, and was equally beloved and esteemed, because she was the very counterpart of the king in every respect; for whatever good qualification was found wanting in one, the other was certain to indemnify the omission. It was plainly manifest that heaven approved of the career in life of the virtuous couple; for during their reign the earth produced exuberant crops, the trees fruit ninefold commensurate with their usual bearing, the rivers, lakes, and surrounding sea teemed with abundance of choice fishes, while herds and flocks were unusually prolific, and kine and sheep yielded such abundance of rich milk, that they shed it in torrents upon the pastures; and furrows and cavities were always filled with the pure lacteal produce of the dairy. All these were blessings heaped by heaven upon the western districts of *Innis Fodhla*, over which the benignant and just Conn swayed his sceptre, in approbation of the course of government he had marked out for his own guidance. It is needless to state that the people who owned the authority of this great and good sovereign were the happiest on the face of the wide expanse of earth. It was during his reign, and that of his son and successor, that Ireland acquired the title of the 'happy isle of the west' among foreign nations. Conn Mór, and his good Queen Eda, reigned in great glory during many years: they were blessed with an only son, whom they named Conn-eda, after both his parents, because the Druids foretold, at his birth, that he would inherit the good qualities of both. According as the young prince grew in years, his amiable and benignant qualities of mind, as well as his great strength of body and manly bearing, became more manifest. He was the idol of his parents, and the proud boast of his people; he was beloved and respected to that degree that neither prince, lord nor plebeian swore an oath either by the sun, moon, stars, or elements, except by the head of Conn-eda. This career of glory however was doomed to meet a powerful but temporary impediment, for the good Queen Eda took a sudden and severe illness, of which she died in a few days, thus plunging her spouse, her son, and all her people, into a depth of grief and sorrow from which it was found difficult to relieve them.

The good king and his subjects mourned the loss of Queen Eda for a year and a day; and, at the expiration of that time, Conn Mór reluctantly yielded to the advice of his Druids and counsellors, and took to wife the daughter of his Archdruid. The new queen appeared to walk in the footsteps of the good Eda for several years, and gave great satisfaction to her subjects. But, in course of time, having had several children, and perceiving that Conn-eda was the favourite son of the king, and the darling of the people, she clearly foresaw that he would become successor to the throne after the demise of his father, and that her son would certainly be excluded. This excited the hatred and inflamed the jealousy of the Druid's daughter against her stepson to such an extent, that she resolved, in her own mind, to leave nothing in her power undone to procure his death, or even exile from the kingdom. She began by circulating evil reports of the prince; but, as he was above suspicion, the king only laughed at the weakness of the queen; and the great princes and chieftains, supported by the people in general, gave an unqualified contradiction; while the prince himself bore all his trials with the utmost patience and always repaid her bad and malicious acts towards him with good and benevolent ones. The enmity of the queen towards Conn-eda knew no bounds, when she saw that the false reports she circulated could not injure him, because he was a public man whose character was too well known and appreciated to suffer the least injury from the poisoned sting of calumny. As a last resource, to carry out her wicked projects, she determined to consult her *Cailleach-chearc* (henwife), who was a reputed enchantress.

Pursuant to her resolution, by the early dawn of morning she hied to the cabin of the *Cailleach-chearc*, and divulged to her the cause of her trouble. 'I cannot render you any help,' said the *Cailleach*, 'until you name the *duais*' (reward). 'What *duais* do you require?' asked the queen impatiently. 'My *duais*,' replied the enchantress, 'is to fill the cavity of my arm with wool, and the hole I shall bore with my distaff with red wheat.' 'Your *duais* is granted, and shall be immediately given you,' said the queen. The enchantress thereupon stood in the door of her hut, and bending her arm into a circle with her side, directed the royal attendants to thrust the wool into her house through her arm; and she never permitted them to cease until all the available space within was filled with wool. She then got on the roof of her brother's house, and, having made a hole through it with her distaff, caused red wheat to be spilled through it, until that house was filled up to the roof, so that there was no room for another grain within. 'Now,' said the queen, 'since you have received your *duais*, tell me how I can accomplish my purpose.' 'Take this chess-board and chess, and invite the prince to play with you; you shall win the first game. The condition you shall make is, that whoever wins a game shall be at liberty to impose whatever *geasa* (conditions) the winner pleases upon the loser. When you win, you must bind the prince under the penalty either to go into *ionarbadh* (exile), or procure for you, within the space of a year and a day, the three golden apples that grow in the garden, the *each dubh* (black steed), and *coilean con na mbuadh* (hound of supernatural powers), called Samer, which are in the possession of the king of the Firbolg race, who resides in Loch Erne. Those two things are so precious, and so well guarded, that he never can attain them by his own power; and, if he would rashly attempt to seek them, he should lose his life.'

The queen was greatly rejoiced at the advice, and lost no time in inviting Conn-eda to play a game at chess, under the conditions she had been instructed to arrange by the enchantress. The queen won the game, as the enchantress had foretold; but so great was her anxiety to have the prince completely in her power, that she was tempted to challenge him to play a second game, which Conn-eda, to her astonishment, and no less mortification, easily won. 'Now,' said the prince, 'since you have won the first game, it is your duty to impose your *geis* first.' 'My *geis*,' said the queen, 'which I impose upon you, is to procure me the *each dubh* (black steed), and *coilean con na mbuadh* (hound of supernatural powers), which are in the keeping of the king of the Firbolgs, in Loch Erne, within the space of a year and a day; or, in case you fail, to go into *ionarbadh* (exile), and never return, except you surrender yourself to lose your head and *comhead beatha*' (preservation of life). 'Well, then,' said the prince, 'the *geis* which I bind you by is, to sit upon the pinnacle of yonder tower until my return, and to take neither food nor nourishment of any description, except what red wheat you can pick up with the point of your bodkin; but, if I do not return, you are at perfect liberty to come down at the expiration of the year and a day.'

In consequence of the severe *geis* imposed unexpectedly upon him, Conn-eda was very much troubled in mind; and, well knowing he had a long journey to make before he would reach his destination, immediately prepared to set out on his way, not, however, before he had the satisfaction of witnessing the ascent of the queen to the place where she was obliged to remain exposed to the scorching sun of summer, and the blasting storms of winter, for the space of one year and a day, at least. Conn-eda being ignorant of what steps he should take to procure the *each dubh* and *coilean con na mbuadh*, though he was well aware that human energy would prove unavailing, thought proper to consult the Great Druid, Fionn Badhna, of Sliabh Badhna, who was a friend of his, before he ventured to proceed to Loch Erne. When he arrived at the *bruighean* of the Druid, he was received with cordial friendship, and the *failte* ['welcome'], as usual, was poured out before him; and, when he was seated, warm water was fetched, and his feet bathed, so that the fatigue he felt after his journey was greatly relieved. The Druid, after he had partaken of refreshments, consisting of the newest of food and the oldest of liquors, asked him the reason for paying the visit, and more particularly the cause of his sorrow; for the prince appeared exceedingly depressed in spirit. Conn-eda told his friend the whole history of the transaction with his step-mother, from the beginning to the end; which, when the Druid heard it, caused him to compress his lips and nod his head very significantly, but he made no answer. 'Can you not assist me?' asked the prince, with downcast countenance, having observed the motions of the Druid. 'I cannot, indeed, assist you at present,' replied the Druid, 'but I will retire to my *grianan* ['sun-room' or study], at sun-rising on the morrow, and learn by virtue of my druidism what can be done to assist you.' The Druid, accordingly, as the sun rose on the following morning, retired to his *grianan*, and consulted the god he adored, through the

power of his *druidheacht* ['druidry']. When he returned, he called Conn-eda aside on the plain, and addressed him thus: – 'My dear son, I find you have been bound under a severe – an almost impossible – *geis*, intended for your destruction; no person on earth could have advised the queen to impose it, except the Cailleach of Loch Corrib, who is the greatest Druidess now in Ireland, and sister to the Firbolg king of Loch Erne. It is not, I am sorry to have to inform you, in my power, nor in that of the deity I adore, to interfere in your behalf; but go directly to Sliabh Mis, and consult *Eán chinn-duine* (the bird with a human head), and if there be any possibility of relieving you, that bird shall do it; for there is not a bird in the western world so celebrated as that bird, because it knows all things that are past, all things that are present, and exist, and all things that shall hereafter exist. It is difficult to find access to his place of concealment, and more difficult still to obtain an answer from him; but I will endeavour to regulate that matter for you; and that is all I can do for you at present.'

The Archdruid then instructed him thus: – 'Take,' said he, 'yonder little shaggy steed, and mount him immediately; for in those days the bird will make himself visible, and the little shaggy steed will conduct you to his place of abode. But lest the bird should refuse to reply to your queries, take this precious stone (*leag longmhar*), and present it to him; and then little danger and doubt exists but he will give you a ready answer.' The prince returned heartfelt thanks to the Druid; and, having saddled and mounted the little shaggy horse without making much delay, received the precious stone from the Druid, and, after having taken his leave of him, set out on his journey. He suffered the reins to fall loose upon the neck of the horse, according as he had been instructed, so that the animal took whatever road he chose.

It would be tedious to relate the numerous adventures he had with the little shaggy horse, which had the extraordinary gift of speech, and was a *draoidheacht* horse, during his journey.

The prince having reached the hiding-place of the strange bird at the appointed time, and having presented him with the *leag longmhar*, according to Fionn Badhna's instructions, and proposed his questions relative to the manner he could best arrange for the fulfilment of his *geis*, the bird took up the jewel from the stone on which it was placed, in his mouth, and flew to an inaccessible rock at some distance, and, when there perched, he thus addressed the prince: – 'Conn-eda, son of the king of Cruachan,' said he, in a loud croaking human voice, 'remove the stone just under your right foot, and take the ball of iron and the *corna* (cup) you shall find under it; then mount your horse, cast the ball before you, and, having so done, your horse will tell you all the other things necessary to be done.' The bird, having said this, immediately flew out of sight.

Conn-eda took great care to do everything according to the instructions of the bird. He found the iron ball and *corna* in the place which had been pointed out. He took them up, mounted his horse, and cast the ball before him. The ball rolled on at a regular gait, while the little shaggy horse followed on the way it led, until they reached the margin of Loch Erne. Here the ball rolled into the water, and became invisible. 'Alight now,' said the *draoidheacht* pony, 'and put your hand into mine ear; take from thence the small bottle of *íce* (all-heal) and the little wicker basket which you will find there, and remount with speed, for just now your great dangers and difficulties commence.' Conn-eda, ever faithful to the kind advice of his *draoidheacht* pony, did what he had been advised. Having taken the basket and bottle of *íce* from the animal's ear, remounted and proceeded on his journey, while the water of the lake appeared only like an atmosphere

The horse sprang from the earth, and flew like an arrow over the burning mountain.

93

above his head. When he entered the lake the ball again appeared, and rolled along until it came to the margin, across which was a causeway, guarded by three frightful serpents; the hissings of the monsters were heard at a great distance, while, on a nearer approach, their yawning mouths and formidable fangs were quite sufficient to terrify the stoutest heart. 'Now,' said the horse, 'open the basket, and cast a piece of the meat you find in it into the mouth of each serpent; when you have done this, secure yourself in your seat in the best manner you can, so that we may make all due arrangements to pass those *draoidheacht peists*. Take the pieces of meat you shall find in the basket, and, with a straight hand and well-directed aim, cast one into the mouth of each *peist*. If you do so unerringly we shall pass them safely, otherwise, we are lost. Conn-eda flung the pieces of meat into the jaws of the serpents with unerring aim. 'Bear a benison and victory,' said the *draoidheacht* steed, 'for you are a youth that will win and prosper.' And, on saying these words, he sprang aloft, and cleared in his leap the river and ford, guarded by the serpents, seven measures beyond the margin. 'Are you still mounted, Prince Conn-eda?' asked the steed. 'It is only half my exertion to remain so,' replied Conn-eda. 'I find,' said the pony, 'that you are a young prince that deserves to succeed, – one danger is now over, but two others still remain.' They proceeded onwards after the ball until they came in view of a great mountain flaming with fire. 'Hold yourself in readiness for another dangerous leap,' said the horse. The trembling prince had no answer to make, but seated himself as secure as the magnitude of the danger before him would permit. The horse in the next instant sprung from the earth, and flew like an arrow over the burning mountain. 'Are you still alive, Conn-eda, son of Conn Mór?' inquired the faithful horse. 'I am just alive, and no more, for I am greatly scorched,' answered the prince. 'Since you are yet alive, I feel assured that you are a young man destined to meet supernatural success and benisons,' said the druidic steed. 'Our greatest dangers are over,' added he, 'and there is hope that we shall be able to overcome the next, and last danger.' After they proceeded a short distance, his faithful steed, addressing Conn-eda, said, 'alight now, and apply a portion of the contents of the little bottle of *íce* to your wounds.' The prince immediately followed the advice of his monitor; and, as soon as he rubbed the *íce* (all-heal) to his wounds, he became as whole and fresh as ever he had been before. After having done this, Conn-eda remounted, and, following the track of the ball, soon came in sight of a great city surrounded by high walls. The only gate which was visible was not defended by armed men, but by two great towers, which emitted flames that could be seen at a great distance. 'Alight on this plain,' said the steed, 'and take a small knife from my other ear; with this knife you shall kill and flay me. When you have done this, envelope yourself in my hide, and you can pass the gate unscathed and unmolested. When you get inside you can come out at pleasure; because, when once you enter, there is no danger, and you can pass and repass whenever you wish; and let me tell you that all I have to ask of you, in return for any little service I may have rendered you, is that you, when once you get inside of the gates, will immediately return, and drive away any birds of prey that may be fluttering around to feed on my carcass, and more, that you will pour any little drop of that powerful *íce*, if such still remain in the bottle, upon my flesh, to preserve it from corruption. When you do this in memory of me, if it be not too troublesome, dig a pit and cast my remains into it.'

'Well,' said Conn-eda, 'my noblest steed, because you have been so faithful to me hitherto, and because I had the pleasure, as well as the happiness, to meet with you, and you still would have rendered me further service, I consider such a proposal insulting to my feelings as a man, and totally at variance with the spir-it which can feel the value of gratitude, not to speak of my feelings as a prince. You, that propose to sacrifice your life for my welfare and benefit, – what a hor-rid revolting proposal your good nature prompts you to make, – a proposal which shall never be sanctioned by me, much less its details be carried into exe-cution. Ah, you, who have been my dearest companion, faithful friend and infal-lible counsellor, to demand such a sacrifice at my hands! But as a prince I am able to say, "come what may, – come death itself in its most hideous forms and ter-rors, – I never will sacrifice private friendship to personal interest, no matter what the urgencies or provocations may be." Hence I am, I swear by my arms of val-our, prepared to meet the worst, – even death itself, – sooner than violate the principles of humanity, honour and friendship! My life, in corroboration of what I state as a prince and a hero, shall be sacrificed before I will lay a single finger upon my noble steed and counsellor, to injure his life. Come, O death, come in your most hideous forms, and you will find what an Irish prince, filled with grate-ful feelings, can endure, with not only patience, but cheerfulness! Well, let me say, your death would lead me to victory. But what would that victory be but a tri-umph over a weak woman? What a sacrifice you propose!' 'Pshaw, man! Heed not that: do what I advise you, and prosper.' 'Never! Never!' exclaimed the prince. 'Well, then, son of the great western monarch,' said the horse, with a tone of sor-row, 'if you do not follow my advice on this occasion, I can tell you that both you and I shall perish, and shall never meet again; but, if you act as I have instructed you, matters shall assume a happier and more pleasing aspect than you may imagine. I have not misled you heretofore, and if I have not, what need have you to doubt the most important portion of my counsel? Do exactly as I have direct-ed you, else you will cause a worse fate than death to befall me. And, moreover, I can tell you that, if you persist in your resolution, I have done with you for ever.'

When the prince found that his noble steed could not be dissuaded from his purpose, he took the knife out of his ear with reluctance, and with a faltering mind and trembling hand, essayed experimentally to point the weapon at his throat. Conn-eda's eyes were bathed in tears; but no sooner had he pointed the druidic *scian* to the throat of his good steed, than the dagger, as if impelled by some druidic power, stuck in his neck, and in an instant the work of death was done, and the noble animal fell dead at his feet! When the prince saw his noble steed fall dead by his hand, he cast himself on the ground, and cried aloud until his consciousness was gone. When he recovered, he perceived that the steed was quite dead; and, as he thought there was no room left for hope of resuscitating him, he considered it the most prudent course he could adopt, to act according to the advice he had given him. After many misgivings of mind, and abundant showers of tears, he essayed the task of flaying him, which was that of only a few minutes. When he found he had the hide separated from the carrion, he, in the derangement of the moment, enveloped himself with it, and proceeding towards the magnificent city in rather a demented state of mind, entered it without any molestation or opposition. It was a surprisingly populous city, and an extremely wealthy place; but its beauty, magnificence, and wealth had no charm for Conn-eda, because the thoughts of the loss he sustained in his dear steed were para-mount to those of all other earthly considerations.

He had scarcely proceeded more than fifty paces from the gate, until the last request of his beloved *draoidheacht* steed forced itself upon his mind, and com-pelled him to return to perform the last solemn injunction imposed upon him. When he came to the spot upon which the remains of his beloved *draoidheacht* steed lay, an appalling sight presented itself: ravens and other carnivorous birds of prey were tearing and devouring the flesh of his dear steed. It was but short work to put them to flight; and, having uncorked his little jar of *íce*, he deemed it a labour of love to embalm the now mangled carrion with the precious ointment. The potent *íce* had scarcely touched the inanimate flesh, when, to the surprise of Conn-eda, it commenced to undergo some strange change, and in a few minutes, to his unspeakable astonishment and inexpressible joy, it assumed the form of one of the handsomest and noblest young men imaginable, and, in the twinkling of an eye, the prince was locked in his embrace, smothering him with kisses, and drowning him with tears of joy. When one recovered from his ecstasy of joy, and the other from his surprise, the strange youth thus addressed the prince: – 'Most noble and puissant prince, you are the best sight I ever saw with my eyes, and I the most fortunate being in existence for having met you! Behold in my person, changed to the natural shape, your little shaggy *draoidheacht* steed! I am brother of the king of this city; and it was the wicked Druid, Fionn Badhna, who kept me so long in bondage; but he was forced to give me up when you came to *consult him*, as my *geis* was then broken; yet I could not recover my pristine shape and appearance, unless you had acted as you have kindly done. It was my own sister that urged the queen, your stepmother, to send you in quest of the steed and powerful puppy hound, which my brother has long had in keeping. My sister, rest assured, had no thought of doing you the least injury, but much good, as you shall find hereafter; because, if she were maliciously inclined towards you, she could have accomplished her end without any trouble. In short, she only wanted to free you from all future danger and disaster, and recover me from my relentless enemies, through your instrumentality. Come with me, my friend and deliverer, and the steed, and the puppy hound of extraordinary powers, and the golden apples, shall be thine, and a cordial welcome shall greet you in my brother's abode; for you deserve all this, and much more.'

The exciting joy felt on the occasion was mutual, and they lost no time in idle congratulations, but proceeded on to the royal residence of the king of Loch Erne. Here they were both received with demonstrations of joy by the king and his chieftains; and, when the purport of Conn-eda's visit became known to the king, he gave a free consent to bestow on Conn-eda the black steed, the *coilean con na mbuadh*, called Samer, and the three golden apples of health that were growing in his garden, under the special condition, however, that he would consent to remain as his guest until he would set out on his journey, in proper time to fulfil his *geis*. Conn-eda, at the earnest solicitation of his friends, consented, and remained in the royal residence of the Firbolg king of Loch Erne, in the enjoyment of the most delicious and fascinating pleasures during that period.

When the time of his departure came, the three golden apples were plucked from the crystal tree in the midst of the pleasure garden, and deposited in his bosom; the puppy hound, Samer, was leashed, and the leash put into his hand; and the black steed, richly harnessed, was got in readiness for him to mount. The king himself helped him on horseback, and both he and his brother assured him that he might not fear burning mountains or hissing serpents, because none would impede him, as his steed was a passport to and from his subaqueous kingdom at every time. And both he and his brother extorted a promise from Conn-eda, that he would visit them once every year, at least.

Conn-eda took his leave of his dear friend, and the king, his brother; the parting was a tender one, soured by regret on both sides. He proceeded on his way, without meeting anything to obstruct him, and, in due time, came in sight of the *dún* of his father, where the queen had been placed on the pinnacle of the tower, in the full hope that, as it was the last day of her imprisonment there, the prince would fail to make his appearance, and thereby forfeit all pretensions and right to the crown of his father for ever. But her hopes were doomed to meet a disappointment; for when it had been announced to her by her couriers, who had been posted to watch the arrival of the prince, that he approached, she was incredulous; but when she saw him mounted upon a foaming black steed, richly harnessed, and leading a strange kind of animal of the dog kind by a silver chain, she at once knew he was returning in triumph, and that her schemes laid for his destruction were frustrated. In the excess of grief at her disappointment, she cast herself from the top of the tower, and was instantly dashed in pieces. Conn-eda met a welcome reception from his father, who mourned for him as lost to him for ever, during his absence; and when the base conduct of the queen became known, the king and his chieftains ordered her remains to be consumed to ashes, for her perfidy and wickedness.

Conn-eda planted the three golden apples in his garden, and instantly a great tree, bearing similar fruit, sprung up. This tree caused all the district to produce an exuberance of crops and fruits, so that it became as fertile and plentiful as the dominions of the Firbolgs, in consequence of the extraordinary powers possessed by the golden fruit. The hound, Samer, and the steed, were of the utmost utility to him; and his reign was long and prosperous, and celebrated among the old people for the great abundance of corn, fruit, milk, fowl and fish that prevailed during this happy reign. It was after the name of Conn-eda the province of Connacht, or *Conneda, Connacht*, was so called.

NOTES

Source: *The Cambrian Journal*, Vol. II (1855), 100–115.

Reading this story, which dates from the tenth century in its original form, one can see how these earlier stories evolved into the recognizable folk-tales of a later period. Here Conn-eda is given an impossible task by his wicked stepmother, aided by an old wise woman. Conn is then helped by a Druid, and a magical talking horse whose character and actions all occur in later fairy-tale narratives. The *Cailleach* (old woman) who advises his stepmother is actually a very ancient figure in Irish myth – a 'mountain mother' or creatrix; while the various druids are part of the archetypal fund of such characters who occupy so many of the bardic tales of this era. The *Fir Bolg* king, who in this instance plays the role of helper and friend to Conn-eda, is one of the primal race of beings who once inhabited Ireland, and who are generally portrayed as monstrous and fearsome. His appearance in this gentler light suggests the intrusion of later characteristics into the story.

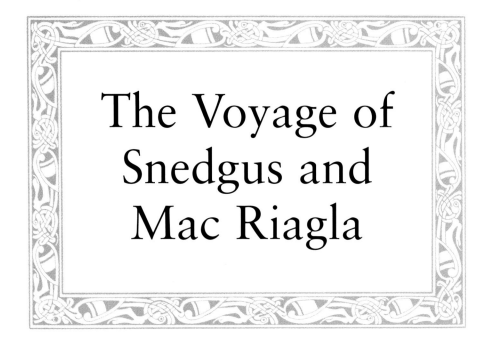

The Voyage of Snedgus and Mac Riagla

HE MEN OF ROSS were under great oppression after the decease of Domnall son of Aed son of Ainmire; and this was the cause of their oppression. When Ireland was taken by Mael Coba's sons after Domnall, Domnall's sons, even Donnchad and Fiacha, were in the sovranty of Cenél Conaill and the Men of Ross, – Donnchad over Tir-connell and Fiacha over the Men of Ross.

Great was their oppression under Fiacha, for neither weapon nor coloured raiment was allowed to any of them; (and they felt this the more) since they had never before that been subject to a king; and exceeding was the soreness of their servitude.

A year was Fiacha in sovranty over them. At the end of the year comes Fiacha to Boyne-mouth, and the Men of Ross are summoned to him. He said to them: 'Do service still more.'

'We cannot do more', say they.

Said he to them,: 'Let each and all of you put your spittle on my palm.'

It was put, and thus was the spittle, half of it (composed) of blood.

Then he said: 'Your service is not proper yet, for *all* the spittle is not blood. Cast the hills into the hollows that they may be (level) land. Plant trees in the plains that they may be forests!'

It was then that a deer passed near them. All the king's household go after the deer. Then the Men of Ross took his own weapons from the king, for none of them had a weapon, and so they killed him.

That deed was evil in his brother Donnchad's eyes, and he came and took them all prisoners, and puts them into one house to be burnt alive.

Then he himself said: 'It is not meet for me to do this deed without counsel from my soul-friend, from Colomb cille.'

So he sends messengers to Colomb cille. And Snedgus and Mac Riagla come from Colomb cille, having (this) counsel for Donnchad, to wit, to cast sixty couples of the Men of Ross on the sea, and that God would pass His judgment upon them.

Small boats are given to them, and they are set upon the sea, and men go to watch them, so that they should not return.

They voyaged to an island, where they found warriors with the heads of cats.

98

(Then) Snedgus and Mac Riagla turn back to go to Iona, to Colomb cille.

As they were in their coracle they bethought them of wending with their own consent into the outer ocean on a pilgrimage, even as the sixty couples had gone, though these went not with their own consent.

So they turn right-hand-wise; and wind wafts them for a while north-west-wards into the outer ocean.

After a space of three days a longing of great thirst seizes them, insomuch that they could not endure it.

It was then that Christ took pity on them, and brings them to a stream well-tasting like new milk, and therewith they are satisfied. They render thanks to God and say: 'Let us leave our voyage to God, and let us put our oars into our boat.' And thereafter their voyage was left alone, and their oars were put into their boat.

And in time they arrived at an island with a fence of silver over the midst thereof, and a fish-weir therein; and that weir was a wide plank of silver, and against the weir huge salmon were leaping. Bigger than a bull-calf was each of these salmon, and thereof they were satisfied.

Thereafter they voyaged to another island, and in that island they found many warriors with heads of cats upon them. One Gaelic champion was therein, and he came down to the strand and made them welcome, and said to them: 'Of the men of the Gael am I,' saith he. 'We came here a boat's crew, and thereof remaineth none save me alone. They were martyrized by the outlanders who inhabit this island.' And he puts food for them (the clerics) into the boat, and they leave a blessing and take a blessing.

Thereafter the wind wafts them to an island wherein was a great tree with beautiful birds (on its branches). Atop of it was a great bird with a head of gold and with wings of silver; and he tells them tales of the beginning of the world, and tells them of Christ's birth from Mary Virgin, and of His Baptism and His Passion and His Resurrection. And he tells tidings of Doom; and then all the birds used to beat their sides with their wings, so that showers of blood dropt out of their sides for dread of the signs of Doom. 'Communion and Creature' was that blood. And the bird bestows on the clerics a leaf of the leaves of that tree, and the size of the hide of a large ox was that leaf. And the bird told the clerics to take that leaf and place it on Colomb cille's altar. So that is Colombcille's flabellum to-day. In Kells it is.

Melodious was the music of those birds a-singing psalms and canticles, praising the Lord. For they were the birds of the Plane of Heaven, and neither trunk nor leaf of that tree decays.

Thereafter the clerics bade farewell to the birds, and they voyage to a fearful land, wherein dwelt men with heads of hounds, with manes of cattle upon them. By God's command, a cleric came to them out of the island to succour them, for they were in danger there, without food; and he gives them fish and wine and wheat.

Thereafter they voyage till they reached a land wherein dwelt men with heads of swine upon them; and they had great bands of reapers reaping the corn in the midst of the summer.

Afterwards they went thence in their boat, and sing their psalms, and pray to God, till they reached a land wherein dwelt a multitude of men of the Gael; and the women of the island straightway sang a *sianan* [a kind of 'mouth-music'] to them, and the clerics deemed it melodious.

'Sing ye still', saith the cleric, saith he; 'here is the *sianan* of Ireland!'

'Let us go, O clerics!' say the women, 'to the house of the King of the island, for therein we shall have welcome and refreshment.'

The women and the clerics enter the house; and the king made the clerics welcome, and they put away their weariness there, and he asked them: 'What is your race, O clerics?'

'Of the men of Ireland are we', say the clerics, 'and of Colomb cille's community.'

'How fares it in Ireland?' saith he, 'and how many sons of Domnall are alive?' saith the King.

The cleric answered: 'Three sons of Domnall's are alive; and Fiacha son of Domnall fell by the Men of Ross, and for that deed sixty couples of them were set on the sea.'

'That tale is true for you, O clerics! It is I that killed the son of the King of Tara, and we it is that were set on the sea. And well for us was that, for we shall abide here till the Judgment shall come; for good are we without sin, without wickedness, without fear of our crime. Good is the island wherein we are, for in it are Elijah and Enoch, and noble is the dwelling wherein is Elijah.'

And he made the clerics very welcome, and said: 'There are in this land two lakes, a lake of water and a lake of fire, and they would have come long ago over Ireland had not Martin and Patrick been praying for them (the Irish).'

'We would fain see Enoch,' say the clerics.

'He is in a secret place until we shall all go to the battle, on the Day of Judgment.'

Thereafter they voyage from that land, and were in the roaring waves of the sea for a long time, until great relief came to them from God, for they were weary. And they beheld a great lofty island, and all therein was delightful and hallowed.

Good was the King that abode in the island, and he was holy and righteous; and great was his host, and noble was the dwelling of that King, for there were a hundred doors in that house, and an altar at every door, and a priest at every altar offering Christ's Body.

So the clerics entered that house, and each of them (host and guests) blessed the other; and thereafter the whole of that great host, both woman and man, went to communion at the Mass.

Then wine is dealt out to them, and the king saith to the clerics: 'Tell the men of Ireland,' saith he, 'that a great vengeance is about to fall on you. Foreigners will come over sea and inhabit half the island; and they will lay siege to you. And this is what brings that vengeance upon them (the Irish), the great neglect they shew to God's Testament and to His teaching. A month and a year ye shall be at sea, and ye shall arrive, safely; and (then) tell all your tidings to the men of Ireland.'

NOTES

Source: Whitley Stokes (translator), in *Revue Celtique*, Vol. XIX (1887).

Another of the cycle of *immrama*, this intriguing text, dating from the fourteenth century, offers another kind of Otherworld voyage – one that has been adapted by a Christian storyteller as a means of exemplifying not only Christian doctrine but also the imagery of Biblical traditions. The appearance of Columb Cille (Columba) links the story with the Irish monastic tradition, and the mention of Biblical characters, such as Enoch and Elijah, ties it firmly into the Christian mythos of the Middle Ages. The character of Domnall son of Aed is almost certainly that of a real person, who seems to have died around AD 642, placing the events of the story in the middle of the seventh century. The Men of Ross, whose vengeful acts motivate the story, were a tribe whose territory is believed to have comprised the parishes of Carrickmacross and Clonany, in the area roughly occupied by parts of Meath and Louth today.

The Adventures of Art Son of Conn

ONN CÉTCHATHACH, son of Feidlimid Rechtmar, son of Tuathal Techtmar, son of Feradach Findfechtnach, son of Crimthand Nia Nair, son of Lugaid Riabh nDerg, son of the three white triplets, even Bres and Nar and Lothar, the names of the son of Ethach Find, was once at Tara of the kings, in the noble conspicuous dwelling of Ireland, for a period of nine years, and there was nothing lacking to the men of Ireland during the time of the said king, for, indeed, they used to reap the corn three times in the year. And his helpmate was Eithne Taebhfada, daughter of Brislind Binn, the king of Norway. He loved her dearly.

After their living a long time together the woman died, even Eithne, and was buried with honour in Tailltiu; for Tailltiu was one of the three chief burial-places of Ireland, namely, the Fair of Tailltiu, and the Brugh, and the cemetery of Cruachan. And he was dejected on account of his wife Eithne's death, and it weighed so heavily on him, that he was unable any longer to rule or govern the kingdom. And there was nothing lacking to Ireland at that time but one thing only, that the king of Ireland should not have found a helpmate worthy of him in her stead.

One day, however, he was all alone; and he went straight out of Tara until he came to Ben Edair meic Etgaith. There he bewailed and lamented his wife and helpmate. It was on that very day the Tuatha De Danann happened to be gathered in council in the Land of Promise, because of a woman who had committed transgression, and whose name was Bécuma Cneisgel, daughter of Eogan Inbir, that is, the wife of Labraid Luathlamar-Claideb, and Gaidiar Manannan's son it was that had committed the transgression. And this was the sentence passed on her as regards herself: to be driven forth from the Land of Promise, or to be burned according to the counsel of Manannan, and Fergus Findliath, and Eogan Inbir, and Lodan son of Lir, and Gaidiar, and Gaei Gormsuilech, and Ilbrec son of Manannan. And their counsel was to banish her from the Land of Promise. And Manannan said not to burn her lest her guilt should cleave to the land or to themselves.

Messengers came from Labraid to the house of Oengus of the Brugh, his own son-in-law; for it was a daughter of Labraid's who was the wife of Oengus of the Brugh, and her name was Nuamaisi. And it was for this reason messengers were despatched, in order that Bécuma Cneisgel should not find a place for her head in any of the *sidh*-mounds of Ireland. Accordingly she was banished beyond the expanse of the sea and the great deep; and it was into Ireland in particular she was sent, for the Tuatha De Danann hated the sons of Mil after they had been driven out of Ireland by them.

It is thus the maiden was. She had a lover in Ireland, even Art son of Conn Cétchathach, and Art did not know that he was her lover. As for the maiden, she found a coracle which had no need of rowing, but leaving it to the harmony of the wind over sea she came to Ben Edair meic Etgaith. Thus was the maiden. She had a green cloak of one colour about her, with a fringe of red thread of red gold, and a red satin smock against her white skin, and sandals of *findruine* [white-silver] on her, and soft, yellow hair, and a grey eye in her head, and love-ly-coloured teeth, and thin red lips, black eyebrows, arms straight and fair of hue, a snowy white body, small round knees, and slender choice feet, with excellence of shape, and form, and complexion, and accomplishments. Fair was the attire of that maiden, even Eogan Inbir's daughter. One thing only, however, a woman was not worthy of the high-king of Ireland who was banished for her own misdeed.

When she came Conn was on Ben Edair, sorrowful, restless, and lamentful, bewailing his wife. The maiden recognized him as the high-king of Ireland, and she brought her coracle to land and sat down beside Conn. Conn asked tidings of her. The maiden answered, and said that she was come from the Land of Promise in quest of Art, whom she had loved from afar, because of the tales about him. And she said that she was Delbchaem daughter of Morgan. 'I would not come between thee and thy choice of courtship,' said Conn, 'though I have no wife.' 'Why hast thou no wife?' said the maiden. 'My helpmate died,' replied Conn. 'What then shall I do?' said the maiden; 'is it with thee or with Art that I shall sleep?' 'Make thine own choice,' replied Conn. 'This is my choice,' said the maiden. 'Since thou dost not accept me: let me have my choice of courtship in Ireland.' 'I see no defects in thee for which it were right to refuse thee, unless they are concealed in thee.'

Then the maiden asked her own judgment of Conn, and it was granted her. And they made a union, Conn and the maiden, and she bound him to do her will. And her judgment was that Art should not come to Tara until a year was past. And his mind was vexed because of this, namely, the banishing of his son from Ireland without cause. After that they both set out for Tara; and the maiden left her coracle in the clefts of the rocks in shelter and concealment, for she knew not when she might need that coracle again.

Art was at Tara then playing *fidchell* [a game distantly related to chess], and Cromdes, Conn's druid, along with him. And the druid said: 'a move of banishment of thine, my son, and because of the woman thy father marries thou art being banished.' The king and his wife arrived at the place, and his son is brought to him straightway. And Conn said to Art: 'Leave Tara and Ireland for a year, and make thy preparation at once, for I have pledged myself to this.' And the men of Ireland deemed it a great wrong that Art should be banished for the sake of a woman. Notwithstanding, Art left Tara that night, and Conn and Bécuma were a year together in Tara, and there was neither corn nor milk in Ireland during that time. And the men of Ireland were in the greatest difficulty about that matter. And the druids of all Ireland were sent with the help of their science and their true wisdom to show what had brought that dreadful evil into Ireland. And it was declared to them; and the druids related to the king of Tara and the nobles of Ireland the cause of the evil. Because of the depravity of Conn's wife and her unbelief it was sent. And it was related, through whom their deliverance would be possible, namely, that the son of a sinless couple should be brought to Ireland and slain before Tara, and his blood mingled with the soil of Tara. This was told to Conn, and he knew not in what place that boy was. And he assembled the men of Ireland in one place, and said to them: 'I will go in quest of that sinless boy; and do you give the kingdom of Ireland to Art yonder so long as I am away, and, moreover, let him not leave Tara while I am absent until I come again.'

Then Conn proceeded straight to Benn Edair, and he found a coracle there. And he was a fortnight and a month on the sea wandering from one isle to another without knowledge or guidance save that of trusting to the course of the stars and the luminaries. And seals and leviathans, and adzeheads and porpoises, and many strange beasts of the sea rose up around the coracle, and swiftly uprose the waves, and the firmament trembled. And the hero began all alone to navigate the coracle until he came to a strange isle. He landed and left his coracle in a secret lonely place. And it is thus the island was, having fair fragrant apple-trees, and many wells of wine most beautiful, and a fair bright wood adorned with clustering hazel-trees surrounding those wells, with lovely golden-yellow nuts, and little bees ever beautiful humming over the fruits, which were dropping their blossoms and their leaves into the wells. Then he saw nearby a shapely hostel thatched with birds' wings, white, and yellow, and blue. And he went up to the hostel. 'Tis thus it was, with doorposts of bronze and doors of crystal, and a few generous folk within. He saw the queen with her large eyes, whose name was Rigru Roisclethan, daughter of Lodan from the Land of Promise, that is, the wife of Daire Degamra, son of Fergus Fialbrethach from the Land of Wonders. Conn saw there in the midst of the hostel a young man with excellence of shape and form, in a chair of crystal, even Segda Saerlabraid, son of Daire Degamra, that was his name.

Conn sat down on the bedside of the hostel, and was ministered unto, and his feet washed. And he knew not who had washed his feet. Before long he saw a flame arising from the hearth, and the hero was seized by the hand to guide him to the fire, and he went towards the fire. Then food-laden boards of the house with varied meats rose up before him, and he knew not who had given them to him. After a short space he saw a drinking-horn there, and he knew not who had fetched the horn. Then the dishes are removed from him. He saw before him a vat excellent and finely wrought of blue crystal, with three golden hoops about it. And Daire Degamra bade Conn go into the vat and bathe, so that he might put his weariness from him. And Conn did so, and he was put in good spirits, so that he slept. A fair cloak was thrown over the king, and he awoke refreshed. Food and nourishment was set before him. He said that it was *geis* for him to eat by himself. And they answered that there was no *geis* at all among them, save that none of them ever ate with the other. 'Though no one has eaten,' said the young man, even Segda Saerlabraid, 'I will eat along with the king of Ireland, so that he may not violate his *geis*.' And they lay in the same bed that night.

Conn arose on the morrow, and complained to the household of his need and his trouble. 'What is thy need?' said they. 'That Ireland is without corn and milk for a year now.' 'Why hast thou come hither?' 'In quest of your son,' replied

Conn, 'if you are willing; for it has been told us that it is through him our deliverance will come, namely, that the son of a sinless couple should be invited to Tara, and afterwards bathed in the water of Ireland; and it is you that possess the same, so let this young man, even Segda Saerlabraid be given up.' 'Alas,' said Daire son of Fergus Fialbrethach, 'we would not lend our son for the kingship of the world; for never did his father and mother come together except when yonder little boy was made; and moreover our own fathers and mothers never came together save at our making.' 'Evil is the thing ye say,' said the young man, 'not to respond to the king of Ireland; I will go myself with him.' 'Do not say that, son,' said the household. 'I say that the king of Ireland should not be refused.' 'If that is so,' said the household, 'it is thus we shall let thee go from us, under protection of the kings of all Ireland, and Art son of Conn, and Finn son of Cumall, and the men of art, so that thou shalt come back safe to us again.' 'All that shall be given,' said Conn, 'if I can.'

As for Conn and his coracle, after having met the adventure, it was only a sail of three days and three nights for them to Ireland. The men of all Ireland were then gathered in assembly awaiting Conn at Tara. And when the druids saw the young man with Conn, this is the counsel they gave: to slay him and mingle his blood with the blighted earth and the withered trees, so that its due mast and fruit, its fish, and its produce might be in them. And Conn placed the young man he had brought with him under the protection of Art and Finn, and the men of art, and the men of Ireland. Then, however, the latter did not accept that, but the kings accepted it at once, even Conn, and Finn, and Art Oenfer, and they were all outraged as regards the youth.

As soon as they had finished this counsel, the young man cried out with a loud voice: 'O men of Ireland, leave me alone in peace, since ye have agreed to slay me. Let me be put to death, as I shall say myself,' said the youth. Just then they heard the lowing of a cow, and a woman wailing continually behind it. And they saw the cow and the woman making towards the assembly. The woman sat down between Finn and Conn Cétchathach. She asked tidings of the attempt of the men of Ireland, that the innocent young man should be put to death in despite of Finn, and Art, and Conn. 'Where are those druids?' 'Here,' said they. 'Find out for me what those two bags are at the cow's sides, namely, the bag at each side of her.' 'By our conscience,' said they, 'we know not indeed.' 'I know,' said she, 'a single cow that has come here to save that innocent youth. And it is thus it will be done to her: let the cow be slaughtered, and her blood mixed with the soil of Ireland and with the doors of Tara, and save the boy. And moreover, there is something which it were more fitting for you to take heed to, that is, when the cow is cut up, let the two bags be opened, and there are two birds inside, a bird with one leg, and a bird with twelve legs.'

And the cow is slaughtered and the birds taken out of her. And they were beating their wings in the presence of the host. 'It is thus we shall discover which is the stronger if they encounter.' Then the one-legged bird prevailed over the bird with twelve legs. The men of Ireland marvelled at that. Said the woman, 'Ye are the bird with the twelve legs, and the little boy the bird with one leg, for it is he who is in the right.' 'Take those druids there,' said the maiden, 'for it were better for them to die, and let them be hanged.' And the young man was not put to death. Then the woman rose up and called Conn aside, and spoke as follows: 'Put this sinful woman away from thee, even Bécuma Cneisgel, daughter of Eogan Inbir, and wife of Labraid Luathlamar-Claideb, for it is through transgression she has been driven out of the Land of Promise.' 'That is good counsel,' said Conn,

'if I could put her away; but since I cannot, give us good advice.' 'I will,' said the woman, 'for it is worse it will be, a third of its corn, and its milk, and its mast to be lacking to Ireland so long as she will be with you.' And she took leave of them then and went off with her son, even Segda. And jewels and treasures were offered to them, but they refused them.

Bécuma chanced to be out on the green then, and she saw Conn's son playing *fidchell* there. It was not agreeable for Art to see his enemy. 'Is that Conn's son Art?' said she. 'It is indeed,' said they. '*Geis* to him,' said she, 'unless he play *fidchell* with me for stakes.' And this was told to Art son of Conn. And a *fidchell* was brought to them then, and they played, and Art won the first game. 'This is a game on thee, girl,' said Art. 'That is so,' said she. 'And *geis* on thee,' said he, 'if thou eat food in Ireland until thou procure the warrior's wand which Cúrói son of Dare had in his hand when taking possession of Ireland and the great world, and fetch it to me here.'

Then the girl proceeded to the dewy light-bespeckled brugh, wherein was Oengus, with his dear wife at his side, even Nuamaisi daughter of Labraid. However she searched most of the *sidh* mounds of Ireland, and found no tidings of the wand until she came to the *sidh* of Eogabal, and a welcome was given her here *from* Aine, daughter of Eogabal. For indeed they were two foster-sisters. 'Thou wilt get thy quest here,' said she; 'and take yonder thrice fifty youths with thee until thou come to the stronghold of Cúrói on the top of Sliabh Mis.' And they found it there, and she was rejoiced thereat.

Thereupon she set out for Tara, and she brought the wand to Art, and laid it upon his knees. The *fidchell* was brought to them, and they play. And the men of the *sidh* began to steal the pieces. Art saw that, and said, 'The *sidh* men are stealing the pieces from us, girl; and it is not thou that art winning the game, but they.' 'This is a game on thee,' said the girl. 'It is so indeed.' said the young man; 'and give thy judgment.' 'I will,' said she; 'even this, that thou shalt not eat food in Ireland until thou bring with thee Delbchaem, the daughter of Morgan.' 'Where is she?' said Art. 'In an isle amid the sea, and that is all the information that thou wilt get.'

Art set out for Inber Colptha; and he found a coracle with choice equipment on the shore before him. And he put forth the coracle, and travelled the sea from one isle to another until he came to a fair, strange island; and fair was the character of that island, full of wild apples and lovely birds, with little bees ever beautiful on the tops of the flowers. A house, hospitable and noble, in the midst of the island, thatched with birds' wings, white and purple, and within it a company of blooming women, ever beautiful, among them Creide Firalaind, daughter of Fidech Foltlebor.

A hearty welcome was then given to him, and food set before him, and tidings are asked of him. And he said that he was come from Ireland, and that he was the King of Ireland's son, and his name was Art. 'That is true,' said she. After that she put out her hand, and gave him a variegated mantle with adornments of burnished gold from Arabia, and he put it on him, and it was sufficient for him. 'Tis true,' said she, 'that thou art Conn's son Art, and it is long since thy coming here has been decreed.' And she gave him three kisses, dearly and fervently. And she said, 'Look at the crystal bower.' And fair was the site of that bower, with its doors of crystal and its inexhaustible vats, for, though everything be emptied out of them, they are ever full again.

He remained a fortnight and a month in that island, after which he took leave of the girl, and related his errand. 'Tis true,' said she, 'that is thine errand; and it

'There is a dark house in the mysterious wood at the head of the path, with seven hags and a bath of lead awaiting thee, for thy coming there has been fated.'

107

will be no little time until the maiden will be found, for the way is bad thither, and there is sea and land between thee *and her*, and, even if thou dost reach it, thou wilt not go past it. There is a great ocean and dark between thee and deadly and hostile is the way there; for that wood is traversed as though there were spear-points of battle under one's feet, like leaves of the forest under the feet of men. There is a luckless gulf of the sea full of dumb-mouthed beasts on this side of that immense wood. And an immense oak forest, dense and thorny before that mountain, and a narrow path through it, and a dark house in the mysterious wood at the head of the same path, with seven hags and a bath of lead awaiting thee, for thy coming there has been fated. And there is somewhat more grievous still, even Ailill Dubhdedach son of Mongan Minscothach. And weapon cannot harm him. And there are two sisters of mine there, daughters of Fidech Foltlebor, Finscoth and Aeb their names. There are two cups in their hands – a cup filled with poison, and one filled with wine. And the cup which is on thy right hand drink therefrom when thou hast need. And near at hand is the stronghold of the maiden. Thus it is, with a palisade of bronze round about it, and a man's head on every stake of it, after being slain by Coinchend, save on one stake alone. And Coinchend daughter of the king of the Coinchind, the mother of the girl, even Delbchaem daughter of Morgan.'

Art then set out after he had been instructed by the girl until he came to the crest of that hapless sea full of strange beasts. And on all sides the beasts and great sea-monsters rose up around the coracle. And Art son of Conn donned his battle attire, and engaged them warily and circumspectly. And he began to slaughter them and maim them until they fell by him.

After that he came to the forest wild where the Coincuilind and the wicked, perverse hags were, and Art and the hags encountered. It was not a fair encounter for him, the hags piercing and hacking at him until morning. Nevertheless the armed youth prevailed over that hapless folk. And Art went on his way using his own judgment until he came to the venomous icy mountain; and the forked glen was there full of toads, which were lying in wait for whoever came there. And he passed thence to Sliabh Saeb beyond, wherein were full many lions with long manes lying in wait for the beasts of the whole world.

After that he came to the icy river, with its slender narrow bridge, and a warrior giant with a pillar-stone, and he grinding his teeth on it, namely, Curnan Cliabhsalach. Nevertheless they encountered, and belike indeed Art overcame the giant, so that Curnan Cliabhsalach fell by him. And he went thence to where Ailill Dubhdedach son of Mongan was. And 'tis thus that man was, a fierce champion was he; no weapon would harm him, or fire burn him, or water drown him. Then Art and he took to wrestling, and they made a manly combat, a stern, heroic, equally-sharp fight. And Ailill Dubhdedach began abusing Art, and *they were* haranguing one another. But Art overcame the giant, so that his head came off the back of his neck. After that he wrecked the stronghold; and he seized his wife, and he sought to do her injury until she told him the way to Morgan's stronghold, and the Land of Wonders.

It was there Coinchend Cendfada, Morgan's wife, was; and she had the strength of a hundred in battle or conflict. She was the daughter of Conchruth, king of the Coinchind. And the Druids had foretold her that if ever her daughter should be wooed, in that same hour she would die. Therefore, she put to death everyone that came to woo her daughter. And it was she that had organized the hags with the bath of lead to meet him, and Curnan Cliabhsalach son of Duscad, the door-keeper of Morgan's house. And it was she that had put Ailill

Dubhdedach in the way of Art son of Conn, because Art would come on that expedition to woo her daughter, as it had been foretold him. And it was she that had contrived the icy bridge, and the dark forest with the Coincuilind and the evil toads, and the mountain full of lions, and the hapless sea-gulf.

Thus came Art to the stronghold which he was in quest of, even Morgan's stronghold, and pleasant it was. A fair palisade of bronze was round about it, and houses hospitable and extensive, and a stately palace in the midst of the stead. An ingenious, bright, shining bower set on one pillar over the stead, on the very top, where that maiden was. She had a green cloak of one hue about her, with a gold pin in it over her breast, and long, fair, very golden hair. She had dark-black eyebrows, and flashing grey eyes in her head, and a snowy-white body. Fair was the maiden both in shape and intelligence, in wisdom and embroidery, in chastity and nobility. And the maiden said: 'A warrior has come to the stead to-day, and there is not in the world a warrior fairer in form, or of better repute.' 'It is true,' said she, 'he is Art; and it is long since we have been preparing for him. And I will go into a house apart,' said she, 'and do thou bring Art into the bower; for I fear lest the Coinchend may put him to death, and have his head placed on the vacant stake before the stronghold.'

With that Art went into the bower, and when the women-folk saw him they made him welcome, and his feet were bathed. After that came the Coinchend, and the two daughters of Fidech along with her, Aebh and Finscoth, for to pour out the poison and the wine for Art.

As for the Coinchend: the amazon arose and put on her fighting apparel, and challenged Art to combat. And it was not Art who refused a fight ever. So he donned his fighting gear, and before long the armed youth prevailed over the Coinchend; and her head came off from the back of her neck, and he placed it on the vacant stake in front of the fortress.

Now concerning Art son of Conn and Delbchaem daughter of Morgan. That night they lay down merry, and in good spirits, the whole stronghold in their power, from small to great, until Morgan king of the Land of Wonders arrived; for indeed he was not there at the time. Then, however, Morgan arrived, full of wrath, to avenge his fortress and his good wife on Art son of Conn. He challenged Art to combat. And the young man arose, and put on his battle-harness, even his pleasant, satin mantle, and the white light-speckled apron of burnished gold about his middle. And he put his fine dark helmet of red gold on his head. And he took his fair, purple, embossed shield on the arched expanse of his back. And he took his wide-grooved sword with blue hilt, and his two thick-shafted, red-yellow spears, and they attacked each other, Art and Morgan, like two enormous stags, or two lions, or two waves of destruction. And Art overcame Morgan, and he did not part from him until his head had come off his neck. After which Art took hostages of Morgan's people, and also possession of the Land of Wonders. And he collected the gold and silver of the land also, and gave it all to the maiden, even Delbchaem daughter of Morgan.

The stewards and overseers followed him from the land, and he brought the maiden with him to Ireland. And they landed at Ben Edair. When they came into port, the maiden said: 'Hasten to Tara, and tell to Bécuma daughter of Eogan that she abide not there, but to depart at once, for it is a bad hap if she be commanded to leave Tara.'

And Art went forward to Tara, and was made welcome. And there was none to whom his coming was not pleasing, but the wanton and sorrowful Bécuma. But Art ordered the sinful woman to leave Tara. And she rose up straightway lamenting in the presence of the men of Ireland, without a word of leave-taking, until she came to Ben Edair.

As for the maiden Delbchaem, the seers, and the wise men, and the chiefs were sent to welcome her, and they came to Tara luckily and auspiciously. And the nobles of Ireland asked tidings of his adventures from Art; and he answered them, and made a lay.

Thus far the Adventures of Art son of Conn, and the Courtship of Delbchaem daughter of Morgan.

NOTES

Source: R.I. Best (translator), in *ERIU*, Vol. 3 (1906), 149–73.

This powerful and complex text dates from a fifteenth-century manuscript known as the *Book of Fermoy*. Though no earlier version exists, it is clearly a very ancient story, full of violence, passion and magic. There are several echoes of the Merlin story as told by the seventh-century monk Nennius in his *Historia Brittonum*. In this, the young Emrys (Merlin) is brought to be sacrificed so that the tyrant Vortigern's castle will stand. As in the present story, the youth is saved by the unriddling of a mystery – in Nennius' account this is the real reason why Vortigern's castle will not stand more than a night (two dragons, used much as are the birds in the story here). In Nennius, however, it is the child himself, rather than his mother, who resolves the mystery.

It is the story of Delbchaem which is at the heart of the tale. Cast out from the Otherworld for daring to love a mortal, she brings the curse of her presence to the mortal world, and through her understanding of the laws of *geasa* (prohibitions) which operated in ancient Ireland is able to cause a great deal of trouble until all is finally resolved with the intervention of other of the *sidhe*.

This is one of the most detailed working out of a story of human-mortal relationships, and it tells us a good deal, not only about the appearance of the Otherworld but also about its own laws and code of conduct. Despite the long lists of unfamiliar names that cluster thickly on certain pages, the story is well worth reading for the sometimes disturbing account of the Otherworld it presents.

Cormac's Adventures in the Land of Promise

ORMAC'S CUP WAS a cup of gold which he had. The way in which it was found was thus:

One day, at dawn in Maytime, Cormac son of Art son of Conn the Hundred-Fighter was alone on Mur Tea in Tara. He saw coming towards him a calm, grey-haired warrior, with a purple, fringed mantle around him, a ribbed, goldthreaded shirt next his skin, and two blunt shoes of white bronze between his feet and the earth. A branch of silver with three golden apples was on his shoulder. Delight and amusement enough it was to listen to the music made by the branch, for men sore-wounded, or women in child-bed, or folk in sickness would fall asleep at the melody which was made when that branch was shaken. The warrior saluted Cormac. Cormac saluted him. 'Whence hast thou come, O warrior?' said Cormac.

'From a land,' he replied, 'wherein there is nought save truth, and there is neither age nor decay nor gloom nor sadness nor envy nor jealousy nor hatred nor haughtiness.'

'It is not so with us,' said Cormac. 'A question, O warrior: shall we make an alliance?'

'I am well pleased to make it.' So they became allies.

'Give me the branch!' said Cormac.

'I will give it,' said the warrior, 'provided the three boons which I shall ask in Tara be granted to me in return.'

'They shall be granted,' said Cormac.

Then the warrior bound Cormac to his promise, and left the branch and went away; and Cormac knew not whither he had gone. Cormac returned to the palace, and the household marvelled at the branch. Cormac shook it at them, and cast them into slumber from that hour to the same time on the following day.

At the end of a year the warrior came and asked of Cormac the consideration agreed upon for his branch. 'It shall be given,' said Cormac.

'I will take thy daughter Ailbe today,' said the warrior. So he took the girl with him. The women of Tara uttered three loud cries after the daughter of the king of Erin. But Cormac shook the branch at them, so that he banished grief from them all and cast them into sleep.

A month later the warrior returned and took with him Cairbre Liffecair the son of Cormac. Weeping and sorrow ceased not in Tara at the loss of the boy, and that night no one ate or slept, and they were in grief and exceeding gloom. But Cormac shook the branch at them, and their sorrow left them.

The same warrior came a third time.

'What askest thou today?' said Cormac.

'Thy wife,' said he, 'even Ethne Taebfada daughter of Dunlang king of Leinster.' Then he took the woman away with him.

That thing Cormac could not endure. He went after them, and every one followed him. A great mist was brought upon them in the midst of the plain, and Cormac found himself alone. There was a large fortress in the midst of the plain with a wall of bronze around it. In the fortress was a house of white silver, and it was half-thatched with the wings of white birds. A fairy host of horsemen were at the house, with lapfuls of the wings of white birds in their bosoms to thatch the house. A gust of wind would blow and would carry away all of it that had been thatched. Cormac saw a man kindling a fire, and the thick-boled oak was cast upon it, top and butt. When the man came again with another oak, the burning of the first oak had ended. Then he saw another royal stronghold, and another wall of bronze around it. There were four palaces therein. He entered the fortress and saw the vast palace with its beams of bronze, its wattling of silver, and its thatch of the wings of white birds. Then he saw in the enclosure a shining fountain, with five streams flowing out of it, and the hosts in turn drinking its water. Nine hazels of Buan grew over the well. The purple hazels dropped their nuts into the fountain, and the five salmon which were in the fountain severed them and sent their husks floating down the streams. Now the sound of the falling of those streams was more melodious than any music that men sing.

He entered the palace. There was one couple inside awaiting him. The warrior's figure was distinguished owing to the beauty of his shape, the comeliness of his form, and the wonder of his countenance. The girl along with him, mature, yellow-haired, with a golden head-dress, was the loveliest of the world's women. Cormac's feet were washed by invisible hands. There was bathing in a pool without the need of attendance. The heated stones of themselves went into and came out of the water.

As they were there after the hour of nine they saw a man coming into the house. A wood-axe was in his right hand, and a log in his left hand, and a pig behind him. ''Tis time to make ready within,' said the warrior; 'because a noble guest is here.'

The man struck the pig and killed it. And he cleft his log so that he had three sets of part-cleavings. The pig was cast into the cauldron.

'It is time for you to turn it,' said the warrior.

'That would be useless,' said the kitchener; 'for never, never will the pig be boiled until a truth is told for each quarter of it.'

'Then,' said the warrior, 'do thou tell us the first truth.'

'One day,' said he, 'when I was going round the land, I found another man's cows on my property, and I brought them with me into a cattle-pound. The owner of the cows followed me and said that he would give me a reward for letting his cows go free. I gave him his cows. He gave me a pig and an axe and a log, the pig to be killed with the axe every night, and the log to be cleft by it, and there would then be enough firewood to boil the pig, and enough for the palace besides. And, moreover, the pig would be alive the next morning and the log be whole. And from then till today they have been like that.'

'True, indeed, is that tale,' said the warrior.

The pig was turned in the cauldron and only one quarter of it was found boiled.

'Let us have another tale of truth,' said they.

'I will tell one,' said the warrior. 'Ploughing-time had come. When we desired to plough that field outside, it was found ploughed, harrowed and sown with wheat. When we desired to reap it, the crop was found stacked in the field. When we desired to draw it into that side out there, it was found in the enclosure all in one thatched rick. We have been eating it from then till today; but it is no whit greater nor less.'

Then the pig was turned in the cauldron, and another quarter was found to be cooked.

'It is now my turn,' said the woman. 'I have seven cows and seven sheep. The milk of the seven cows is enough for the people of the Land of Promise. From the wool of the seven sheep comes all the clothing they require.'

At this story the third quarter of the pig was boiled.

'It is now thy turn,' they said to Cormac.

So Cormac related how his wife and his son and his daughter had been taken from him, and how he himself had pursued them until he arrived at that house.

So with that the whole pig was boiled.

Then they carved the pig, and his portion was placed before Cormac. 'I never eat a meal,' said Cormac, 'without fifty in my company.' The warrior sang a song to him and put him asleep. After this he awoke and saw fifty warriors, and his son and his wife and his daughter, along with him. Thereupon his spirit was strengthened. Then ale and food were dealt out to them, and they became happy and joyous. A cup of gold was placed in the warrior's hand. Cormac was marvelling at the cup, for the number of the forms upon it and the strangeness of its workmanship. 'There is something about it still more strange,' said the warrior. 'Let three falsehoods be spoken under it, and it will break into three. Then let three true declarations be made under it, and it will unite again as it was before.' The warrior spoke under it three falsehoods, and it broke into three parts. 'It would be well to utter truth,' said the warrior, 'for the sake of restoring the cup. I declare, O Cormac,' said he, 'that until today neither thy wife nor thy daughter has seen the face of a man since they were taken from thee out of Tara, and that thy son has not seen a woman's face.' The cup thereupon became whole.

'Take thy family now,' said the warrior, 'and take the cup that thou mayst have it for discerning between truth and falsehood. And thou shalt have the branch for music and delight. And on the day that thou shalt die they all will be taken from thee. I am Manannan son of Lir,' said he, 'king of the Land of Promise; and to see the Land of Promise was the reason I brought thee hither. The host of horsemen which thou beheldest thatching the house are the men of art in Ireland, collecting cattle and wealth which passes away into nothing. The man whom thou sawest kindling the fire is a thriftless young chief, and out of his housekeeping he pays for everything he consumes. The fountain which thou sawest, with the five streams out of it, is the Fountain of Knowledge, and the streams are the five senses through which knowledge is obtained. And no one will have knowledge who drinks not a draught out of the fountain itself and out of the streams. The folk of many arts are those who drink of them both.'

Now on the morrow morning, when Cormac arose, he found himself on the green of Tara, with his wife and his son and daughter, and having his Branch and Cup.

Source: Tom Peete Cross and Clark Harris Slover (editors), *Ancient Irish Tales*, Dublin: Figgis, 1936.

Once again in this story we have an appearance of the Silver Branch. As in 'The Voyage of Bran', it has a powerful effect on mortals, being able to cast them into a deep slumber, soothe them in time of trouble, and even heal them through the peace of forgetfulness. Its effects are strong even when wielded by a mortal – in this case Cormac, who receives a double bounty of magical objects in this text; not only the Branch, but also the wonderful four-sided cup of truth, which breaks apart when a falsehood is uttered in its presence, and reunites its broken parts whenever a truth is spoken. Good use of this is made in the story, as a device for telling a number of smaller anecdotes within the framework of the greater. The visit to the Otherworld is detailed and delightful in its references to the feasting and entertainment offered by the immortals. There is also a moral twist to the story, especially in the small tales within the main narrative. The author seems to be at pains to show the fairy people in a favourable light, as mischievous, ultimately powerful, but essentially good.

Cormac himself is the son of Art, who features in 'The Adventures of Art Son of Conn' (page 102). Both are recognized as great rulers, whose dealings with the Otherworld made them wise beyond the abilities of most mortals.

The Adventures of Nera

NE HALLOWEEN AILILL and Medb were in Rath Cruachan with their whole household. They set about cooking food. Two captives had been hanged by them the day before that. Then Ailill said: 'He who would now put a withe round the foot of either of the two captives that are on the gallows, shall have a prize for it from me, as he may choose.'

Great was the darkness of that night and its horror, and demons would appear on that night always. Each man of them went out in turn to try that night, and quickly would he come back into the house. 'I will have the prize from thee', said Nera, 'and I shall go out.' 'Truly thou shalt have this my gold-hilted sword here', said Ailill.

Then this Nera went out towards the captives, and put good armour on him. He put a withe round the foot of one of the two captives. Thrice it sprang off again. Then the captive said to him, unless he put a proper peg on it, though he be at it till the morrow, he would not fix his own peg on it. Then Nera put a proper peg on it.

Said the captive from the gallows to Nera: 'That is manly, O Nera!' 'Manly indeed!' said Nera. 'By the truth of thy valour, take me on thy neck, that I may get a drink with thee. I was very thirsty when I was hanged.' 'Come on my neck then!' said Nera. So he went on his neck. 'Whither shall I carry thee?' said Nera. 'To the house which is nearest to us', said the captive.

So they went to that house. Then they saw something. A lake of fire round that house. 'There is no drink for us in this house', said the captive. 'There is no fire without sparing in it ever.' 'Let us therefore go to the other house, which is nearest to us', said the captive. They went to it then and saw a lake of water around it. 'Do not go to that house!' said the captive. There is never a washing- nor a bathing-tub, nor a slop-pail in it at night after sleeping. 'Let us still go to the other house', said the captive. 'Now there is my drink in this house', said the captive. He let him down on the floor. He went into the house. There were tubs for washing and bathing in it, and a drink in either of them. Also a slop-pail on the floor of the house. He then drinks a draught of either of them and scatters the last sip from his lips at the faces of the people that were in the house, so that they

The bull calf and the Whitehorn of Ai meet in the plain of Cruachan.

all died. Henceforth it is not good to have either a tub for washing or bathing, or a fire without sparing, or a slop-pail in a house after sleeping.

Thereupon he carried him back to his torture, and Nera returned to Cruachan. Then he saw something. The dun was burnt before him, and he beheld a heap of heads of their people cut off by the warriors from the dun. He went after the host then into the cave of Cruachan. 'A man on the track here!' said the last man to Nera. 'The heavier is the track', said his comrade to him, and each man said that word to his mate from the last man to the first man. Thereupon they reached the *sid* of Cruachan [the Otherworld] and went into it. Then the heads were displayed to the king in the *sid*. 'What shall be done to the man that came with you?' said one of them. 'Let him come hither, that I may speak with him', said the king. Then Nera came to them and the king said to him: 'What brought thee with the warriors into the *sid*?' said the king to him. 'I came in the company of thy host', said Nera. 'Go now to yonder house', said the king. 'There is a single woman there, who will make thee welcome. Tell her it is from me thou art sent to her, and come every day to this house with a burden of firewood.'

Then he did as he was told. The woman bade him welcome and said: 'Welcome to thee, if it is the king that sent thee hither.' 'It is he, truly', said Nera. Every day Nera used to go with a burden of firewood to the dun. He saw every day a blind man and a lame man on his neck coming out of the dun before him. They would go until they were at the brink of a well before the dun. 'Is it there?' said the blind man. 'It is indeed', said the lame one. 'Let us go away', said the lame man.

Nera then asked the woman about this. 'Why do the blind and the lame man visit the well?' 'They visit the crown, which is in the well', said the woman, 'a diadem of gold, which the king wears on his head. It is there it is kept.' 'Why do those two go?' said Nera. 'Not hard to tell', said she, 'because it is they that are trusted by the king to visit the crown.' 'One of them was blinded, the other lamed.' 'Come hither a little', said Nera to his wife, 'that thou mayst tell me of my adventures now.' 'What has appeared to thee?' said the woman. 'Not hard to tell', said Nera. 'When I was going into the *sid*, methought the rath of Cruachan was destroyed and Ailill and Medb with their whole household had fallen in it.' 'That is not true indeed', said the woman, 'but an elfin host came to them. That will come true', said she, unless he would reveal it to his friends. 'How shall I give warning to my people?' said Nera. 'Rise and go to them', said she. 'They are still round the same caldron and the charge has not yet been removed from the fire.' Yet it had seemed to him three days and three nights since he had been in the *sid*. 'Tell them to be on their guard at Halloween coming, unless they come to destroy the *sid*. For I will promise them this: the *sid* to be destroyed by Ailill and Medb, and the crown of Briun to be carried off by them.'

These are the three things, which were found in it: the mantle of Loegaire in Armagh, and the crown of Briun in Connaught, and the shirt of Dunlaing in Leinster in Kildare.

'How will it be believed of me, that I have gone into the *sid*?' said Nera. 'Take fruits of summer with thee', said the woman. 'Then he took wild garlic with him and primrose and golden fern. And I shall be pregnant by thee', said she 'and shall bear thee a son. And send a message from thee to the *sid*, when thy people will come to destroy the *sid*, that thou mayest take thy family and thy cattle from the *sid*.'

Thereupon Nera went to his people, and found them around the same caldron; and he related his adventures to them. And then his sword was given to him, and he stayed with his people to the end of a year. That was the very year, in which Fergus mac Roich came as an exile from the land of Ulster to Ailill and Medb to

Cruachan. 'Thy appointment has come, O Nera', said Ailill to Nera. 'Arise and bring thy people and thy cattle from the *sid*, that we may go to destroy the *sid*.'

Then Nera went to his wife in the *sid*, and she bade him welcome. 'Arise out to the dun now', said the woman to Nera, 'and take a burden of firewood with thee. I have gone to it for a whole year with a burden of firewood on my neck every day in thy stead, and I said thou wert in sickness. And there is also thy son yonder.' Then he went out to the dun and carried a burden of firewood with him on his back. 'Welcome alive from the sickness in which thou wast!' said the king. 'I am displeased that the woman should sleep with thee without asking.' 'Thy will shall be done about this', said Nera. 'It will not be hard for thee', said the king. He went back to his house. 'Now tend thy kine today!' said the woman. 'I gave a cow of them to thy son at once after his birth.' So Nera went with his cattle that day.

Then while he was asleep the Morrigan took the cow of his son, and the Donn of Cualgne bulled her in the east in Cualgne. She (the Morrigan) then went again westward with her cow. Cuchulaind overtook them in the plain of Murthemne as they passed across it. For it was one of Cuchulaind's *gessa* that even a woman should leave his land without his knowledge. It was one of his *gessa* that birds should feed on his land, unless they left something with him. It was one of his *gessa* that fish should be in the bays, unless they fell by him. It was one of his *gessa* that warriors of another tribe should be in his land without his challenging them, before morning, if they came at night, or before night, if they came in the day. Every maiden and every single woman that was in Ulster, they were in his ward till they were ordained for husbands. These are the *gessa* of Cuchulaind. Cuchulaind overtook the Morrigan with her cow, and he said: 'This cow must not be taken.'

Nera went back then to his house with his kine in the evening. 'The cow of my son is missing', said he. 'I did not deserve that thou shouldst go and tend kine in that way', said his wife to him. On that came the cow. 'A wonder now! Whence does this cow come?' 'Truly, she comes from Cualgne, after being bulled by the Donn of Cualgne', said the woman. 'Rise out now, lest thy warriors come', she said. 'This host cannot go for a year till Halloween next. They will come on Halloween next: for the fairy-mounds of Erinn are always opened about Halloween.'

Nera went to his people. 'Whence comest thou?' said Ailill and Medb to Nera, 'and where hast thou been since thou didst go from us?' 'I was in fair lands', said Nera, 'with great treasures and precious things, with plenty of garments and food, and of wonderful treasures. They will come to slay you on Halloween coming, unless it had been revealed to you.' 'We shall certainly go against them', said Ailill. So they remain there till the end of the year. 'Now if thou hast anything in the *sid*', said Ailill to Nera, 'bring it away.' So Nera went on the third day before Halloween and brought her out of the *sid*. Now as the bull calf went out of the *sid*, the calf of the cow of Aingene (Aingene was the name of his son), it bellowed thrice. At that same hour Ailill and Fergus were playing draughts, when they heard something, the bellowing of the bull calf in the plain. Then said Fergus:

> I like not the calf
> bellowing in the plain of Cruachan,
> the son of the black bull of Cualgne, which approaches,
> the young son of the bull from Loch Laig.
>
> There will be calves without cows
> on Bairche in Cualgne,
> the king will go a long march
> through this calf of Aingene.

Aingene was the name of the man and Be Aingeni the name of the woman, and the appearance which this Nera saw on them was the same as that which Cuchulaind saw in the Tain Bo Regamna.

Then the bull calf and the Whitehorn of Ai meet in the plain of Cruachan. A night and a day they were there fighting, until at last the bull calf was beaten. Then the bull calf bellowed when it was beaten. 'What did the calf bellow?' Medb asked of her neat-herd, whose name was Buaigle. 'I know that, my good father Fergus', said Bricriu, 'it is the strain which thou sangest in the morning.' On that Fergus glanced aside and struck with his fist at Bricriu's head, so that the five men of the draught-board that were in his hand, went into Bricriu's head, and it was a lasting hurt to him. 'Tell me, O Buaigle, what did the bull say?' said Medb. 'Truly, it said', answered Buaigle, 'if its father came to fight with it, that is the Donn of Cualgne, it would not be seen in Ai, and it would be beaten throughout the whole plain of Ai on every side.' Then said Medb in the manner of an oath: 'I swear by the gods that my people swear by, that I shall not lie down, nor sleep on down or flockbed, nor shall I drink butter-milk nor nurse my side, nor drink red ale nor white, nor shall I taste food, until I see those two kine fighting before my face.'

Thereafter the men of Connaught and the black host of exile went into the *sid*, and destroyed the *sid*, and took out what there was in it. And then they brought away the crown of Briun. That is the third wonderful gift in Erinn, and the mantle of Loegaire in Armagh, and the shirt of Dunlaing in Leinster in Kildare. Nera was left with his people in the *sid*, and has not come out until now, nor will be come till Doom.

NOTES

Source: Kuno Meyer (translator), in *Revue Celtique*, Vol. XV (1898), 214–28.

This strange, oblique tale is really a prequel to the more famous epic of the *Tain*, or, as it is also known, 'The Cattle Raid of Culaigne'. In the latter story, the Brown Bull of Culaigne, or, as it is called here, 'the Donn', is stolen by Queen Medb and her followers, prompting a war as the Ultonians set out to recover it. In the present text, we see that Nera's visit to the Otherworld, in which there is a great displacement of both time and space, sets the origins of the struggle in context, which is in reality a struggle not between human forces but between the fairy race and the mortal world for the possession of the Bull, which we see here guarded by the blind and lame men. There is, indeed, the echo of an even more primal struggle here, and it has been suggested that beneath the layers of story may lie hidden a fragmentary creation text, in which the battling of the two bulls brings the earth into being.

The beginning of the tale, with its terrifying account of Nera's visit to the gallows, and his subsequent journey in search of water for the dead man, must be one of the most memorable in the whole of Celtic literature. Originally this was probably a separate story, but the author of the text, translated here, has cleverly made it the starting point for Nera's adventures, as he sees a vision of his slain comrades and is prompted to enter the realm of the *sidhe* (or *sid* as it is referred to here).

The appearance of the Morrigan, who is the great battle goddess of the Celts, is almost unexplained here, and suggests that there may once have been more of the story than has currently survived; but, however it came to be there, her presence adds a note of epic mythology to the struggle between mortals and fairy people that lies at the heart of this story.

Gold Apple,
Son of the King
of Erin

HERE WAS A KING in Erin long ago who had a Queen and one son. The Queen died when the son was still young, and the King gave his word to the Queen on her death bed that he would never put her son under a stepmother's rule; that he would not marry till the boy was 21 years of age.

In time the great men were complaining and saying that life in the castle was lonely; that it was not well for a King to be in his kingdom without a Queen. Their talk went so far that one day when the King was going to hunt he called out in anger: 'I will marry the first woman I meet.'

The King was not long on the road when whom should he meet but the ugliest hag he had ever set eyes on, terrible to look at, more like a beast than a woman.

'Will you marry me?' asked the hag.

'I will not, indeed,' said the King.

With her malice and enchantment the hag fastened the horses to the road and the men to the horses and kept a strong wind blowing with sleet and snow, in their faces, till noon of the following day, when she came before them a second time.

'Good morning to you, worthy King,' said the hag.

'Good morning to you,' said the King.

'Well, will you marry me to-day?'

'By my honour I will not,' said the King.

She kept him and his men there till the third day, with the same treatment.

'Why not marry her?' asked the attendants. 'Take her to the castle, throw her into a dark room by herself; give her one day some small bite to eat, and the next leave her fasting. You need never look after her.'

'Good morning,' said the woman on the third day. 'Will you marry me?'

'I will,' said the King.

He took the hag and rode home, married her, took her to the darkest room in the castle, and left her there. One day she got a small bite, the next she got no bite at all, had to fast for herself.

One morning the King was riding away from the castle; when at some distance he turned in the saddle the woman was looking from the window, and she outside the wall to her waist; and what was she but the finest and fairest woman that the King had ever laid eyes on, or that any man could see.

The King turned home that minute, went to the dark room, brought out the woman, kissed and embraced her, said he was sorry to leave her in darkness so long.

The two were spending their time after that in enjoyment and pleasure, and the son of the dead Queen away in a castle by himself, with men to attend him.

The Queen went out walking one day and got a fall while passing the house of a henwife, a widow. A second day she went the same way and got a worse fall. She went after that a third day and got the worst fall of all. The henwife had laid a curse on her and she had no power to rise the third time.

'Bad luck to you,' said the henwife, 'lie there till I raise you.'

'Bad luck to yourself,' said the Queen; 'why are you cursing me?'

'I had everything from the woman that was in it before you, a bite of everything that was in the King's house, from you I have nothing.'

'Was there a woman in it before me?'

'There was,' said the henwife, 'and the King has a fine son.'

'It's going from me that the wealth is,' said the Queen, 'and I don't know where 'tis going.'

'If you show me kindness I will let you know where 'tis going.'

'What would be kindness for you?' asked the Queen.

'The full of my yellow horn of butter, as much meal as would go in my cap, as much wool as would go under my armpit.'

'I will give you all these,' said the Queen.

'Will you, surely?' asked the henwife.

'I will,' said the Queen; 'and how much would these three things be?'

'As much butter as seven dairies would make in seven years; as much wool as would be sheared from seven hundred sheep in seven years; as much wheat as seven ploughmen would plough land for in seven years.'

'Oh, you asked too much, but I have promised and must give.'

'Will you give them to-day?' asked the henwife.

'I will,' said the Queen, and all the old woman had asked for was brought to her.

'I will tell you now,' said the henwife. 'The King has a son living in a castle by himself, the name of that son is Gold Apple, and it is to him that everything goes that is going from you.'

'How could I see that son?'

'I'll give you chicken's blood in a bottle, go home and be ailing, take some of the blood in your mouth, spit it out, tell the King that you are dying, that nothing will cure you but a sight of his son. He'll be denying the son and saying that he never had a wife, and never had a son, but you are to say that you'll not rise till he brings you Gold Apple, his son, and the son of his first wife. He will deny in every way, but at last he will bring him.'

The Queen obeyed the henwife in all things. The King brought his son after many denials and struggles.

In a short time the Queen played chess for a sentence with her stepson, played twice, won one game and lost one.

'What is your sentence on me,' asked the stepson.

'I put you under sentence,' said she, 'not to sleep two nights on one bed, nor eat twice off one table till you bring me the head of the eight-legged dog.'

'I put you under sentence,' said Gold Apple, 'to go to the top of this castle the moment I start, and stay there till I bring the head.'

'Relieve me,' cried the Queen, 'and I will relieve you from your sentence.'

'I will not relieve you,' said the King's son. 'I shall see many things on the way if I live; if I live you will suffer till I come, if I die you will die on the top of the castle.'

When the King came home that evening the son broke a rafter in the roof of the castle with a sigh that went from him.

'That was the sigh of a King's son under sentence,' said the father.

'It was,' said Gold Apple.

'What is the sentence?' asked the King.

'To bring the head of the eight-legged dog to my stepmother.'

'Stop at home,' said the King. 'I will give you a new table every day and a fresh bed every night; stay under the sentence.'

'No,' said the son. 'If I come back I can talk about many things; if I die I shall not die the second time.'

Next morning Gold Apple made ready for the road and away with him. The moment he started the stepmother mounted the castle.

The King's son travelled till twilight, when he saw a small hut at the corner of a forest. The hut was so small and poor looking that he almost missed seeing it, but when he went in it was the finest castle that he had ever set eyes on. A woman was sitting on the floor and combing her hair. At one side of the fire was a gold chair and a chair of silver at the other side.

'Well,' said the King's son to himself, 'it is better for me to sit on the gold chair.' With that he sat down on the gold chair. When the woman heard the noise she parted her hair from before her eyes and looked at him, then she rose and gave him a blow of her hand across the face that drove the life half way out of him.

'You'll get more than that when the giant comes,' said she.

The giant came quickly. 'I find the smell of a stranger,' said he, 'and I know not who he is or what he wants.'

'I am here,' said Gold Apple, 'whatever you wish to do to me, do it.'

When the giant looked at the King's son he was delighted and began to embrace him and kiss him, saying:

'You are Gold Apple, only son of my sister and the King of Erin. What brought you this way to us?'

Gold Apple told the whole story.

'Ah, then God help you,' said the uncle. 'It would be every bit as well for you to be striving to count all the stars in the sky as to go looking for that head, for the daughter of Rí Fó Thuinn (King Under the Wave) has the dog, and there are seventy-seven poles behind her father's castle, and the head of a king's son born of an honourable Queen on each pole of them but one, and that pole is for your head, if you go there. I'll give you a new bed and table every day if you will stay with me.'

'I will go on,' said Gold Apple, 'while alive I shall be living, if I die I shall have no more to do.'

'Are you going?' asked the uncle, next morning.

'I am,' said the King's son.

The uncle brought out one apple and said: 'Put this in your pocket, and never use it till you are in great need. You will reach my brother's house to-night, but be careful not to pass it.'

Gold Apple was making his way that day, walking as fast as he could until twilight, when he saw a small, poor hut at one side of the road in the corner of a wood. He did not think much of the hut, at first hardly noticed it, but when he went in he saw the finest castle and richest that he had seen or that any man could find. On each side of the fire was a chair, one of gold, one of silver. He sat down on the gold chair. In the middle of the room, sitting on the floor, was a woman with her hair down over her face and she combing it. The woman rose when Gold Apple sat in the chair, and struck him a much harder blow than the woman in the first castle.

'You'll be treated still worse when the giant comes,' said she.

'If the giant is harder on me than what you are he'll not leave much life in me.'

The giant came soon. 'It's the smell of a stranger that's in the castle!' cried he, 'and I cannot tell who he is till I see him.'

'Whatever is to be done to me, I am here,' said the King's son.

The giant shook hands with his sister's son, kissed and embraced him in the same way as the first uncle. 'Tell me what brought you and where you are going, tell all.'

Gold Apple told the whole story.

'Oh, then, my poor sister's son, you might as well be throwing stones at the moon as going for that head. My two brothers and I lost all we had, lost our lands and our cattle striving to get that dog and here we are now poor and weak. The daughter of Rí Fó Thuinn has that dog. There are seventy-seven poles behind her father's castle and the head of a king's son on each pole except one. Stay with me here, I will give you a fresh table and bed every day.'

'I will not stay. I must go on till I get what I came for or be killed while I'm getting it.'

Next morning the uncle said: 'Here is an apple which you will use only when great need is on you. You'll be in my brother's house to-night, however you'll pass from that out.'

The King's son walked off, keeping the two apples carefully. Between light and dark he saw a hut in a forest at some distance from the road. Inside this hut he found a woman combing her hair. When she put her hair aside she began to cry.

'Well, kind woman, will you tell why you are crying?' asked Gold Apple.

'I will,' said she. 'I pity such a fine young man as you, and you waiting for the cruel and painful death that will meet you when the giant comes.'

Soon after the voice of the giant was heard: 'I find the smell of a stranger!' shouted he, 'and I cannot tell whether it is better to put him under my feet or to swallow him; he's too big for one bite and too small for two.'

'I am here for whatever is waiting for me,' said Gold Apple.

The moment the giant saw the son of his sister and the King of Erin he kissed and embraced him and asked: 'What brought you or where are you going?'

Gold Apple told his whole story.

'God help you, poor sister's son. My two brothers and I lost what we had in striving to get what you are looking for. Stay with me; you'll have a pleasant life here. Go no further.'

'While I live I will live like a man; when I am dead I shall not meet death a second time.'

They made three parts of that night, and when morning came and with it the time for parting the giant said: 'Here is an apple for you, but spare it till great need comes. You'll be in your grandfather's house to-night.'

'Do not go for a while yet,' said the giant's wife. (She had made a cake, kneaded with milk from her own breast.) 'There is a dog in that house who never lets a man come to the door, but takes the life from every stranger. That dog is ever on the watch for fear that some man might come to the house unobserved. When at some distance throw the cake to the dog. If he smells it there's no fear of you; if he does not your chance is a bad one. The old man is very old; there is no knowing how old he is; his name is Crusty White Gray.'

Gold Apple left a blessing with his uncle and hurried on till he faced the house of the old man. Out came the dog. The King's son threw the cake at the beast from a distance. The dog saw the cake, did not stop at first, but ran back in a moment, smelled a little, ran forward, turned back again; this time he ate the cake.

When the dog had the cake eaten he was so glad and had such welcome for Gold Apple that the King's son had to keep him off with his sword.

Gold Apple entered the house, and the dog went before him. The old man rose up to kill the dog. 'Why let some herder into my house to take the life from me?' cried he to the dog.

'Oh,' said Gold Apple, 'don't kill the dog, I am not a shepherd, nor am I some herder, but the son of your daughter from Erin.'

"Tis easily known that a friend came and the dog to let him in. Oh, but I am glad to see you.'

They made three parts of that night, and during the evening a foster daughter of the old man talked long with Gold Apple and pleased him. He told her his story.

'It is useless for you to go alone,' said she. 'In the morning when I give you your breakfast stick your fork in the meat and don't taste it. The old man will ask you why you are not eating; do you say, "I will not eat till you give me the asking of a gift." "Anything I have to give I will give you, save one thing, the hound," is what the old man will tell you. Do you say then, "That is the only gift I want." He will say, "I cannot part with the hound or give him to any man." Do you rise up boldly and in anger, throw down the table, walk out, and say when you are going: "To be refused for a dog by my grandfather!"'

Next morning Gold Apple did all as the girl had advised. When the old man refused and Gold Apple walked out the girl rose up and said: 'I will walk away from you and leave this house forever if you refuse the dog to Gold Apple.' The old man gave the dog then. The young woman went out and said to Gold Apple in parting:

'Take care not to speak to the dog till he speaks to you, then talk without hindrance.'

The King's son walked on till the mid-afternoon. 'Gold Apple,' said the dog, 'why not shorten the day and the road?'

'Why, I thought the like of you never had talk or knowledge.'

'I have then,' said the dog, 'and I will give you a proof of it. We'll be at the castle of Rí Fó Thuinn to-night; there is a great assembly there to hunt to-morrow in Gleann Doracha (Glen of Darkness), and there is not a better place in the world for hunting or fowling than that very same glen. When you reach the hall door of the castle strike with the knocker. A man will come out and ask, "Who is there?" You'll say, "I am a hunter from Erin, and have brought my hound with me."'

All happened as the dog said. When the messenger announced Gold Apple. 'There are too many here now,' said one man. 'Oh, let him in,' said another; 'we'll be making game of himself and his wild dog from Erin.'

They let him in.

Said the dog to Gold Apple: 'When hunting to-morrow sit you above on the edge of the valley and keep me close to you till I wag my tail and beg you to let me out. If I were let out in the first of the hunt I should kill all there is in the glen, and might kill yourself if I could not find game enough.'

Gold Apple went out, sat on the edge of the glen, and as each man passed he beckoned to the King's son to go on. In the middle of the afternoon the dog stood up and begged. Gold Apple unleashed him, and away the hound rushed. In the end he brought more beasts and birds than all the dogs together.

In the evening every one was praising the dog, saying that it was wonderful how much game he had taken.

'Now,' said the dog on the way home, 'do not go out to-morrow at all. Be very tired, and say that you are sick. Everybody will be coming and asking me of you. Do not give me to any man till the King comes. Give me to him then, and tell him not to let me go earlier than you did to-day. If he does I'll not leave a thing living in the glen. When we are coming home be outside, and tell me what passed between you and the King's daughter.'

Next morning Gold Apple feigned sickness; would not go hunting. Every man wanted to borrow his hound, but he would give him to no man till the King asked. The King got the dog with the warning to keep him till late in the day. The King went to hunt, and Gold Apple walked out to meet the King's daughter. Toward evening the King was returning, and Gold Apple was outside waiting to talk with the dog.

'You saw the King's daughter?' asked the hound.

'I did,' said Gold Apple; 'she was pleasant and kind to me.'

'Well, I will go to the garden,' said the dog, 'and hear what she will say to her maid. The Princess has a suitor, and he will try to kill you this evening.'

The King's daughter went to walk with her maid.

'Which is the better man?' asked the maid.

'Oh, Gold Apple,' said the Princess. 'I could love that man and spare him.'

'He is only a stranger; no one knows where he came from or where he is going,' said the maid.

'I know him,' answered the Princess.

'Now,' said the hound when he came back to Gold Apple and told what he had heard, 'in the evening you'll take me to the castle to show me to all the great people; there will be a large company in it. The Princess would spare you, and has put away the eight-legged dog, but the suitor will bring the dog in a box to the Princess – the dog can make himself big or little – and will let him jump to the floor before she can stop him, and the suitor will say: "Here is a better dog than that hound from Erin." The dog will be going around till he comes up in front of you to cut your throat with a bite. You must keep out your hands well before you to guard yourself, seize the dog, throw him over your head, and say: "Whichever dog is better let him win." I will seize him then and you will see the end.'

That was done. The dogs fought till they made bits of everything in the castle. The people rushed out, escaping in every direction. The dogs left the castle and fought for three nights and three days on the field outside. Then they made two hawks of themselves, rose in the air, and flew away fighting.

On the seventh day Gold Apple went out, lamenting and weeping for the loss of his dog. In the evening of that day he saw the hound coming in his own shape and the head of the eight-legged dog in his mouth.

'Now,' said the hound, 'you are safe. The stepmother will have great welcome before you, and will ask have you the head. You will say, "I have." "Give it here," she will say then. "If I was bound to bring the head I was not bound to give it," will be your answer. But before you go put me in a coffin and bury me in this place, for I am dying now after the terrible battle.'

The hound died, Gold Apple buried him, and went back to his stepmother, carrying the head of the eight-legged dog. She welcomes him greatly. 'Have you the head?' 'I have,' answered he.

She stooped forward to grasp the head, Gold Apple punched her in the body with his thumb, and she fell like an empty bag of wet paper. She dropped dead. Gold Apple turned back to his grandfather's house now. He and the foster daughter were talking in the evening, and heard the old man moaning and complaining. 'It is sad for me,' said he, 'to be as I am in my old age, and my sons wasting away under enchantment, tearing each other to pieces in the form of wild dogs, and the means of salvation near me.'

'What is that?' asked Gold Apple.

'Nothing,' said the old man.

'It must be something,' said Gold Apple.

'There is,' said the old man, 'a horn under a stone there behind, and with it a branch. When the horn is sounded all the birds of the world will come, and when the branch is placed on a dead, sick, or wounded man it will cure him. The Queen of Lonesome Glen took from me the ring of youth, the pot of health, and the rod of enchantment; while I had them I was able to live as well as any man ever could, and my sons were living with me, but that Queen came with great forces and fought long against me and my sons, and never stopped till she took those three things from us and turned two of my sons into dogs, one into the eight-legged-dog and the other into the dog that followed you. We hid the horn and the branch from her under the stone, and she could not find them. We are waiting and expecting this long time for a man to come and knock satisfaction out of the Queen of Lonesome Glen through the use of the branch and the horn and bring back the three things to us.'

Next morning Gold Apple went to the stone, turned it over, found the horn and branch, and brought them in to Crusty White Gray.

'Do you think that you would be well if this branch were rubbed on you?' asked Gold Apple.

'I should be as well and strong as ever. I should not have the good looks, though. To get those I should have the ring of youth.'

Gold Apple rubbed the old man with the branch. He was as strong and healthy as ever, but looked old. The King's son blew the horn now, and one-third of what birds were in the world came to him. They cursed and abused him for calling them. 'What do you want of us, and why do you trouble us?' asked the birds.

'Do you know where Lonesome Glen is?'

'We do not, and cannot tell you. We are looking for that place ourselves more anxiously than you are.'

He blew the horn a second time, and the second third of all the birds in the world came. They gave the same answer. He blew the third time and put the same question to the third third. He blew the fourth blast, and the biggest and strongest bird, the eagle, came.

'What do you want of me and why have you called me?'

'I want knowledge from you. Where is Lonesome Glen and how can I go to it.'

'It is easy for me to tell you that, for the fastenings of my nest are in the chimney of the castle of Lonesome Glen, and if I had a-plenty of food I would bear you on my back to that place.'

'I will get food for you,' said Gold Apple.

He found a fine bullock, killed him, and gave the eagle plenty. They started early next morning and were rising till the eagle went high. He began to go down at nightfall, and was dropping lower till daylight, when he was over the sea.

'Well,' said the eagle, 'I must leave you here on a rock till I find food for myself.'

'Wait, I may have something,' said the King's son. He gave the eagle one apple. The eagle ate it and said: 'I am stronger now than when I ate the bullock yesterday.'

He was rising and travelling till nightfall, then descending till daylight, when he said: 'I must leave you on a rock and go to find food.'

'Wait,' said the King's son. 'Eat this apple.'

'The apple is very good and wholesome,' said the eagle. 'I am stronger now than I was yesterday.' He travelled in the same way till daylight of the third day.

'I have another apple; it may serve you.'

'If you have another apple, that will do.' He gave the apple. 'I am stronger than yesterday,' said the eagle. 'We shall be in Lonesome Glen to-morrow.'

The following morning they were in Lonesome Glen, and the eagle said to Gold Apple: 'When you are walking along in front of the castle open your breast and expose the love spot that is on it. The Queen will see the spot and fall in love with you, and send out a messenger to bring you. When you go in you will sit at her side, look at her sweetly, smiling, striving to get the ring of youth, and if you get that you will get every other thing.'

The eagle went about his own business, and everything happened as he said. The Queen fell deeply in love with Gold Apple. 'I will give you the ring,' said she, 'if you will bring it back to me and stay here yourself, and do you give your word of honour on that?'

'I do,' said Gold Apple. When he got the ring, he said: 'I want the rod of enchantment and the pot of health.'

She gave him these also. 'Now,' said she, 'when you are in Erin you'll need another thing. Here is a cloth for you. When you spread the cloth you'll have everything to eat and drink that you can wish for. Here is a mirror, too, and if you are a hundred and twenty years old you'll be young when you look in it; and here is a rod; if you hold it before you there will be a firm road over the ocean and across the wild waves, and you'll go in safety. When you have passed the road will close behind you and vanish in the water.'

He took the things and went his way. He kept the rod before him and never stopped till he went to the kingdom of Rí Fó Thuinn. He went to the buried hound which had killed the eight-legged dog, opened the grave and took the hound out, rubbed the body with the branch, and the hound was made living, gave him a blow of the rod of enchantment and made a man of him. He put for a moment the ring of youth on each finger of the right hand and made him young, he rubbed him with cure from the pot of health and made him well and strong.

The hound was a splendid champion now and went with the King's son to Erin. Gold Apple used the ring of youth on the old man and he was made as good as ever. 'It is too bad,' said Gold Apple, 'that we have the head of the eight-

The biggest and strongest bird, the eagle, bears Gold Apple on his back to Lonesome Glen.

legged dog in Erin and the body in another place. We must put them together.' They took the head out of a grave where Gold Apple had buried it; took it in a cloth and went away to where the body was buried, put the body and head together, used the branch, the rod, the pot of health, and the ring of youth. The eight-legged dog was a man young and well. 'I am a long time fasting,' said the champion.

Gold Apple had forgotten the cloth till then. He took it out, they ate their fill, and then made off for Erin. Gold Apple, Crusty White Gray, and his five sons lived together and rejoiced for a long time. Gold Apple had forgotten his mirror and rod, till one night when he dreamed of them. He was growing old then. Next morning he opened the box in which they were, looked at the mirror, and was young and strong. Then he said:

'It is a long time that I am away from Lonesome Glen. I will go there.' So he set out, holding the rod in front of him. A firm road rose up before and sank down behind him. He travelled till he reached Lonesome Glen, where he found a great welcome. In the castle they made three parts of that night with great pleasure and good cheer. Next morning the Queen sent out a bellman, calling all to the wedding, gentle and simple, rich and poor. There were seven hundred guests at the short table, eight hundred at the long table, nine hundred at the round table, and a thousand in the grand hall.

NOTES

Source: J. Curtin, *Hero Tales of Ireland*, London: MacMillan, 1894.

It will be seen at once that this story is related to that of 'The Story of Conn-eda, or the Golden Apples of Loch Erne' (page 89). In the latter, we find many of the same elements, including the evil queen, the wicked henwife, and the trilogy of giants and their wives; here, however, these elements are subtly altered, the pattern played with by a master storyteller.

In the beginning we have the age-old theme of the king who promises not to remarry but ends up doing so – in this instance 'the first woman he sees' – with unfortunate results. Here the woman is a haglike creature who requests him to marry her, rather like the loathsome lady Dame Ragnell in the medieval poem 'The Wedding of Sir Gawain'. In both instances, she turns out to be fair rather than foul, but promptly seems to lose her magical powers in the face of the henwife, who soon has her agreeing to her formulaic demands.

The story then follows the general shape of 'Conn-eda', but with noteworthy differences. For example Gold Apple, the hero (whose name must surely derive from the title of the Conn-eda tale 'The Golden Apples of Loch Erne) has to find an eight-legged dog instead of performing the three impossible tasks of the alternative version. The battle of the dogs, who are really men in that shape, is typical of many magical duels fought between either druids or enchanters.

The description of the horn which calls all the birds of the air to congregate is reminiscent of the episode in the Celtic Arthurian tale 'The Lady of the Fountain' from the *Mabinogion,* in which the knight Colgrevant (and later the hero of the story) find their way to the mysterious Fountain of Baranton in the enchanted woodland of Broceliande, and, on pouring water from a basin over a huge emerald rock, witness the arrival of thousands of birds, which settle like leaves on a tree.

In this story, Gold Apple has to attain another triad of objects – the Ring of Youth, the Pot of Health, and the Rod of Enchantment, which here replace the more usual cup and bottle and endlessly-restoring loaf of bread found in other stories (see, for example, 'Coldfeet and the Queen of Lonesome Island' in J. Matthews *Classic Celtic Fairy Tales*, Blandford, 1997). Here better use is made of them – and of the further series of gifts which Gold Apple obtains in the closing pages of the story.

In an unusual detail, we find Gold Apple turning the tables on the Queen of the Lonesome Glen (probably the same character as in the story mentioned above) through the use of a love spot on his breast. This recalls the same blemish which is on the face of Diarmuid O'Duibne, the Fenian hero, who had to wear a hat pulled down over his face in order to prevent every woman he met from falling in love with him. As in each of the stories included here, we learn even more about the nature of the Otherworld and its inhabitants from the adventures of Gold Apple.

The Adventure of Cian's Son Teigue

T WAS ONCE UPON A TIME when Teigue son of Olioll Olom's son Cian was on his 'next heir's circuit' into the west of Munster, and his own kindly brethren: *Airnelach* and *Eoghan* along with him. And that was the very time and hour in which came *Cathmann* son of *Tabarn* – a man that was king of the beauteous land of Fresen: a country lying over against Spain to the south-east – out of the coasts of Fresen then this same Cathmann (with a strength of nine first-rate ships' crews) came on a roving commission, scouring the sea to make discovery, until they made the land in Munster's western part where, in or about Berehaven (to be precise), they caught the country napping, and so slipped ashore, the whole fleetful of them; by whom the country was spoiled and ravaged, nor were the inhabitants ever aware of them until they had surrounded their prey, both human and of kine: Teigue's entire family being taken, and himself by sheer weapon-play coupled with resolution hardly escaping away from them. There namely were captured *Líban*, daughter of Conor Red-brows and wife of Cian's son Teigue, with both his brethren: Airnelach and Eoghan; and among all the various denominations of captives and of booty away they were carried, in the hands of robbers and trusting to the clemency of *allmarachs* [a poor look-out], until they reached Spain and the coasts of Fresen. Teigue's wife, Cathmann takes off to himself for the purposes of his bed and most privy couch; his two kinsmen he relegates to servitude and hardship: Eoghan, to work a common ferry across a fjord on the coast; Airnelach, to pull firewood and to keep up fire for the people at large; while for their support was given them barley seed only, with muddy turbid water.

Teigue's concerns must be told now: whom grief and discouragement affected, for sake of his brethren and his wife ravished from him by Allmarachs. Forty warriors of his people however had likewise escaped unslain by these, having on the contrary themselves killed of them a man apiece, and one individual of the over-sea men they brought in in hand. This fellow told them the particulars of that land out of which they had been attacked; and the project which Teigue formed in consequence was to build and fit out (suitably to a long passage) a smart, strongly put together currach of five-and-twenty thwarts, in which should be forty ox-hides of hard bark-soaked red leather. Then he provided all due items of his currach's necessaries: in the way of thick tall masts, of broad-bladed oars, of pilots fully qualified, and of thwarts solidly well laid and fitted in their berths, in such fashion that in all respects this currach was as it should be, and thoroughly staunch.

With mighty effort now they ran down and bravely launched the craft: some stout hands in her, all standing by to meet the huge green billows, to deal with the lofty rising of the salmon-bearing, strong-crested sea, with the rude broken race of the spring tide. With victuals and all stores they filled their currach so that, though they kept the sea for a whole year, they had had as much as would keep them of meat and drink, and of right good raiment. The young men then being at all points ready, Teigue said: 'Men! Take your currach to sea, and let us be off in quest of our own that for now already some time are away from us.'

Forth on the vast illimitable abyss they drive their vessel accordingly, over the volume of the potent and tremendous deluge, till at last neither ahead of them nor astern could they see land at all, but only colossal Ocean's superficies. Farther on, they heard about them concert of multifarious unknown birds and hoarse booming of the main; salmons, irridescent, white-bellied, throwing themselves all around the currach; in their wake huge bull seals, thick and dark, that ever cleft the flashing wash of the oars as they pursued them and, following these again, great whales of the deep; so that for the prodigiousness of their fashion, motion and variety, the young men found it a festive thing to scrutinise and watch them all: for hitherto they had not used to see the diverse oceanic reptiles, the bulky marine monsters. For the space of twenty days with twenty nights thus they continued rowing on the sea, and then sighted bold land having a fair and favourable coast. They hold a straight course for the same till they reach it, then all hands land and there they beach their currach; they light fires, their provisions are passed out to them, and these the warriors despatch redoubtably. On the beautiful green grass they make themselves beds, and from that moment to the bright hour of sunrise on the morrow enjoy themselves in sleep. Next day, Teigue being early risen prepares to perambulate and to search out the land, to make a circuit and find out whether in the island were any inhabiting of either men or beasts. He takes on him his armature of battle therefore, and thirty warriors of his people fully weaponed start with him; they go right ahead and explore the whole island, but signs of human habitation find not any whatsoever nor, save only all flocks of sheep, aught else. The size of these creatures was unutterable: they were not less than horses of the largest, the entire island too being full of their wool. One parlous great flock in particular they found there, of gigantic rams which a single special one exceeded all: nine horns bedecked him and on our heroes he charged, violently butting. In irritation Teigue's people turn on him and between them and him a fight comes off, in which the ram at this first burst staves in some five of their shields; but then Teigue poises that throwing javelin of his that might not be eluded, and at the ram delivers a lucky cast, so killing him. Now the full burthen of those nine-and-twenty others that were present, that is what he was to carry. They brought him to the currach, prepared him deftly, and brandered him till he was meat fit for the young men to consume. For its beauty, its extraordinary nature and the richness of it, they gather great store of the wool and put it into the currach. For three nights they were in the island, and a wether it was that nightly provided our fine fellows. Human bones too of enormous size they found there, but what death had carried off the owners was unknown to them:

whether it were men that had slain, plague or pestilence exterminated, or in fact the rams that had killed them.

They leave the island and pull ahead, upon which course that they held they light on a pair of most peculiar islands, containing a multitude of very special birds of the blackbird sort: some of them possessing the bulk of eagles or of cranes, and they red (but with green heads on them) while eggs they had that were pied of blue and of pure crimson. Of which eggs certain from among the navigators ate somewhat, and on the instant an integument of feathers would sprout out all over every one that so fed; but when they bathed, such plumage would as quickly drop from them. Now the Allmarach that they had with them, he it was that had given them this course, for on some former occasion he as he cruised had followed this same track of theirs.

Again they pull away, for six weeks (during which spell they never made a landfall), until the Allmarach said: 'we are all adrift, and carried into the deep illimitable ocean of the great abyss!' Then the blast with its coarse utterance rose; great uproar was wrought in the sea, so that it was turned into heaving hills, into great mountains ill to climb; and at encounter of all this dirty weather, of these heavy squalls: things which hitherto they had not practised to endure, much fear occupied the people of Cian's son Teigue. But he fell to stir up and to incite them, telling them to meet the sea like men, and he said: 'Do valiantly – fight for your lives against the ocean's heavy seas that rise at you along the currach's sides!' He by himself took the craft's one side, all his people manned the other, and Teigue prevailed against the whole of them: he alone sufficing to pull the currach round on the other twenty-nine, while he contrived to bale and keep it dry besides. After this they got a turn of fair wind and hoisted their sail, whereby the currach shipped less water on them; then the sea moderated, abating its hubbub till finally it lay fair flat calm, and until on every hand about them there was chorus of birds unknown and multiform. They now descry land with a good coast, of a pleasing aspect, and at the sight become joyful and of good courage. They close in with it, and find a fine green-bosomed estuary with spring-well-like sandy bottom having silver's pure-white refulgence; with salmons variegated and gaudy, decked in choice shades of crimson red; delicate woods with empurpled tree-tops fringing the delightful streams of this country into which they were come. 'A beauteous land is this, young men,' said Teigue: 'and I could give him joy whose natural lot in life it were to dwell on in the same!'

And he went on: 'a lovely land and a fruitful, I say, is this into which we are come; land we then, haul ye up your currach and dry it out!' which done, a score of stalwart warriors set out on their rambles, leaving other twenty to mind the currach. Now, for all they had had of cold, of strain on their endurance, of foul weather and of tempest, yet neither for meat nor for fire did they, after reaching the coast on which they thus were landed, feel any craving at all: the perfume of that region's fragrant crimsoned branches being by way of meat and satisfying aliment all-sufficient for them. Through the nearest part of the forest they take their way, and come by-and-by upon an orchard full of red-laden apple-trees, with leafy oaks too in it, and hazels yellow with nuts in their clusters. 'I marvel, men,' quoth Teigue, 'at that which I perceive: in our own land at this present instant we have winter, and here, in this country, summer!' Extraordinary was the amenity of that spot to which they had attained now; but they quit it, and happen on a wood: great was the excellence of its scent and perfume, round purple berries hung on it, and every one of them was bigger than a man's head. Birds beautiful and brilliant feasted on these grapes; fowls they were of unwonted kind: white, with scarlet heads and with golden beaks. As they fed, they warbled music and minstrelsy that was melodious and superlative, to which patients of every kind and the repeatedly wounded would have fallen asleep.

Still they advance, and so to a wide smooth plain clad in flowering clover all bedewed with honey: a perfectly flat and even plain it was, without either rise or fall of surface except three prominent hills that it bore, each one of these having on its side an impregnable place of strength. Said plain they traverse so far as the nearest hill, and there find a white-bodied lady, fairest of the whole world's women, who said: 'I hail thine advent and, Teigue son of Cian, thou shalt have victual and constant supply!' 'The same to thee, if that be lawful for me; but, gentle and sweet-worded woman, what is thy name?' 'I am *Gothnia's* daughter, wife of *Sláinghe* son of *Dela* son of *Loth,*' she answered. 'Queen,' said Teigue, 'that thou sayest there is good: set me now forth, I pray thee, every colony that ever settled Ireland, and the tongues that served them all, from *Cesair's* time to her plantation by Milesius' sons.' And so she sang a lay that told all of those things.

Then he said: 'woman, that is well; knowledge thou hast and genuine instruction; tell me therefore what is this regal and great fortalice upon the high hill's face, with round about it a bulwark of white marble?' 'That,' she answered, 'is the fort of the royal line.' 'What line is that?' 'Of Ireland's kings: from Heremon son of Milesius to Conn of the Hundred Battles, who was the last to pass into it.' Teigue asked: 'what is this country's name?' '*Inis locha* or "loch island" this is,' she said: 'over which they are two kings that reign, as *Ruadrach* and *Dergeroiche* sons of Bodhb.' 'And who dwells in yon middle fort that has a colour of gold?' 'It is not I that will tell it thee; but to that same intermediate fort betake thyself, and there thou shalt learn it;' with which the lady departed from them to the fort of white marble. Teigue with his people moved on till they gained the middle hold, where again they found a queen of gracious form and she draped in vesture of a golden fabric. 'All hail, Teigue!' said she, and: 'lady, I thank thee for the same,' he returned. 'Long time it is since 'twas foretold for thee to come on this journey, Teigue.' 'Thy name, lady?' 'Cesair, daughter of Noah's son *Bethra,* people call me; I am the first woman that reached Ireland before the Flood, and with me three men: Bith, Fintan, Ladra; but ever since we came out of that dark unquiet land, in this one here we bide in everlasting life.' 'Thou art a knowledgeable expert woman so,' said Teigue. 'Proficient I am indeed,' she answered, 'in every people and generation that ever, down to this very day, took Ireland.' 'This island's name, what is it?' 'Thou askest that thou knowest already.' 'But,' said Teigue, 'I know not whether it be the same tale with thee and with her whom previously we have addressed.' 'The same verily,' she said: '*inis derglocha* or "red loch island" is this one's name; because of a red loch that is in it, containing an island surrounded with a palisade of gold, its name being *inis Patmos*, in which are all saints and righteous that have served God. These latter, men's eyes never have beheld, for between radiance of the Divinity and the constant discourse which God and the Angels hold with them, our vision may not dwell nor even but impinge on them.'

'Let us now learn from thee, woman,' said Teigue, 'who dwells in this *dún* that we see with a golden rampart.' 'Soon said,' was her answer: 'all kings, and rulers, and noble men of ordained rank that from our own time back to that of Milesius' sons have held Ireland's supreme power – they 'tis that are in yonder *dún*: both Partholan and Nemid, both Firbolgs and *tuatha dé Danann.*' 'Woman, that is well,' Teigue said: 'knowledge thou hast, and right instruction.' 'Truly,' said Cesair, 'I am well versed in the World's history: for this precisely is the Earth's fourth paradise; the others being *inis Daleb* in the world's southern, and *inis Escandra* in its boreal part (to the northward of "the black watery isle"), Adam's paradise, and this island in which ye are now: the fourth land, I say, in which Adam's seed dwell – such of them as are righteous.' 'And in that notable *dún* we see encircled with a silver rampart, who inhabits?' 'It is not that I know not,' she replied, 'but I will not tell you; go to yonder hill however, there shall ye learn all.' They proceeded to the third hill, on the summit of which was a seat of great beauty and, on its very apex, a gentle and youthful couple clad in outward semblance that was fresh and recent. Smooth heads of hair they had, with sheen of gold; equal vestments of green wrapped them both; and all might deem it to have been from but the one father and the one mother that they sprang, seeing that dissimilarity of form or fashion between them there was none. Round the lower part of their necks chains of red gold were wound and, above these, golden torques clasped their throats.

'What, gentle queen,' he enquired, 'is thy cognomen; whence thy race?' 'Soon told,' she answered: 'my name is Veniusa, and daughter I am to Adam – for four daughters we are in the four mysterious magic countries which Cesair declared to thee: Veniusa, Letiusa, Aliusa and Eliusa our names are, whom though the guilt of our mother's transgression suffers not to abide together in one place, yet for our virginity and for our purity that we have dedicated to God we are conveyed into these separate joyful domiciles.' 'Who is that so comely stripling by thy side?' 'Him let himself proclaim to thee,' said she, 'for he has both speech and eloquence.' Now the youth was so, that in his hand he held a fragrant apple having the hue of gold; a third part of it he would eat, and still, for all he consumed, never a whit would it be diminished. This fruit it was that supported the pair of them and, when once they had partaken of it, nor age nor dimness could affect them. The young fellow answered Teigue, saying: 'I am son to Conn of the Hundred Battles.' 'Art thou then Connla?' 'I am indeed; and this young woman of the many charms it was that hither brought me.' 'That,' said Teigue, 'is both likely and as it should be.' 'I had bestowed on him true affection's love,' the girl explained, 'and therefore wrought to have him come to me in this land; where our delight, both of us, is to continue in looking at and in perpetual contemplation of one another: above and beyond which we pass not, to commit impurity or fleshly sin whatsoever.' 'That,' quoth Teigue again, 'is a beautiful, and at the same a comical thing! And who occupies yon grand *dún* that we see, girt with a silver rampart?' 'In that one,' she replied, 'there is not any one.' 'Why, what means that?' Teigue asked. 'For behoof of the righteous kings that after acceptance of the Faith shall rule Ireland it is that yonder *dún* stands ready; and we are they who, until such those virtuous princes shall enter into it, keep the same: in the which, Teigue my soul, thou too shalt have an appointed place.' 'And how may that be contrived?' 'Believe thou in the Omnipotent Lord,' she said, 'and even to the uttermost Judgment's time thou shalt win that mansion, with God's Kingdom afterwards.' 'I confess, I adore, I supplicate him!' responded Teigue. 'Come we now away,' the girl said, 'till we view the disposition of yonder abode.' 'Were it permitted us, I would go,' said Teigue, and she assented: 'so it is.' Then Teigue with his people (said pair accompanying them) drew near to the *dún* where the girdle of marble was, and it was but hardly if the beautiful green grass's heads were bowed beneath that couple's smooth soft-white footsoles. They pass under the arched doorway with its wide valves and portal-capitals of burnished gold; they step on to a shining well-laid pavement, tessellated of pure white, of blue, of crimson marble, and so on till they gain the vast lordly edifice in which was to be the happy and splendid company of kings. A jocund

*The navigators
wash their
feathered-skins
in the river.*

137

house was that, and one to be desired: there was a silver floor, with four choice doors of bright gold; gems of crystal and of carbuncle in patterns were set in the wall of *finndruine* ['white gold'], in such wise that with flashing of those precious stones day and night alike shone. The girl takes in hand to deliver them the plan and whole description of the dwelling, saying: 'here we are stationed, to await all monarchs, provincial kings, and tribal chiefs in Ireland.'

Obliquely across the most capacious palace Teigue looked away, and marked a thickly furnished wide-spreading apple-tree that bore blossom and ripe fruit both. 'What is that apple-tree beyond?' he asked, and she made answer: 'that apple-tree's fruit it is that for meat shall serve the congregation which is to be in this mansion, and a single apple of the same it was that brought Connla to me.'

She continued to Teigue: 'here make we a halt, here let us pause; for not mine it is to declare to thee the manner of thy life's ending, but one that will do so thou shalt have.' Thereupon the two part from them; howbeit the exhilarating properties of the house were such that, after their leaving them, Teigue and his people experienced neither melancholy nor sorrow.

Soon they marked towards them a whole array of feminine beauty, and among them a lovely damsel of refined form: the noblest and most desire-inspiring of the whole world's women to survey, who when she was come on the ground said: 'I welcome thee, Teigue!' 'I thank thee for it,' he returned: 'and, maiden, who art thou?' 'Cleena Fairhead, daughter of Genann mac Creon of the *tuatha dé Danann*, sweetheart of Eochaid Redweapon's son Ciabhan of the curling locks; for now some time I am in this island, and from me "Cleena's Wave" in the borders of Munster is denominated. Also, that which for meat and sustenance serves us all is the fruit of the same apple-tree which but a while ago thou sawest.' To Teigue and party it was a pleasant thing, and a pastime, to listen to her parlance; then he said: 'it is time for us to set about going in quest of our people.' 'The longer ye bide and tarry with us,' the young woman said, 'the better shall we be pleased.' Even as they exchanged these words they saw enter to them, through the side of the house three birds: a blue one, with crimson head; a crimson, with head of green; a pied one having on his head a colour of gold, and they perched upon the apple-tree that stood before them. They eat an apple apiece, and warble melody sweet and harmonized, such that the sick would sleep to it. 'Those birds,' Cleena said, 'will go with you; they will give you guidance, will make you symphony and minstrelsy and, until again ye reach Ireland, neither by land nor by sea shall sadness or grief afflict you. Take with thee,' she continued, 'this fair cup of emerald hue, in which are inherent many virtues: for among other things though it were but water poured into it, incontinently it would be wine.' 'Where was it fashioned?' he enquired. 'Soon said: a whale it was which in this haven where ye landed the sea cast ashore; we cut him up, and in his heart's core was found that goblet, the name of which is *an biasdain*, [product of the *biast* or bestia]. From that, let not thine hand part; but have it for a token: when it shall escape from thee, then in a short time after shalt thou die; and where thou shalt meet thy death is in the glen that is on Boyne's side: there the earth shall grow into a great hill, and the name that it shall bear will be *croidhe eisse*; there too (when thou shalt first have been wounded by a roving wild hart, after which Allmarachs will slay thee) I will bury thy body; but thy soul shall come with me hither, where till the Judgment's Day thou shalt assume a body light and ethereal. This armature as well take thou about thee and, how many soever the battles and the single combats thou shalt fight, though thy body be hurt yet shall thy soul be whole.'

Subsequently they depart out of the bright radiant mansion, the girl going with

them to convey them to the landing-place where they had left their comrades and
currach. To these latter she gave very courteous greeting, for which they thanked
her in kind; she asked them then how long they had been in the country, and: 'in
our estimation,' they replied, 'we are in it but one single day.' She however said:
'for an entire twelvemonth ye are in it; during which time ye have had neither meat
nor drink nor, how long soever ye should be here, would cold or thirst or hunger
assail you.' 'Happy he that should for ever live on in that life!' Teigue's people
cried, but he said: 'ungrateful and irksome to us though it be to depart, yet were
it time that in earnest we went to work to leave the bright land in which we are.'

Their sharp fast currach now they drive ahead over the great deep's convexi-
ty; and the birds struck up their chorus for them, whereat, for all they were so
grieved and sad at renouncing that fruitful country out of which they were thus
come, these modulations gladdened and soothed them that they became merry
and of good courage all. But when they looked astern they saw not the land from
which they came, for incontinently an obscuring magic veil was drawn over it.

For the space of a day and a half now they carry on and sail the sea, they being
all the time sunk in slumber of deepest sleep, till they reached the land of Fresen;
then they perceive that they are come into port and have taken the ground, and
the birds desist and are silent. The young men rose and in all haste landed; which
done, they took counsel how they should proceed in the quest for Teigue's wife and
kinsfolk, and he said: 'I will go alone to search out and to explore the country.'
His arms and armature were brought to him; the fearless hero set out and stoutly
walked the land until he came to an arm of the sea [fjord] that was betwixt them
and as he now discovered the king's hold. Then to the shore's very edge he went
down to examine it; there he saw a currach lying off all ready for him, and asked
to have the craft put across for him. The young man in charge of the ferry rose,
came to meet him, and fell to curiously consider him; whose form of speech when
he heard, his heart warmed to the hero's whole guise and to his manner of address.
Strenuously he pulled in the currach to him, and as quickly stepped ashore; but
Teigue had recognised him when as yet he was afloat. Yet, though Teigue, even for
Teigue it had been no easy matter for him to discern his own brother: for that good
warrior's form and fashion were all changed with this drudgery of the sea, he not
having from his youth up had experience of such service. For all which, the heroes'
hearts however had acknowledged each other; earnestly now and passionately
they kissed, and side by side upon the sandy beach sat down. Of Eoghan, for he it
was, Teigue sought tidings concerning Airnelach and the woman, his own wife.

This ended, a second time Teigue began to question Eoghan: how was the
keep, as regards both strength and power to hold out; or had the king any that
were moved by ill-will or irritation at him: one that disputed his realm with him,
or had in hand to contrive the monarch's detriment?' 'Surely he has, warrior,' said
Eoghan: 'and a propitious hour is this in which ye are come, seeing that 'tis not
long since it was mooted to assault this hold.' 'Who would execute this enter-
prise?' 'Two most noble sons of kings that are in this land, being of the monarch's
own blood and kinship: Eochaid Redweapon namely, and Tuire called *tortbhuil-
leach* or "of the ponderous blows," two sons of Cathmann the king's brother,
who for a year past vex this land with marauding and with acts of outlawry. But
yesterday they were on this coast; I was summoned to confer with them, and in
respect of this strong place they examined me. They solicited me instantly,
reminding me of my cause of enmity against the king, of my dishonour at the
hands of him that held me in bondage and in hardship. Nor did I for my part
deny but that I would perform that of which they spoke: to deliver the monarch

to his enemies. I went therefore to report the matter to Airnelach, and said young men we trysted for this night and in this spot, in order to carry the fastness and overpower the king. This secret design we imparted to the queen also, and for the same her spirit was rejoiced: for the gentle lady loved not Cathmann, neither had renounced her first loving love for thee. When therefore we found her mind and our own inclinations to coincide with those of the gallant company of depredators (the king's near kinsmen I mean), accompanied as they were with a strong force, the resolve to which we came was to attack the monarch this very night. Since then the lady's wedding-feast is all ready, and the end of that respite which she craved of Cathmann now at hand, thus it is that thou must do: go amongst thy people to hurry them up. For myself, I will repair to yonder wood, in which are the king of Fresen's two sons: Eochaid and Tuire as before, and to them will impart all thy description, and how that to take vengeance for thy wife and kindred ravished from thee thou art come into this land, as well as to take us out of this bondage and misery in which we are. Also, to those braves I will promise this country's royal rule; and will tell them to come at this night's first beginning to meet thee, and so on to the fastness to deliver a combined assault.'

Here Teigue bade Eoghan wind up this conversation, confer again with both Airnelach and the lady, and return to him with the result; but first he related to his brother somewhat of his passage, of his perilous things and of his wonders. Then they, being thus in perfect agreement, parted.

Touching Teigue now: he being jocund and of good cheer sought his people, and the young men were gladdened when they saw him draw near the strand, because in consideration of the length of time that he had been away from them apprehension had possessed them and they wearied for him. They questioned him of the land; pleasantly he fell to tell them all about it, and from first to last rehearsed to them his whole adventure. With this recital they were invigorated hugely, and their spirits rose when they heard that in the region Eoghan and Airnelach still lived before them.

And Teigue continued: 'rise ye now, my good people, and let us go to meet them that have trysted us.' Round about Teigue then, to keep him well, that tough band rose and in one course reached the hard at which Eoghan plied the ferry. The very first of night it was with them then; and at the one instant Teigue arrived at the strand, Eochaid and Tuire on the other shore opposite them. In familiar wise they discoursed each other across the fjord, and to Teigue with his strong men the Fresenachs accorded welcome. They [the Gaels] being busy with these speeches saw Eoghan in his boat heading for them; he came where Teigue was, and imparted the news of the fort: that he had had speech of Airnelach and the woman, the whole community meanwhile being seated in order to the enjoying of that great feast; that the monarch's banqueting-hall was ordered, the nobles of the land of Fresen tranquilly in act of battening there and, the bulk of [liquid] provision being now served out, that they were well drunken and made hilarious uproar. He told Teigue that now was the time to storm the citadel, and by his means the farther heroes were ferried across to their allies so that all together they were on the fort's side of the arm. Which royal youths when they had joined Teigue entered into conditions and fellowship with him, and struck their hands in his; he on his side giving them guarantees that might not be transgressed, to the effect that, supposing them to come victorious off from this operation, the kingdom should be handed over to them. Now the warriors' number upon the ground, they being drawn up together, was seven hundred, and (for the present) so much for them.

Concerning the Allmarach that accompanied Teigue on this expedition – the

Venusia and
Connla.

141

same that in the matter of the original contention had by our heroes been captured in the Irish countries – he it was that on this cruise gave Teigue his course, and piloted him. He now had been present at Teigue and the king's sons' making of their compact together, nor took they any heed at all either to watch or to ward him. When therefore he heard a project for the monarch's violent death put into working order, natural fondness and affection filled his heart, and away round the rear of that noble party he stole off in hot haste to the fort with intent to warn the king in advance of the others, and so arrived. But just as he won to the door of the king's own mansion, he saw towards him a man: Airnelach son of Cian, and the same questioned him what haste or hurry ailed him. 'Great cause indeed there is for it, seeing that Cian's son Teigue with his merry men out of Ireland's lands comes at you to take vengeance on you for his wife and kin. Tuire and Eochaid too are with him, wherefore suffer me to pass on to the king with a warning.' When Airnelach heard that, round the Allmarach's shoulders he locked both his long strong arms, ejected him through the fortress' gate, took him out on the green, and speedily beheaded the riever; this done, Teigue and his reached the same green; Airnelach went to meet them, and to them all administered friendship's kisses. Headlong then they made for the fastness and (for at this season never a guard was mounted at the gate) got in. In this one rush they penetrated right up to the main building [the king's own], round about which they emitted whoops such as would make the inmates to jump smartly and to its sides they applied firebrands and torches.

As concerning them of the mansion: when they heard those diverse loud unfriendly shouts, promptly they rose and took to them their arms, their manifold weapons of edge and point; but the manner of them that were in the fort at large was this: that they were in a condition of drunkenness and bewilderment. Now the noblest and most excellent that at this instant kept the king company were Illann called *áithesach* or 'the exultant' (the monarch's only son) and Conan called *codaitchenn* or 'hardhead' (chief of his household), having along with them twelve hundred of the land of Fresen's champions. These came then, and thus they found the king: in his own privy chamber, with his fighting harness on him. Through the *bruiden's* ['hall'] doors they burst out, and by them the fires were quenched, slaughter and losses wrought on the assailants. By no manner of means might this punishment and these losses be endured by the Eirennachs from the Allmarachs: again they assailed the *bruiden* to its peril, and were as rudely met by the Allmarachs. At this point Teigue enjoined his people to show hardihood and valiance, and in the bicker to outdo all the rest [their allies]; dourly, grimly the Eirennachs answered, and went to work cutting off the Allmarachs. Then it was that Cian's son Eoghan *coscarach* and Conan Hardhead, chief of the monarch's household, encountered in the press and fought an unintermittent, brave, and bitter fight; but upon Eoghan's other side there came nine warriors of Conan's poll-guard to destroy him, yet the end of the tussle was that by Eoghan's hand Conan and his nine fell expeditiously. As for Eoghan himself however, he had but taken Conan's head and uttered his triumph-cry when he too fell in the same blood-litter. When Illann saw these deaths his anger rose, and his soul grew high as he beheld his people slain and brought to naught, and he made his way to range through the whole battle. Tuire Hardhitter made for him, and presently they closed on the field: the set-to was an even one, for in the mêlée both champions together fell. Teigue and Eochaid Redweapon seeing these deaths, and their own next-of-kin in dire straits, discharged themselves upon the Allmarachs and with terrible carnage punished them to such pitch that in this onset two hundred fell by them. Here then the Allmarachs failed to make a stand against our young men; so that a chance at the *bruiden* was had, and Teigue with his Eirennachs about him made his way to the king's chamber, in which he was. Eochaid and Airnelach pursued the Allmarachs whom, so long as ever they stuck up to the young men to bandy blows with them, they kept on thinning out and violently slaughtering. Upon their return they found Teigue and Cathmann laying on each other in the fair midst of the *bruiden:* in which bout Cathmann gave Teigue thirty wounds, but Teigue 'brought the upper earth to bear on him' [i.e. manœuvred to get the advantage of higher ground], which is so much as to say that his body's president, his head to wit, he made to part company with his carcase; whereupon, and after Cathmann's head duly taken, he 'gave the cry.'

When the queen, Liban daughter of Conor Redbrow, heard the triumph-shouts and learned these killings, without delay or dilly-dally she came to her spouse, and for her dear love rejoiced and was glad exceedingly; that she saw her hero was to the gentle lady matter of thankfulness indeed. To the far end of a fortnight they abode in that fort, and in the result of it all Eochaid Redweapon was made king over the fair realms of Fresen. To Teigue they yielded pledges and hostages. Then he constrained his people that they should depart, telling them to face the sea cheerily; out of the strong place he carried away precious things, treasures, other good booty, forby Liban his wedded wife and his two brethren: Eoghan and Airnelach.

 # NOTES

Source: Standish H. O'Grady (editor), *Silva Gadelica*, Edinburgh: Williams & Norgate, 1892.

This remarkable, late tale is a classic of the *immrama* type. Beginning as a quest to regain Teigue's lost wife and family, it quickly becomes an excuse to visit another series of islands inhabited by strange creatures. This time the description of the Otherworld has been greatly influenced by Christian traditions. The four-aspected view of the Otherworld, which is repeated in a number of texts, has for its fourth aspect a paradisal realm which will be occupied by those of the new faith. This shows a remarkable understanding of the original concept of the Otherworld and the way it could be expressed in Christian terms. The remaining descriptions of the castles first encountered by Teigue and his men when they arrive are consistent with the older traditions. Thus *Inis Locha* is a familiar name for the Irish Otherworld,

and the names of those who live there, from the sons of Bodhb to Cessair, are all recognizable from a wide spectrum of Irish traditions. Indeed Teigue encounters a veritable armada of famous characters, heroes and gods, who would all have been well known to those who heard or read the story. (Even Connla the Fair, from the fourth tale in this collection, puts in a brief appearance, and we learn how he was summoned to the Otherworld).

The work preserves a great deal of the age-old lineage of people and kings, derived from a number of sources. Thus Cessair is said to be the daughter of Noah's first son – a curious tradition which made the early Irish descendants of the Biblical patriarch! The original text is interspersed, according to the style of the bardic storyteller, with verses which are unfortunately not fully translated into English. The fragments which were included in the version printed here have therefore been omitted for ease of reading.

The
Tuairisgeal

HERE WAS A KING over Erin before this, who had only one son. He determined to give him a full and perfect education, such as would become a king's son, in respect of every kind of learning that was going in his day.

For this purpose, he sent him to school for a period of seven unbroken years, after which he spent a year at home.

He next sent him there for another seven years, and then he spent, in like manner, a whole year at home.

Again he sent him there for another seven years, and his training being then perfected and finished, he finished with training.

In a moorland glen, the King built a beautiful castle, six storeys high, and when the lad came home, he took him to see the castle. While they were looking at the edifice, the lad, in the twinkling of an eye, took a standing leap, and alighted on the highest storey. When he came down, his father and he returned home.

The castle pleased the lad exceedingly, but he did not disclose that to his father. And so it was, that on the-morrow, he betook himself to the glen.

In the glen and at the castle, a Red-Headed Olach met him, and said to him: –

'Wilt thou play a game of chess to-day, thou Son of Erin's King?'

'I will, I will, why should I not do so in the kingdom of my father and my grandfather?' said the Son of the King.

They began playing at chess, and they were hard at it from the rising to the going down of the sun, and the play went against the Red-Headed Olach.

'Claim and take from me the stakes of thy gaming,' said the Red-Headed Olach.

'I will, I will,' said the King of Erin's Son. 'The stakes are that one side of this glen be stocked with black cattle, every one of them having red ears.'

He returned home that night, and told his father what had happened.

'It is well if it last,' quoth the King.

Early in the morning, he betook himself to the glen, to inspect the castle and the herds he had won yesterday, and at the castle, the Red-Headed Olach meets him.

'Wilt play a game at chess to-day, thou Son of Erin's King?' said the Red-Headed Olach.

'I will, I will – why should I not play to-day as I played yesterday, in the kingdom of my father and my grandfather?' said the Son of the King of Erin. They began playing, and they were hard at it from the rising to the going down of the sun, and the play went against the Red-Headed Olach.

'Claim and take from me the stakes of thy gaming,' said the Red-Headed Olach.

'I will, I will,' said the Son of Erin's King. 'The stakes are that the other side of the glen be stocked with red cattle, having black ears.'

He returned home that night, and told his father what had happened.

'It is well if it last,' said the King.

He went to bed, and in the dead of night, who should come into his room but the most beautiful woman he had ever seen, and he falls deeply in love with her.

'Neither mistress nor wedded wife will I ever have but thee,' said he.

'I will never marry thee,' said she. 'Thou art going to-morrow to the glen, and I have come to put thee on thy guard; thou wilt lose the game – good night to thee.'

Early in the morning he arose, and betook himself to the glen, and the Red-Headed Olach met him where he usually did.

'Wilt play a game at chess to-day, thou Son of the King of Erin?' said the Red-Headed Olach.

'I will, I will – why should I not play to-day as I played yesterday, in the kingdom of my father and my grandfather?' said the Son of the King of Erin, but at nightfall, the game went against the Son of the King.

'Claim and take from me the stakes of thy gaming,' said the Son of the King of Erin.

'I will, I will,' said the Red-Headed Olach, 'it is high time for me to do so.

So I lay it upon thee as crosses and spells,
That thou be a bald-headed, scabby leper,
Until thou find out for me
How the Great Tuairisgeal met his death,
And bring his sword of light also
With thee here to me.'

'Release me from thy spells,' said the Son of Erin's King, 'for I have never even heard mention of such a person.'

'I will neither release thee, nor bind thee, except as already said,' said the Red-Headed Olach.

'If that be how matters are,' said the Son of Erin's King,

Be thy face to the western airt,
And thy back to the eastern,
And have thou never a morsel of food,
Save what the north wind drives
From off that glen of barley down yonder,
And have thou never a drop of water,
Save what the east wind drives
From off the fresh-water loch up there,
    Till I return.

'Release me from thy spells, and I will release thee from mine,' said the Red-Headed Olach.

'I will neither release thee nor bind thee, except as already said,' said the Son of the King of Erin.

'Well, then, if that be the way of it,' said the Red-Headed Olach, 'come back and tell thy story on this hillock, even though my bones be so scattered that one of them be in Erin, one in Albyn, and one in England.'

There was no help for it, so he returned home, and told his father what had happened; and it was no wonder that the King was sorrowful and tearful. There was neither rest nor sleep for the lad that night, but before the birds of the air had tasted water [*i.e.*, early in the morning], he arose and put –

His little pleated gauzy shirt,
Of yellow silk,
About his fair body.
He put a defensive coat of satin
Over the little golden shirt.

He put on a great sleeved mail hauberk,
An elfin hauberk, much-pierced, much-decorated,
A stout hauberk much-engraved,
Upon which had been arduously lavished
The labours of two smithies,
In order to protect his body
And his fair bosom,
(And in order that for him might be readily impassioned
The love of women and of maidens),
A hauberk that sea could not drown,
Nor fire burn.

He drew his slender steel blade
Out of the fine pine chest,
And off he set with mighty steps,
With lusty, vaulting strides,
Speeding recklessly over the land he knew,
And blithely speeding over the land he knew not,
And larger than any bluff hummock of the hills
Were the masses of earth that his two heels spurned up behind him as he went,
And anon he had gone right up, he had gained the shoulder of the little glen,
Faring forth to seek the death-story of the Tuairisgeal!

And that night he came to the house of the Great Gruagach, Son of the King of Sorcha.

'Hail to thee, thou Son of the King of Erin,' said the Gruagach, 'long has it been in the prophecies that thou shouldst spend a night in my house. Shall I be any the worse of asking thee what the aim and end of thy journeying and thy travelling may be?'

'Thou shalt be none the worse of asking,' said the Son of Erin's King, 'not thou. I am travelling to try if I can find out how the Great Tuairisgeal met his death.'

'Well then,' said the Gruagach, 'the realm of many a king and a knight have I travelled, but never have I heard mention of the Great Tuairisgeal – nevertheless come in, for to-night thou shalt take thy rest here with me. I have a brother, who, it may well be, is even more addicted to roving than I am myself. Perhaps thou wilt get tidings from him about the Tuairisgeal, and perhaps not, but in any case, come in.'

The Son of the King of Erin went in; hospitably was he received and right well was he entertained; but never mind, on the morrow, he rose early in the morning, and prepared to start off.

The Gruagach was afoot, and while bidding the lad farewell and wishing him success, he said to him, that between him and the house of his next eldest brother, there was a distance that would take a day and a year to walk. – 'But,' said he, 'I possess some Soles-of-Ease, and they will bring thee there by nightfall. When thou gettest there, thou shalt turn their face towards this house, and they will come back home of themselves.'

He put the Soles-of-Ease on, and arrived at the house of the next eldest brother before nightfall. He sent the Soles-of-Ease home as the Gruagach had asked him.

The next eldest brother saluted him, and said to him, 'Long has it been in the prophecies that thou shouldst spend a night in my house. Shall I be any the worse of asking thee what the aim and end of thy journeying and thy travelling may be?'

'Thou shalt be none the worse of asking,' said the Son of Erin's King, 'not thou. I am travelling to try if I can find out how the Great Tuairisgeal met his death.'

'Well then,' said he 'the realm of many a king and a knight have I travelled, but of the Great Tuairisgeal have I never heard mention. Nevertheless, come in.'

He then told him that he had a young brother, more addicted to roving then he himself. 'He is in the habit,' said he, 'of putting a circuit about the earth twice a year, and if thou get no information from him about the Tuairisgeal, thou mayst as well return home. There is a day and a year's walking between thee and him, but I possess some Soles-of-Ease, and they will bring thee there by nightfall. When thou gettest there, set their faces towards this house, and they will come back of themselves.'

Early on the morning of the morrow, he made him ready, and put on the Soles-of-Ease. He set out. When he arrived at his destination, and he was not long in doing so, he sent the Soles-of-Ease back home, as he had been asked.

The youngest brother saluted him, and said to him, 'Long has it been in the prophecies, thou Son of Erin's King, that thou shouldst spend a night in my house. Shall I be any the worse of asking thee what the aim and end of thy journeying and thy travelling may be?'

'Thou shalt be none the worse of asking,' said the Son of Erin's King, 'not thou. I am travelling to try if I can find out how the Great Tuairisgeal met his death.'

'Well then,' said he, 'the realm of many a king and a knight have I travelled, but never have I heard mention of the Great Tuairisgeal. However, come in.'

Hospitably was he received, and right well was he entertained, as was meet and fitting for a king's son, and early in the morning when he was ready to go, the young Gruagach said to him,

'There is no help for it, thou Son of the King of Erin. Thou must repair to the glen up yonder. There thou wilt see a multitude of horses and fillies, leaping and frisking. But when night, with open jaws begins to approach, a washing fairy-woman will come to drink a draught from the well. She will put her right teat on her left shoulder, and her left teat on her right shoulder. Lay hold of the nipple of

147

*Through a hole
in the roof
comes a Claw-
Hand, and
whisks the child
away.*

the breast, and convey it to thy mouth, and call upon heaven and earth to witness, that thou art a foster-child of her right breast.'

All this did the hero do accordingly. He repaired to the glen, came to the well, saw the *bean-nighe* or washing-fairy, seized her as the young Gruagach had desired him, and called upon heaven and earth to witness that he was a foster-child of her right breast.

'Many a wretched foster-child have I had,' said the *bean-nighe*, 'but what is it that thou dost desire?'

'What I desire,' said he, 'is the story of the death of the Great Tuairisgeal.'

The *bean-nighe* took a bridle out of her pocket, and shook it, and a dun shaggy filly came forth from among the herd of horses, and put her head into the bridle. 'Mount her back,' said the *bean-nighe;* 'I need not to be telling thee anything – take the advice of thy female companion, the filly, and she will tell thee what thou oughtest to do.' The dun shaggy filly also spoke to him.

'Mount my back,' said she, 'this is no time for delay.'

He mounted the back of the shaggy filly, and oh! Son of my heart! – Never had there been such fast travelling and such running as on that night – for the March-wind that was before them, they were aye leaving behind them, and the March-wind that was behind them, could not overtake them. – At last, they came to a loch.

'This loch,' said the filly, 'is seven miles long in each direction, and seven miles in depth. This is not the time for going round, but I will clear it with a leap. If thine errand prosper with thee, thou wilt have ridden well.'

She took a preparatory run, and leaped.

When they landed on the other side, he was only just hanging on by her tail.

'Thou didst hold on well,' said she, 'have courage – but dost thou know where thou now art? – Thou art in the territories of the King of the Inneidh. He is holding a race to-day, he and many of the nobles. And many a horse and a filly has he. There is a barrel of gold and a barrel of silver at each goal. When we arrive, the King will come up to the place where thou wilt be, and will ask thee how much thou art going to add to the stakes. Say thou that thou hast neither gold nor silver about thee, but that thou wilt pledge thine own head; but whatever they may offer thee for me, take nothing, not a thing, except the Old King of the Inneidh, and remember that.'

All these things took place accordingly.

'What racing-wager wilt thou lay?' said the Young King.

'With your leave, O King,' said he, 'neither gold nor silver have I – when on a journey, it is not my wont to carry with me more than will barely suffice my needs; but I am willing to wager my head.'

'That will suffice,' said the Young King of the Inneidh.

Then the contest began. They let the horses go, but before the other horses were half-way over the course, the dun filly overturned the barrel of gold, and likewise, the barrel of silver.

The Young King of the Inneidh then came over to the Son of the King of Erin, and said to him, 'What thou hast there is the steed of a king and of a knight, not the steed of a poor man; for her I will give thee her weight in gold.'

'I will not take anything for the dun filly, not a thing except the Old King of the Inneidh,' he answered.

'It is not for that ragged little filly that we would sell the Old King of the Inneidh at all, nor is it to be expected that we would,' said the Young King.

'Well then, if not, I shall keep my filly to myself,' said the Son of Erin's King.

The nobles of the Inneidh put their heads together, and the plan which grew out of their deliberations and which was designed for the purpose of pleasing the Young King, was, to sell the Old King, seeing that the Old King had become useless in any case.

The lad found it hard, as hard indeed it was, to part with the dun filly, but he had no alternative. She, however, urged him to take the rein or bridle with him, and to shake it at the very first emergency that should come upon him.

Then was the Old King of the Inneidh brought forth, swaddled in a woolly fleece and lying in a wicker basket – The lad hoisted the basket on to his back, and then he and the dun filly parted.

On and on he travelled, afar, afar, as far as ocean and as far as the remoteness, with the Old King on his back in the basket. At last, he came to a great forest.

'When going through this forest, it was my custom to alight from my horse in order to gather a switch with which to urge him on: let me descend, I would leave my farewell blessing with the forest,' said the Old King of the Inneidh.

'Thou has kept away from the place for a long time,' said the King of Erin's Son.

They were pressing on and on in this way, when the King said again, 'There is a great river hereabouts, and I have never passed this way without drinking a draught from it; let me alight.'

'Thou hast kept away from it for a long time,' said the King of Erin's Son. Had he allowed him to alight, he would have had the strength of a hundred men, and he therefore shook the rein or bridle.

It was not long before he saw the dun filly coming. Up she came, and he sprang on to her back.

On and on they pressed, and what should they come to but a fire, and there they stopped.

'O,' said she, 'wilt thou not roast the soles of the wretch at the fire in order that he tell us a story!' – He did so, and the Old King began –

'My father had three sons, myself and another two. Our mother died young, and our father married again. Our stepmother was not good to us at all, and on a day of days, she was seized with an access of rage, and struck us with the witch-wand, and drove us out in the shape of three wild wolves to the mountain up yonder.

We began to live on the flocks of our father; but in no long time the shepherds found us out, and what happened was, that they sent the chase after us, and drove us over a great rock.

I know not how long we were unconscious; but when I awoke, I found that my brothers had been drowned, and my own ears eaten off. Then I took to the water and swam to the other side of the loch. It fell out that there were many people gathered together when I was reaching land, some shouting that I should be killed, and some desiring that I should be spared, as I might make a pet.

Amongst them there was a gentleman, who had been enjoying the scenery. He takes a fancy to me, and makes a pet of me. He took me home with him, put me on a leash, and had me into his own bed-room. Who should this gentleman be but a king. Everybody was very kind to me, and lack or want had I none.

In the course of time, the queen was drawing near to her delivery, but it happened that the King was out in the hills hunting at the time. A man-child was born to the Queen, but what should come humming round the house but the Harp-of-Music, and under its influence the midwives fall asleep, and then, in through a hole in the roof comes a Claw-Hand, and whisks the child away.

'When the midwives awoke, they knew not at first what to do; but thou knowest that the women were never without resource, and so what they did was, to kill a puppy, and rub its blood over my mouth, and thus they made the King believe that I had killed the child.'

"A bad business," said the King, "bad indeed; but let him do me two more ill turns, and I will kill him."'

'In course of time the queen was again delivered. Again the Harp-of-Music and the Claw-Hand came, and things fell out as they did before, and the King was not at all pleased.'

'There was no help for it, but I determined that I would cut the chain with my teeth, before the queen should be delivered again. But nevertheless, the Harp-of-Music came round about the house once more, the midwives fall into a sound slumber, and in comes the Claw-Hand as usual, and snatches up the child.'

'But that did not discomfit me. I sprang after the Claw-Hand, though it was no trifle, and tore it away from the shoulder. I recovered the child too, and placed them both beside me in the pen.'

'When the women awoke, they rubbed the blood of a kitten over my mouth, that there might be some appearance of blood about me, and when the King returned from hunting in the hills, they told him that the crop-eared wolf had eaten the child.'

'The King became deeply enraged, and no wonder that he was so, and he said to me, "If this be the way matters stand, thou shalt live no longer," and he opened the door of the pen to let me out.'

'Then I fetched out the Claw-Hand and the child, pushing them out before me.'

'And the King understood how things were, and he said to me, "Thou crop-eared wolf, hadst thou been free three years ago, my loss to-day had not been so very heavy as it is – but so long as thou live, thou shalt have thy liberty, and let me see who dares to shake a finger at thee, or find fault with thee"'

'Here the King struck me with the wizard-wand, and I became a man once more as I had been before, and I related every detail of the story just as it happened.'

'Upon receiving my liberty, I dashed out into the open, and with the joy that I felt, I did not know whether I was standing on my head or on my feet.'

'When going past a certain dyke, what should I hear but a heavy groaning; back I turned, and found such a huge urisk of a man lying prone, stretched behind the dyke.'

"Who is there?"' said I.

"It is I," he replied, "the Great Tuairisgeal. Seeing that it is thou who didst tear my claw-hand off my shoulder, put now mould and earth on me."'

"I am unable to dig thee a grave,"' said I.

"Behold my great sword up yonder; with that shalt thou dig my grave – in length make my grave seven times as long as thyself, and in breadth three times as long as thyself."'

'As soon as I had the grave ready, he asked me to measure it. But when I was in it, down straddled that Tuairisgeal into it crosswise, to try if he could smother me; but in spite of any injury I may have received and though hard put to it, I arose after a great struggle and heaped mould and earth on the Tuairisgeal.'

'He told me that the two stolen sons of the King were in a rock over our heads, which would open if I stamped my foot upon it, and that I should find them inside it alive and well. I found them as he had said, and I brought them to the King, and greatly did the King rejoice.'

'Thou wilt find the Great Tuairisgeal's sword under that clump of bulrushes.'

The King of Erin's Son searched under the clump of rushes, and found the sword.

'Throw the wretch into the fire,' said the dun shaggy filly, 'the pursuers are coming – five hundred full-warriors, sixteen giants, and twenty knights. They are coming to capture me. Up, up, and mount my back – there they are in the distance.'

The King of Erin's Son sprang on to the filly's back, and she took to her heels.

'Alas! I am becoming weaker and weaker and more exhausted,' said she presently, 'see if thou canst find a white pebble in the side of my hoof, and throw it behind thee.'

He found it and threw it behind him, and it became a great rocky cliff, seven miles long and seven miles high, and every one of the five hundred full warriors fell down the rock, and the brains were dashed out of them all. The giants and the horses cut a leap, and both they and the knights also fell at the foot of the rock, but the filly did not stand long looking at them.

On and on they galloped at full speed, but at last the filly said, 'O, I am getting weaker and more exhausted, and the pursuers are still coming. See if thou canst find a drop of sweat in the root of my ear, and throw that behind thee.'

He found and threw it, and it became a loch, seven miles long, seven miles broad, and seven miles deep. The pursuers gave a bound, and the giants and the horses and all the knights were drowned, except one black horse and rider.

'The great black horse, my brother, is coming,' quoth the filly, 'and needs must that thou be prompt and skilful, and while he is passing, see whether thou canst cut off the head of him who is riding him.'

The lad made ready, and as the great black horse was going by, the filly gave a side-leap, and the lad cut off the head of the Young King of the Inneidh – for it was he who was on the back of the great black horse.

'Come,' said the great, black horse, 'come off the filly's back, and mount my own.'

'Yes, mount my brother's back,' said she, 'he has as much love for thee as I now have myself.' So he mounted the back of the great black horse, and there was no halting till they came to Erin, the place whence they had started forth.

Then they came to a loch.

'Come now,' said the filly, 'strike off my head and the head of my brother here, and throw them out into the loch.'

'What? I?' said he, 'not I. I am the very man who will not do so – rather would I strike off the head of any man who attempted it.'

'Unless thou strike off our heads, we will strike off thine; wherefore hasten.' So what happened then was, that he struck off their heads, and threw them out into the loch. And then he began to weep and lament, until at last, sleep overcame him.

When he awoke, whom should he see coming towards him but a young man and a beautiful maiden.

They asked what it was that was troubling him.

He told them what had happened – how he had killed the dun filly and the great black horse, and that he feared that good fortune would never attend him again, now that they had gone.

'Wilt thou not take me in place of the filly, and my brother in place of the

black horse?' said the maiden. He gave her thanks, but said he would not take anything at all in their stead.

'Well then,' said she, 'I am the dun shaggy filly, and my brother is the great black horse. We are the children of the King of Spain, but we had been enchanted in the way you saw.'

'If that be so,' said he, 'I will never have mistress or wife but thee.'

'I am willing, then,' said she, 'but I will not marry thee until a year has passed: for I have to go home to see my father and my mother and my friends. But here is a golden ring for thee, and we will make two halves of it. When thou seest me again, the two halves of the ring will unite together, and it will become whole as it was before. And,' said she, 'thou too must go home, but give no kiss to either father or mother, or to any other thing, else, if thou dost – thou wilt no more remember either wife or lover.

Thou must now go to the glen where thou didst leave the Red-Headed Olach, and there, on the hillock, thou shalt tell him about the death of the Great Tuairisgeal. The Red-Headed Olach is now nothing but a heap of reddish-brown bones on the hillock, but while thou art telling him thy tale, he will be reviving again, and while he is reviving, he will be summoning up and gathering to himself his blood and his sinews until he becomes the same as ever he was – but when he is revived so far as to be sitting up and leaning on his elbow, do thou sweep off his head with the sword, otherwise, when he sees his brother's sword, he will be so transported with rage, that he will not leave any one in the country alive.'

The King of Erin's Son left a farewell blessing with them, and they went home.

The King of Erin's Son now betook himself to the hillock, and told his story. While he was telling it the Red-Headed Olach was summoning up and gathering to himself his blood, his flesh, and his sinews, until he was himself again, and had revived so far as to be sitting up and leaning on his elbow; but he the King of Erin's Son whirled up the sword, and swept off his head; and then he went home to see his father.

His father was lying on his bed, blind, deaf, and powerless, and had been in that condition lamenting for his son, from the day he had departed, up to then. – 'Two thirds of my sight, and two thirds of my hearing, have come back to me; look ye abroad, for either my son is coming, or else news of him.'

In a little while, he cried –

'I am as strong as ever I was, and will myself go out.'

And so it was that he himself rushed out, and met his son approaching. He fell about his son's neck, but his son would by no means give him or any other person a kiss. But when he was at last seated indoors, and they had heard his story, what should come in but a greyhound bitch which had belonged to him in past time, and she recognized him, and licked him violently on the mouth, and thenceforth he had no remembrance of wife or of sweetheart.

Thenceforward, he dwelt with the King; but at the end of a year, he determined to marry. And whom now was he going to marry but the woman who had come to see him the night before he set out on his travels.

The wedding was being made ready, as it were, tonight. Many were invited to the wedding of the King's Son. When the wedding guests were about to sit down, who should burst in but a fine young fellow, and a lovely maiden with him. She being a maiden and he being a bachelor had been invited because they were strangers.

When the bridegroom drew forth the marriage money, what should come out of his pocket but the piece of the ring which the King of Spain's Daughter had given him. And when she the stranger maiden noticed this, she took out her own piece, and thereupon the two pieces of the ring sprang to meet each other and united, and the ring became as it had been when quite new.

Then he came to himself and remembered, and recognized her; and the upshot was that he and she married; and her brother married her whom the King of Erin's Son had been going to marry. And for them there was made a great wedding, magnificent and merry, one that lasted a day and a year, and never a raised voice or a cross word came between either of the two couples, as long as they lived.

NOTES

Source: J. G. Mackay (editor and translator), in *Transactions of the Gaelic Society of Inverness*, Vol. 34 (1927/28), 1–112.

This story, known and retold in versions across all of Scotland and Ireland, really belongs in the category of folk-tale rather than the more literary productions included in this collection. Not that it is without artifice. In fact, it was recognized by storytellers everywhere as one of the truly great tales – a long, complex, rhythmical story that manages to encompass, within itself, references to a dozen other tales and themes from the folklore tradition. The tale as a whole defies analysis, except in a broader canvas than is available here, and anyway its editor and translator, J.G. Mackay, gives over 80 pages to a detailed breakdown of the content and alternative versions found in collections all over the Celtic world. Story types worthy of mention here are the werewolf tale, variations of which are found in Wales, Scotland, and Ireland – and which reappear, in sophisticated form, in the Arthurian story 'Arthur and Gorlagon'; and the Calumniated wife, a favourite theme among storytellers, which makes another appearance in this collection in the story of Rhiannon from the *Mabinogion* tale of 'Pwyll in Annwvyn' (page 72).

In its present form, the story dates from the nineteenth century, in a version told by the famous *shanachie* Angus Mackay of Eigg in the Hebrides, but contains material from many earlier sources. Its view of the Otherworld is comprehensive, and completely in line with the other tales in this collection. It is filled with strange and mysterious characters like the Red-Headed Orach, who can reconstitute himself from his own bones, blood and sinews; or the magical dun mare and the black stallion who are really brother and sister in enchanted form.

The Tuairisgeal of the title is almost certainly a kind of giant who lived in caves along the seashore, while his great sword is a type of the Sword of Light so often sought by the heroes of folk-tale and romance. The Soles-of-Ease utilized by the King of Erin's Son are the Celtic equivalent of the seven-league boots familiar to all from fairy tales the world over. Here also the use of the story-within-a-story device is wonderfully adapted to enable the teller not only to include more than one strand of narrative, but to bring together two originally unrelated tales – the quest for the cause of the Tuairisgeal's death, and the story of the werewolf king.

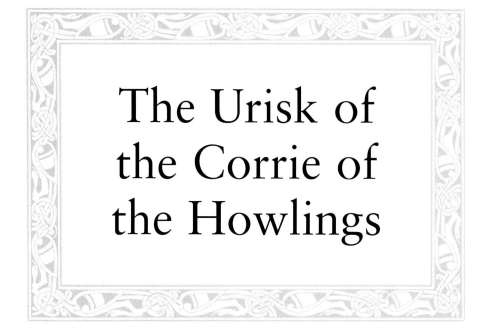

The Urisk of the Corrie of the Howlings

T HAPPENED LONG AGO that the king of Othilam came from the Tower of Athilam to the Glen of the Fawns and Roes to hunt, and his dwelling was

> Under a linen covering laid over a birch branch
> In sight of the silken-flags in the mastheads of his ships.

And it happened on a day of the days, when they were out hunting, that the king's son, Talamsan of the golden locks, strayed from the rest, when he was accompanied by only two gillies and his dog, Luran (Darling), and while they were seeking the way, evening came on them, and it happened that the way home took them through the Corrie of the Howlings, and when they were going by the sheiling of the Carlin of the Mountain-foot, she was out, and said to them 'Turn back, children, for the Corrie is not clear (empty) before you'.

'None but a coward turns back, Crooked Carlin', said Talamsan. 'What cares Talamsan, son of the king of Othilam from the Tower of Athilam, for thyself or for all in the Corrie'.

'High is thy rank, young hero, but the worst of men is he that will not take advice,' said the Carlin.

The heroes went on through the Corrie of the Howlings until they came to The Hollow-of-the-Mounds (Sloc-nam-Meall), and there they beheld the loveliest maiden eye ever looked at.

> Her fascinating blue eye was like a drop of honey
> At the point of a garden sapling.
> Like breast of swan or down of cana [cotton grass, *Eriophorum*]
> Was the hue of her shining bosom.

She had a willow wand in her right hand, and held her left hand behind her. The dog went a step before the men and then stood and began to bark at her.

'Stop thy dog, Talamsan, the dogs of princes are usually held in a leash until the hunt begins', said she.

'Lie down, Luran' said Talamsan.

'That is Luran of thy woe to-night' said the maiden who was no longer a maiden, but a howling, venomous, vindictive hag. The willow wand in her hand became an enchanting beetle, and a fiery, scaly serpent lay coiled in her bosom.

> Her skin was like the hide
> Of the grey buck of the cairns,
> Which stands between the smith and the spark.
> She would crack a nut
> Between her nose and chin.

As soon as she got the dog's name, she called him to her, and he would no longer give heed to his master. What he did was to attack the latter with the Urisk, for it was the Urisk of the Corrie of the Howlings, handsome though she appeared at the first sight which they got of her.

When the gillies saw what happened, they fled home with the melancholy tale that the Urisk of the Corrie of the Howlings had killed Talamsan, the king's son.

On the morrow, the king, accompanied by every man within some miles' distance of him, set out in search of his son. They found the dog, Luran, dead, and without a fibre of hair on him. But they saw not the king's son nor an Urisk, nor anything but a new mound in the Hollow-of-the-Mounds.

The king returned home sadly and sorrowfully. He had of children but Talamsan and one daughter, brown-haired Slender-eyebrow (*Caol-mhala*), and Slender-eyebrow vowed that she would never marry any man but one that would kill the Urisk of the Corrie-of-the-Howlings.

Spotted-knee (*Breac-ghlùn*) son of Torquil, king of Dunadd in Ireland, heard of the vow which brown-haired Slender-eyebrow made. That was Spotted-knee of the seven battles, and seven victories, and seven heroes used to fight on each hand of him.

On a day of the days he landed at the Channel-of-the-Boats (*Amar-nan-Eithear*) and in the evening ascended the steep hill, and since he had only a Carlin (as he thought) to encounter he did not think it worth while taking his heroes with him, but he took the Swift-footed Slender-houghs (*Easgadach*),

> Who would overtake the swift March wind,
> But the swift March wind would not overtake him.

Passing the hill-pasture bothy of the Carlin of the Mountainfoot, the Carlin was out and said: 'Turn back, children, for the Corrie is not clean before you'.

'Go thy way, Crooked Carlin', said Spotted-knee, 'none but a coward turns back. What cares Spotted-knee, son of Torquil, king of Dunadd of the five gables in the north of Ireland, for thyself or all in the Corrie!'

'High is thy rank, Brave Man, but worthless is he that takes not advice' said the Carlin.

When Spotted-knee reached the Corrie of the Howlings he beheld the fairest maiden eye ever gazed on, –

157

Beyond every maiden in appearance,
Surpassing all the women of Ireland.

She had a willow wand in her right hand, and said to him, 'What is thy whence, and which is thy whither? What is the cause of thy journey and travelling?'

'I am', said he, 'Spotted-knee, son of Torquil, king of Dunadd of the five gables in the north of Ireland, and I am going to the Corrie of the Howlings to kill the Urisk of the Hollow-of-the-Mounds at the request of brown-haired Slender-eyebrow, daughter of the king of Othilam in the Tower of Athilam.'

Said the Maiden 'Is it love of maiden or hatred of Urisk that brought Spotted-knee from Erin? If it be hatred of Urisk, his steel will bend against her breast; if it be love of maiden, slippery is the hold of an eel by her tail. There are eight nobles with earls in the Tower of Athilam to night.

Slippery is the threshold in the door of a Tower,
More slippery than that is love for the dead.

I am the daughter of king Stout-spear (*Garbh-shleagh*) in the Hall-of-Luxury (*Talla-nan-Sògh*), and my father's nobles are enjoying a sumptuous-feast to night. Send thy gillie to invite thy heroes, and let all of you come to the Hall-of-Luxury, and you will find such entertainment as thou never hadst on the soil of Erin.'

'Go, Slender-houghs,' said Spotted-knee, whispering in his ear, 'hasten hither the heroes, but let them be in their armour.'

Away went Slender-houghs, but before he had barely gone the Maiden changed her form, and Spotted-knee knew that it was the Urisk he had. Her willow wand became an enchanting beetle, and Spotted-knee drew his spear –

Which was beating on the Urisk's beetle,
And drawing echo from the cliffs of the bens.

But when Slender-houghs and the heroes returned, they found no king's Son, nor Maiden, nor Urisk – nor anything but a new mound in the Hollow-of-the-Mounds.

But this is what happened on a certain day –

When the yellow crested birds sang
Their sweet pipe-music,

that Young Farquhar of the chase came with his hounds in a leash. When he was passing the summer-pasture bothy of the Carlin at the mountain-foot in the evening, the Carlin was out and said –

'Turn back, children; the Corrie is not clean before you.'

'No one ever returned who did not forsake, gentle Nurse of the sheiling,' said Farquhar. 'Wilt thou not come with me seven steps? Give me thy blessing and send me away, and I'll sleep this night under the shade of the Elm in the Glen of the fawns and roes with my three red-haired gillies and my two greedy eager hounds,

And my little rough-haired bitch of the sharp tusk,
That will bring blood on the deer at every bite . . .'

The Carlin answered:

> Did Farquhar cast a longing look
> Towards the maiden of mildest eye?

'I asked neither maiden nor renown,' said Farquhar. 'I am going to the Ben of venison and hunting to chase the buck, the badger and deer before the sun rises to-morrow.'

Then said the Nurse of the sheiling – 'I'll go with thee seven steps, and give thee seven blessings, –

> Farquhar son of Art, son of Allin (Beautiful)
> Daughter of the king of Mann in the Ocean,
> Who came over the waves of Innis-Orc (Orkney Isle),
> Son of the father who never took tribute
> Even from a foe without mercy.

Here is to thee my straight staff of the three branches of the undecaying apple-tree, which a Monk planted and which a Monk cut on the south side of the enclosing wall of the chapel, and which a Monk blessed three times, and before which will bend the edge of the bronze weapon, if its stroke be struck by the wicked. Put off the garter of thy left foot, and put a loan of it round the bitch's neck, take a drop of blood from the right ear of (each one) of the two dogs, and call none of them by his name from the time the sun goes down until the bird tastes the water next day, and my blessing be with thee, and be gone.'

Farquhar went away with his gillies and his dogs, and the night sang music to him. When he reached the Hollow of the Mounds, there met him a maiden, and fair was her appearance –

> Her smooth, full bosom
> Was like purest snow on the ground.
> The tip of her breast
> Was like the briar-rose in the bud,
> In the warm shelter of the bosky grove.

A willow wand was in her right hand, and the dogs began to bark at her.

'Stop thy dogs, hero,' said she.

'I'll neither incite nor hinder them,' said Farquhar.

The dogs had every hair on their bodies standing on end as straight as the bristles of the wild boar. The maiden assumed an angry look and transformed herself into an Urisk as terrible and even more terrible than she was either to Talamsan or to Spotted-knee.

'If thou wilt not stop them, I'll stop them,' said she, as she attacked one of them with the beetle.

Farquhar drew his spear, and the beating began. If there was no howling in the Corrie-of-the-Howlings before, there was abundance of it there that night between the dogs and the Urisk.

> At every bound Bruid (Goader) took
> He returned with blood on his mouth.
> At every wound Speach (Wasp) gave
> The Urisk gave a scream-of-two-screams.

159

The fiery scaly serpent sprang from the bosom of the Urisk, and attacked Farquhar. But he struck her with the staff of the Nurse-of-the-Shieling, and she went into a coil, and then she swelled and burst.

> With the echo of a sound which sent a tremor
> On every hoof in the Glen.

Then she went into a flame of fire, which set the Urisk on fire along with her, and in the twinkling of an eye Farquhar had nothing (left) but a small heap of ashes.

He went under the shelter of the birch, and sleep came upon him, for he was tired, and at day-break he was awakened by Brionn (Brindled) licking his forehead. Then sang

> The yellow crested birds
> Their sweet pipe-music,

and when Farquhar looked about him, he saw that there were many heaps of strange stones in the Hollow-of-the-Mounds. He struck the apple-tree staff on one of the heaps and the heap turned into a man, and Farquhar fled. 'Fly not with the apple-tree staff of virtues, Farquhar' said the man; 'there is need of thee still in the Hollow-of-the-Mounds.'

Farquhar returned and struck the staff on mound after mound, on every mound in the Hollow-of-the-Mounds, and every mound became a warrior, until nine companies of nine heroes were standing at his side, and among them was Talamsan, the son of the king of Othilam, and Spotted-knee, the son of king Torquil, and Farquhar took them all to the Tower of Athilam.

And he got the king's daughter and two obeisances,
And his dwelling in the Tower of Innis Stoth (Island of Spray).
And if they have not died since, they are alive still.

NOTES

Source: James MacDougall (translator), in *Zeitschrift für Celtische Philology*, Vol. I (1897/9).

This is a comparatively late tale, dating from eighteenth-century Scotland – though the names of the various characters are older and suggest a point of origin for the story at least as early as the Middle Ages. The names Othilam and Athilam have been traced to the historical family of the Dukes of Athol, who were widely perceived as 'Kings' of Mann, though their proper title was in reality only 'The Lords of Mann'. This places the story in its present form no earlier than 1735, when the second Duke of Athol formally received this title.

The 'Urisk' of the story, as encountered by Talamsan and Spotted-Knee, is usually described as a surly, boorish man, much like the 'carl' or 'churl' of medieval romance. Here the character has become 'a terrible, venomous hag', who defends the Corrie against mortals. Her power over the hero's dog is the age-old power of the name – to possess which is to have control over its owner. She also carries a willow wand, like that of the fairy women in 'The Sick-bed of Cu Chulainn' (page 48), which has the power to enchant and transform.

As in so many of these stories, the Urisk is finally defeated through the help of another Otherworldly being, the Carlin or Wise Woman, who is treated in cavalier fashion by the first two heroes. Only when the third, Farquhar, speaks kindly to her and asks for her help does he receive the branch of the eternal apple-tree. Here there is a mingling of pagan and Christian imagery in that the apple is an ancient symbol of the Otherworld, which in this story is grown and cut by a monk and adopts a cruciform shape. This again dates the story to a later period, but implies material from an earlier time.

The Corrie itself may be a cauldron, or a whirlpool, like the famous Corrie Vrechan which claimed so many heroes and ships. In the present story, it also seems to represent an aspect of the Otherworld which has to be defended and which may only be penetrated at great cost and with true courage.

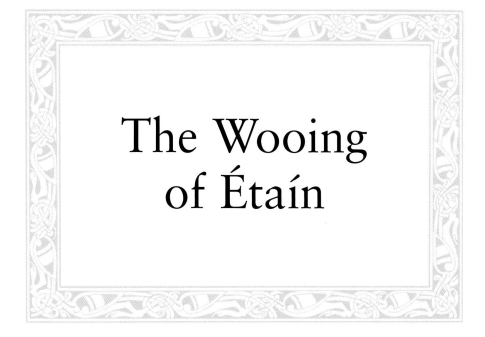

The Wooing of Étaín

HERE WAS A FAMOUS KING of Ireland of the race of the Tuatha Dé, Eochaid Ollathair his name. He was also named the Dagda [The Good God], for it was he that used to work wonders for them and control the weather and the crops. Wherefore men said he was called the Dagda. Elcmar of the Brug had a wife whose name was Eithne, and another name for her was Boand. The Dagda desired her in carnal union. The woman would have yielded to the Dagda had it not been for fear of Elcmar, so great was his power. Thereupon the Dagda sent Elcmar away on a journey to Bres son of Elatha in Mag nInis, and the Dagda worked great spells upon Elcmar as he set out, that he might not return betimes (that is, early) and he dispelled the darkness of night for him, and he kept hunger and thirst from him. He sent him on long errands, so that nine months went by as one day, for he had said that he would return home again between day and night. Meanwhile the Dagda went in unto Elcmar's wife, and she bore him a son, even Aengus, and the woman was whole of her sickness when Elcmar returned, and he perceived not her offence, that is, that she had lain with the Dagda.

The Dagda meanwhile brought his son to Midir's house in Brí Léith in Tethba, to be fostered. There Aengus was reared for the space of nine years. Midir had a great playing-field in Brí Léith. Thrice fifty lads of the young nobles of Ireland were there and thrice fifty maidens of the land of Ireland. Aengus was the leader of them all, because of Midir's great love for him, and the beauty of his form and the nobility of his race. He was also called *in Mac Óc* (the Young Son), for his mother said: 'Young is the son who was begotten at the break of day and born betwixt it and evening.'

Now Aengus quarrelled with Triath son of Febal (or Gobor) of the Fir Bolg, who was one of the two leaders in the game, and a fosterling of Midir. It was no matter of pride with Aengus that Triath should speak to him, and he said: 'It irks me that the son of a serf should hold speech with me,' for Aengus had believed until then that Midir was his father, and the kingship of Brí Léith his heritage, and he knew not then of his kinship with the Dagda.

Triath made answer and said: 'I take it no less ill that a hireling whose mother and father are unknown should hold speech with me.' Thereupon Aengus went to Midir weeping and sorrowful at having been put to shame by Triath. 'What is this?' said Midir. 'Triath has defamed me and cast in my face that I have neither mother nor father.' ''Tis false,' said Midir. 'Who is my mother, from whence is my father?' 'No hard matter. Thy father is Eochaid Ollathair,' said Midir, 'and Eithne, wife of Elcmar of the Brug, is thy mother. It is I that have reared thee unknown to Elcmar, lest it should cause him pain that thou wast begotten in his despite.' 'Come thou with me,' said Aengus, 'that my father may acknowledge me, and that I may no longer be kept hidden away under the insults of the Fir Bolg.'

Then Midir set out with his fosterling to have speech with Eochaid, and they came to Uisnech of Meath in the centre of Ireland, for 'tis there was Eochaid's house, Ireland stretching equally far from it on every side, to south and north, to east and west. Before them in the assembly they found Eochaid. Midir called the king aside to have speech with the lad. 'What does he desire, this youth who has not come until now?' 'His desire is to be acknowledged by his father, and for land to be given him,' said Midir, 'for it is not meet that thy son should be landless while thou art king of Ireland.' 'He is welcome,' said Eochaid, 'he is my son. But the land I wish him to have is not yet vacant.' 'What land is that?' said Midir. 'The Brug, to the north of the Boyne,' said Eochaid. 'Who is there?' said Midir. 'Elcmar,' said Eochaid, 'is the man who is there. I have no wish to annoy him further.'

'Pray, what counsel dost thou give this lad?' said Midir. 'I have this for him,' said Eochaid. 'On the day of Samain let him go into the Brug, and let him go armed. That is a day of peace and amity among the men of Ireland, on which none is at enmity with his fellow. And Elcmar will be in Cnoc Síde in Broga unarmed save for a fork of white hazel in his hand, his cloak folded about him, and a gold brooch in his cloak, and three fifties playing before him in the playing-field; and let Aengus go to him and threaten to kill him. But it is meet that he slay him not, provided he promise him his will. And let this be the will of Aengus, that he be king a day and a night in the Brug; and see that thou yield not the land to Elcmar till he submit himself to my decision; and when he comes let Aengus' plea be that the land has fallen to him in fee simple for sparing Elcmar and not slaying him, and that what he had asked for is kingship of day and night, and,' said he, 'it is in days and nights that the world is spent.'

The Midir sets out for his land, and his foster-son along with him, and on Samain following, Aengus having armed himself came into the Brug and made a feint at Elcmar, so that he promised him in return for his life kingship of day and night in his land. The Mac Óc straightway abode there that day and the following night as king of the land, Elcmar's household being subject to him. On the morrow Elcmar came to claim his land from the Mac Óc, and therewith threatened him mightily. The Mac Óc said that he would not yield up his land until he should put it to the decision of the Dagda in presence of the men of Ireland.

Then they appeal to the Dagda, who adjudged each man's contract in accordance with his undertaking. 'So then this land accordingly belongs henceforth to this youth,' said Elcmar. 'It is fitting,' said the Dagda. 'Thou wast taken unawares on a day of peace and amity. Thou gavest thy land for mercy shown thee, for thy life was dearer to thee than thy land, yet thou shalt have land from me that will be no less profitable to thee than the Brug.' 'Where is that?' said Elcmar.

'Cleitech,' said the Dagda, 'with the three lands that are round about it, thy youths playing before thee every day in the Brug, and thou shalt enjoy the fruits of the Boyne from this land.' 'It is well,' said Elcmar; 'so shall it be accomplished.' And he made a flitting to Cleitech, and built a stronghold there, and the Mac Óc abode in the Brug in his land.

Then Midir came on that day year to the Brug on a visit to his fosterling, and he found the Mac Óc on the mound of Síd in Broga on the day of Samain, with two companies of youths at play before him in the Brug, and Elcmar on the mound of Cleitech to the south, watching them. A quarrel broke out among the youths in the Brug. 'Do not stir,' said Midir to the Mac Óc, 'because of Elcmar, lest he come down to the plain. I will go myself to make peace between them.' Thereupon Midir went, and it was not easy for him to part them. A spit of holly was thrown at Midir as he was intervening, and it knocked one of his eyes out. Midir came to the Mac Óc with his eye in his hand and said to him: 'Would that I had not come on a visit to thee, to be put to shame, for with this blemish I cannot behold the land I have come to, and the land I have left, I cannot return to it now.'

'It shall in no wise be so,' said the Mac Óc. 'I will go to Dian Cécht that he may come and heal thee, and thine own land shall be thine and this land shall be thine, and thine eye shall be whole again without shame or blemish because of it.' The Mac Óc went to Dian Cécht. 'Now see that thou mayest go with me,' said he, 'to save my foster-father who has been hurt in the Brug on the day of Samain.' Dian Cécht came and healed Midir, so that he was whole again. 'Good is my journeying now,' said Midir, 'since I am healed.' 'It shall surely be so,' said the Mac Óc. 'Do thou abide here for a year that thou mayest see my host and my folk, my household and my land.'

'I will not stay,' said Midir, 'unless I have a reward therefor.' 'What reward?' said the Mac Óc. 'Easy to say. A chariot worth seven cumals,' said Midir, 'and a mantle befitting me, and the fairest maiden in Ireland.' 'I have,' said the Mac Óc, 'the chariot and the mantle befitting thee.' 'There is moreover,' said Midir, 'the maiden that surpasses all the maidens in Ireland in form.' 'Where is she?' said the Mac Óc. 'She is in Ulster,' said Midir, 'Ailill's daughter Étaín Echraide, daughter of the king of the north-eastern part of Ireland. She is the dearest and gentlest and loveliest in Ireland.'

The Mac Óc went to seek her until he came to Ailill's house in Mag nInis. He was made welcome, and he abode three nights there. He told his mission and announced his name and race. He said that it was in quest of Étaín that he had come. 'I will not give her to thee,' said Ailill, 'for I can in no way profit by thee, because of the nobility of thy family, and the greatness of thy power and that of thy father. If thou put any shame on my daughter, no redress whatsoever can be had of thee.' 'It shall not be so,' said the Mac Óc. 'I will buy her from thee straightway.' 'Thou shalt have that,' said Ailill. 'State thy demand,' said the Mac Óc. 'No hard matter,' said Ailill. 'Thou shalt clear for me twelve plains in my land that are under waste and wood, so that they may be at all times for grazing for cattle and for habitation to men, for games and assemblies, gatherings, and strongholds.'

'It shall be done,' said the Mac Óc. He returns home and bewailed to the Dagda the strait he was in. The latter caused twelve plains to be cleared in a single night in Ailill's land. These are the names of the plains: Mag Macha, Mag Lemna, Mag nÍtha, Mag Tochair, Mag nDula, Mag Techt, Mag Lí, Mag Line, Mag Murthemne. Now when that work had been accomplished by the Mac Óc he went to Ailill to demand Étaín. 'Thou shalt not obtain her,' said Ailill, 'until thou draw out of this land to the sea twelve great rivers that are in wells and bogs and moors, so that they may bring produce from the sea to peoples and kindreds, and drain the earth and the land.'

He came again to the Dagda to bewail the strait he was in. Thereupon the latter caused twelve great waters to course towards the sea in a single night. They had not been seen there until then. These are the names of the waters: Find and Modornn and Slena and Nas and Amnas and Oichén and Or and Banda and Samaír and Lóche. Now when these works were accomplished the Mac Óc came to have speech with Ailill in order to claim Étaín. 'Thou shalt not get her till thou purchase her, for after thou hast taken her, I shall have no profit of the maiden beyond what I shall obtain forthwith.' 'What dost thou require of me now?' said the Mac Óc. 'I require,' said Ailill, 'the maiden's weight in gold and silver, for that is my portion of her price; all thou hast done up to now, the profit of it goes to her folk and her kindred.' 'It shall be done,' said the Mac Óc. She was placed on the floor of Ailill's house, and her weight of gold and silver was given for her. That wealth was left with Ailill, and the Mac Óc brought Étaín home with him.

Midir made that company welcome. That night Étaín sleeps with Midir, and on the morrow a mantle befitting him and a chariot were given to him, and he was pleased with his foster-son. After that he abode a full year in the Brug with Aengus. On that day year Midir went to his own land, to Brí Léith, and he brought Étaín with him. On the day he went from him the Mac Óc said to Midir, 'Give heed to the woman thou takest with thee, because of the dreadful cunning woman that awaits thee, with all the knowledge and skill and craft that belongs to her race,' said Aengus, 'also she has my word and my safeguard before the Tuatha Dé Danann,' that is, Fuamnach wife of Midir, of the progeny of Beothach son of Iardanél. She was wise and prudent and skilled in the knowledge and magic power of the Tuatha Dé Danann, for the wizard Bresal had reared her until she was betrothed to Midir.

She made her husband welcome, that is Midir. 'Come, O Midir,' said Fuamnach, 'that I may show thee thy house and thy wealth of land.' Midir went round all his land with Fuamnach, and she showed his seizin to him and to Étaín. And after that he brought Étaín again to Fuamnach. Fuamnach went before them into the sleeping chamber wherein she slept, and she said to Étaín: 'The seat of a good woman hast thou come into.' When Étaín sat down on the chair in the middle of the house, Fuamnach struck her with a rod of scarlet quickentree, and she turned into a pool of water in the middle of the house; and Fuamnach comes to her foster-father Bresal, and Midir left the house to the water into which Étaín had turned. After that Midir was without a wife.

The heat of the fire and the air and the seething of the ground aided the water so that the pool that was in the middle of the house turned into a worm, and after that the worm became a purple fly. It was as big as a man's head, the comeliest in the land. Sweeter than pipes and harps and horns was the sound of her voice and the hum of her wings. Her eyes would shine like precious stones in the dark. The fragrance and the bloom of her would turn away hunger and thirst from any one around whom she would go. The spray of the drops she shed from her wings would cure all sickness and disease and plague in any one round whom she would go. She used to attend Midir and go round about his land with him, as he went. To listen to her and gaze upon her would nourish hosts in gatherings and assemblies in camps. Midir knew that it was Étaín that was in that

shape, and so long as that fly was attending upon him, he never took to himself a wife, and the sight of her would nourish him. He would fall asleep with her humming, and whenever any one approached who did not love him, she would awaken him.

After a time Fuamnach came on a visit to Midir, and along with her as sureties came the three gods of Dana, namely Lug and the Dagda, and Ogma. Midir reproached Fuamnach exceedingly and said to her that she should not go from him were it not for the power of the sureties that had brought her. Fuamnach said that she did not repent of the deed she had done, for that she would rather do good to herself than to another, and that in whatsoever part of Ireland she might be she would do naught but harm to Étaín so long as she lived, and in whatsoever shape she might be. She brought powerful incantations and spells from Bresal Etarlam the wizard to banish and warn off Étaín from Midir, for she knew that the purple fly that was delighting Midir was Étaín herself, for whenever he saw the scarlet fly, Midir loved no other woman, and he found no pleasure in music or in drinking or eating when he did not see her and hear the music of her and her voice. Fuamnach stirred up a wind of assault and magic so that Étaín was blown from Brí Léith, and for seven years she could not find a summit or a tree or a hill or a height in Ireland on which she could settle, but only rocks of the sea and the ocean waves, and she was floating through the air until seven years from that day when she lighted on a fringe on the breast of the Mac Óc as he was on the mound of the Brug.

There it was that the Mac Óc said, 'Welcome, Étaín, wanderer careworn, thou that hast encountered great dangers through the cunning of Fuamnach.

The Mac Óc made the girl welcome, that is, the purple fly, and gathered her to his bosom in the fleece of his cloak. He brought her to his house and his sun-bower with its bright windows for passing out and in, and purple raiment was put on her; and wheresoever he went that sun-bower was carried by the Mac Óc, and there he used to sleep every night by her side, comforting her, until her gladness and colour came to her again. And that sun-bower was filled with fragrant and wondrous herbs, and she throve on the fragrance and bloom of those goodly precious herbs.

Fuamnach was told of the love and honour that was bestowed by the Mac Óc on Étaín. Said Fuamnach to Midir, 'Let thy fosterling be summoned that I may make peace between you both, while I myself go in quest of Étaín.' A messenger comes to the Mac Óc from Midir, who went to speak to him. Meanwhile Fuamnach came by a circuitous way until she was in the Brug, and she sent the same blast on Étaín, which carried her out of her sun-bower on the very flight she had been on before for the space of seven years throughout Ireland. The blast of wind drove her along in misery and weakness until she alit on the rooftree of a house in Ulster where folk were drinking, and she fell into the golden beaker that was before the wife of Étar the champion from Inber Cíchmaine, in the province of Conchobar, so that she swallowed her with the liquid that was in the beaker, and in this wise she was conceived in her womb and became afterwards her daughter. She was called Étaín daughter of Étar. Now it was a thousand and twelve years from the first begetting of Étaín by Ailill until her last begetting by Étar.

After that Étaín was brought up at Inber Cíchmaine by Étar, and fifty daughters of chieftains along with her, and he it was that fed and clothed them to be in attendance on Étaín always. On a day it befel that all the maidens were bathing in the estuary when they saw from the water a horseman entering the plain towards them. He was mounted on a broad brown steed, curvetting and pranc-

ing, with curly mane and curly tail. Around him a green mantle in folds, and a
red-embroidered tunic, and in his mantle a golden brooch which reached to his
shoulder on either side. A silvern shield with rim of gold slung over his back, and
a silver strap to it and boss of gold thereon. In his hand a five-pronged spear with
bands of gold round about it from haft to socket. Bright yellow hair he had reaching to his forehead. A fillet of gold against his forehead so that his hair should
not fall over his face. He halted a while on the bank gazing at the maiden, and
all the maidens loved him. Thereupon he uttered this lay:

This is Étaín here to-day
at Síd Ban Find west of Ailbe,
among little boys is she
on the brink of Inber Cíchmaine.

She it is who healed the King's eye
from the well of Loch Dá Líg;
she it is that was swallowed in a drink
from a beaker by Étar's wife.

Because of her the King shall chase
the birds from Tethba,
and drown his two steeds
in the pool of Loch Dá Airbrech.

Full many a war shall be
on Eochaid of Meath because of thee;
there shall be destruction of elfmounds,
and battle against many thousands.

'Tis she that was sung of in the land;
'tis she that strives to win the King;
'tis she who comes to Bé Find,
She is our Étaín afterwards.

The warrior departed from them after that, and they knew not whence he had
come or whither he had gone.

When the Mac Óc came to confer with Midir, he did not find Fuamnach
there, and he (Midir) said to him: 'The woman has played us false, and if she be
told that Étaín is in Ireland she will go to do her ill.' 'Methinks 'tis likely so,' said
the Mac Óc. 'Étaín has been at my house in the Brug since a little while in the
shape in which she was blown from thee, and perhaps it is she that the woman is
making for.'

The Mac Óc returns home and finds the crystal sun-bower without Étaín in
it. The Mac Óc turns upon Fuamnach's traces and came up on her at Aenach
Bodbgna at the house of the druid Bresal Etarlám. The Mac Óc attacked her and
shore off her head, and he brought that head with him to the Brug. . . .

NOTES

Source: Osborn Bergin and R. I. Best, in *ERIU*, Vol. 12 (1938), 137–65.

The *Torchmarc Etaine*, or 'Wooing of Étaín' is an ancient tale of love, war and political struggles carried on by the Otherworldly beings who inhabit the lands of ancient Ireland. It belongs within a mini-cycle of stories featuring Midir 'king of the elfmounds of Bri Leith', who occupies the position within the Irish traditions of a kind of trickster figure. He is also lord of the *Fir Bolg*, the primal race of Ireland.

It will be seen at once that the beginning of the story is a version of that already told in 'The Story of Bóänd' (page 84). Here the story is fleshed out, and the long-term effects of the Dagda's desire for Bóänd worked out in the succeeding account of Étaín and Midir's story. It is fascinating to see the working of tradition in this way – how succeeding generations of storytellers shaped and reworked the older tales. The story, as told here, bears all the hallmarks of an extremely ancient and primal myth, in which the gods (still half-human like the Dagda, who is here identified with a 'king' of the *Tuatha de Danaan* (Tribe of Dana), and only called 'The Good God' as a title rather than an actual name) live and love and fight in a manner not unlike their human counterparts.

Midir's temporary loss of an eye is not only reminiscent of the Norse Baldur myth but also emphasizes the ancient Celtic belief that only a person unblemished in body could rule. If he was in any way damaged, or lost a limb or an eye, the land would suffer accordingly. This theme continued to echo throughout Celtic myth, and reappeared later in the Arthurian cycle in the figure of the Wounded King.

The remainder of the story, with its fantastic account of Étaín's transformation into a fly and her subsequent rebirth over 1,000 years later, is also extremely old. The text ends somewhat abruptly with an alternate suggestion (omitted here for the sake of clarity) in which Midir and Fuamnach are both destroyed by the sea-god Manannan mac Lir. The text is corrupt in several places, and I have edited these for ease of reading. A full account of these textual problems will be found in the original edition.

APPENDIX

Some Names of the Celtic Otherworld

THE CELTIC OTHERWORLD has many names, especially in Ireland, where every hill seems to bear the name of one of the *sidhe*. The following list, based in part on that compiled by David Spaan in 1969, (and gratefully acknowledged), augmented by the present author, lists only some of the huge variety of such names to be found within Celtic literature.

Aenach Bodbgna
Aircthech
Allbine
Annwn
Ben Etair
Brug mac ind Oicc
Brug na Boine
Budi's Land
Caire Cendfinne
Cave of Cruachan
Chocc Baine
Ciuin
Cnoc Ardmulla
Cnoc Miodchaoin
Crithan na Cuan
Domnall's Land
Dun Forgall
dun Inbir
Emain
Emain Ablach
Es Dara
Falias
Fer Menia

Ferdach Isle
Findias
Fururdhocht
Gorias
Ildathach
Imchuin
In Brug
Inis Derglocha
Inis Fianchuire
Inis Subai
Ioruatha
Isle of Ailbe
Isle of Falga
Isle of Grief
Isle of Joy
Isle of Scathach
Isle of Strong Men
Isle of Tethra
Lachtmaig
Lochlann
Mag Argatnel
Mag Denna
Mag Dha Cheo

Mag Findargat

Mag Inis

Mag Luada

Mag Mell

Mag Mon

Mag Mor

Mag Nime

Mag Rein

Murias

Oenech Fidga

Oenech nEmna

Oi Sidh

Paps of Anu

Paradise of Birds

Perilous Glen

Pisear

Plain of Bad Luck

Plain of Cruach

Samera's Land

Sidh

Sidh Aedh

Sidh Aircelltrai

Sidh Almha

Sidh Ane Cliach

Sidh Aodh

Sidh Ban Find

Sidh Boadach

Sidh Bri Ele

Sidh Bri Leith

Sidh Bru Ruair

Sidh Brug na Boinne

Sidh Cleitech

Sidh Cruachan

Sidh Duma Granerit

Sidh ar Femuin

Sidh Fionnachaid

Sidh In Braga

Sidh Leithet

Sidh Lethet Oidni

Sidh Meada

Sidh na mBan Fionn

Sidh Nennta

Sidh Rodruban

Sidh Sliabh Mis

Sidh Tech Duinn

Sidh Truim

Sidh Uaman

Sigear Isle

Slieve Slanga

Sorcha

Talamh na Naomh

Tenmag Trogalge

Tir Mar

Tir Mor

Tir na Fer

Tir na mBan

Tir na mBeo

Tir na n-Altheach

Tir na n-Dionn

Tir na-nIngen

Tir na nOg

Tir n-Uath

Tir Tairngire

Uaimh Bodhbh

Uaimh Cruachan

Further Reading

There are innumerable texts which describe the Celtic Otherworld in varying detail. Some of the best are included here, but there are others. What follows is a selection only of the available texts, together with some of the books which deal with the concept of the Otherworld in some detail. The works by Spaan, Löffler and Patch all include extensive bibliographies.

Alger, W.R., *The Destiny of the Soul*, Boston: Little, Brown, 1888.
Boswell, C.S., *An Irish Precursor of Dante*, London; D. Nutt, 1908.
Brown, A.C.L., *The Origin of the Grail Legend,* Cambridge, Mass.: Harvard University Press, 1943.
Carey, John, The Irish "Otherworld": Hiberno-Latin Perspectives', in *Eigse*, Vol. 25 (1991), 154–59.
Carmichael, A., *Carmina Gadelica*, Edinburgh: Floris Books, 1992.
Chadwick, Nora K., 'The Borderland of the Spirit in Early European Literature', in *Trivium*, Vol. 11, no. 5 (1996/7), 17–37.
Cross, Tom Peete and Slover, Clark Harris, (Eds), *Ancient Irish Tales*, Dublin: Figgis, 1936.
Curtin, J., *Hero Tales of Ireland*, London: Macmillan, 1894.
Dillon, M., *Early Irish Literature*, Chicago: University of Chicago Press, 1972.
Dodds, M., *Forerunners of Dante*, Edinburgh: Williams & Norgate, 1903.
Dunn, J., *The Ancient Irish Epic Tain Bo Cualange*, London: D. Nutt, 1914.
Guest, Lady Charlotte (trans.), *The Mabinogion*, London: J.M. Dent, 1937.
Hamel, A.G. van, *Immrama*, Dublin: Figgis, 1941.
Henderson, G., *Survivals in Belief Among the Celts*, Glasgow: Black, 1911.
Hull, E., 'Old Irish Taboos, or Geasa', in *Folk-Lore*, Vol. XII (1901), 44–66.
Joyce, P.W., *Old Celtic Romances*, London: Kegan Paul, 1894.
Kennedy, P., *The Bardic Stories of Ireland*, Dublin: M'Glashen & Gill, 1871.
Löffler, Christa Maria, *The Voyage to the Otherworld Island in Early Irish Literature* (2 vols), Institute Für Anglistik und Amerikanistik, Universitat Salzburg, 1983.
Matthews, C., *The Celtic Book of the Dead*, London: Thorsons, 1994.
Matthews, John, *The Celtic Shaman*, Shaftesbury: Element Books, 1995.
    (ed.) *Classic Celtic Fairy Tales*, London: Blandford, 1997.
    (ed.) *From The Isles of Dream*, Edinburgh: Floris Books, 1993.
    Taliesin: Shamanism and the Bardic Traditions in Britain and Ireland, London: Thorsons, 1993.
    (ed.) *Within the Hollow Hills*, Edinburgh: Floris Books, 1994.

Meyer, Kuno, (ed.), *The Vision of Mac Conglinne*, London: Kegan Paul, 1892.
    (ed. and trans.), *The Voyage of Bran mac Febal to the Land of the Living
    . . . with an essay on the Irish Version of the Hay Otherworld by Alfred
    Nutt*, London: D. Nutt, 1895–7 (2 vols).
Nennius, *The History of the Britons*, translated by A.W. Wade-Evans, London:
    SPCK, 1938.
O'Grady, Standish H., *Silva Gadelica*, Edinburgh: Williams & Norgate, 1892.
O'Hogain, D., *Myth, Legend and Romance: An Encyclopaedia of the Irish Folk
    Tradition*, London: Ryan Publishing Co., 1990.
Patch, Howard Rollin, *The Otherworld According to Descriptions in Medieval
    Literature*, Cambridge, Mass.: Harvard University Press, 1950.
Rees, A. and B., *Celtic Heritage*, London: Thames & Hudson, 1961.
Rhys, J., Celtic Folk-Lore, Welsh and Manx (2 vols), London: Wildwood House,
    1980.
Spaan, David Bruce, *The Otherworld in Early Irish Literature*, Ann Arbor:
    University of Michigan, 1969.
Stewart, R.J., *Earth Light*, Shaftesbury: Element Books, 1991.
    The Living World of Faery, Glastonbury: Gothic Image Publications, 1995.
    Magical Tales, London: Thorsons, 1990.
    Power Within the Land, Shaftesbury: Element Books, 1992.
    The Underworld Initiation, London: Thorsons, 1985.
Stewart, R.J. and Williamson, R., *Celtic Bards, Celtic Druids*, London:
    Blandford, 1996.
Warner, M., *From the Beast to the Blonde*, London: Chatto & Windus, 1994.
Wentz, W.Y., Evans, *The Fairy Faith in Celtic Countries*, Oxford: Oxford
    University Press, 1911.
Westropp, T.J., 'Brasil and the Legendary Islands of the North Atlantic', in
    Proceedings of the Royal Irish Academy, Vol. XXX (1912), 223–60.
Williamson, R., *The Craneskin Bag*, Edinburgh: Canongate Books, 1993.
Young, E., *Celtic Wonder Tales*, Edinburgh: Floris Books, 1990.
    The Tangle-Coated Horse, Edinburgh: Floris Books, 1991.
    The Wonder-Smith and His Son, Edinburgh: Floris Books, 1992.

Index